The **New Professional's Toolkit**

The **New Professional's Toolkit**

Bethan Ruddock

 facet publishing

© Bethan Ruddock, 2012
Published by Facet Publishing
7 Ridgmount Street, London WC1E 7AE
www.facetpublishing.co.uk

Facet Publishing is wholly owned by CILIP:
the Chartered Institute of Library and Information Professionals.

British Library Cataloguing in Publication Data
A catalogue record for this book is available from the British Library.

ISBN 978-1-85604-768-5

First published 2012

Mixed Sources
Product group from well-managed
forests and other controlled sources
www.fsc.org Cert no. SA-COC-1565
© 1996 Forest Stewardship Council

Text printed on FSC accredited material.

Typeset from author's files in 10/14 pt Palatino Linotype and Frutiger
by Facet Publishing.
Printed and made in Great Britain by MPG Books Group, UK.

Dedication

For John, because everything is.

Contents

Preface

Welcome to the 21st century, where information professionals roam the land. You can find these adaptable creatures in almost every evolutionary niche: health, education, banking and finance, law, the IT industry, government (national and local), schools, universities. Their camouflage skills are excellent; they are often no longer distinguishable by their titles of 'librarian' or 'archivist', instead merging seamlessly with their new environments with titles such as 'transformation manager', 'knowledge strategist' and 'content expert'.

With such a diverse population, it can be hard to pick out distinguishing characteristics that identify information professionals as members of the same tribe. Cardigans, buns and spectacles are no longer considered reliable indicators. Researchers who have spent time close to the tribe claim that the only distinguishing physical characteristic is a certain liveliness, intelligence and curiosity around the eyes. Even in conversations, it is not always possible to spot a well assimilated information professional. They will use the same value terms and keywords as others in their surrounding environment, and will easily pick up on the argot or jargon of their local community.

It is astonishing to think that the vast majority of these information professionals sprang from a relatively limited number of training institutions: library schools as they are often called. One of the continuing mysteries surrounding information professionals is how a generic course, usually lasting no longer than a year or two, can produce so many information professionals who thrive in specialized environments. In fact, new research suggests that much of the development of the information professional takes place in the wild (or on the job), and it is rumoured that one reliable method of identifying information professionals is to search their conversations for the presence of the mysterious phrase, 'I bet you didn't learn that in library school.'

If these indications are correct, then we must accept that there is considerable scope within the information professions for continuous professional development (CPD): self-education, which begins where the more formal library school training left off. Many methods and forms for this CPD have been posited; we have definite evidence of training courses and conferences. These can be distinguished from non-information professional conferences by the nature of the queer plastic objects known as freebies left behind. We also know of the existence of professional organizations, where information professionals could relax in the company of their own kind.

Less well documented are the online discussion groups. Some rumours even have a large band of information professionals living in some semi-mythical second life, where, despite being able to fly, they choose to spend their time dispensing information and advice.

What follows is a find that has shed considerable light on the life of an information professional in the early 21st century. Apparently designed for the instruction of cadet members of the profession, this work seems to be a survival kit for those who have just left the library school training grounds. When information professionals were asked why such revealing and instructive documents about their profession had never come into the public view before, they replied simply, 'They were always there. You just never asked us where to find them.'

Acknowledgements

This book would not have been possible without the help, input, and support of many people. I'd especially like to thank all those who have contributed case studies or other content: Amy Affelt, Jo Alcock, Fiona Bradley, Linda Butt, Lisa Charnock, Linsey Chrisman, Alison Circle, Maria Cotera, Deborah Dalley, Reece Dano, Annette Earl, Kathy Ennis, Rebecca Goldman, Emily Goodhand, Hannah Green, Dick Hartley, Amanda Hill, Emily Hopkins, Lisa Jeskins, Sarah Johnson, Rosie Jones, Bohyun Kim, Lukas Koster, Sue Lawson, Dee Magnoni, Fiona Marriott, Aileen M. J. Marshall, Bronagh McCrudden, David McMenemy, Lynne Meehan, Tim Padfield, Ned Potter, Lee Pretlove, Dimitris Protopsaltou, Lyndsay Rees-Jones, Chris Rhodes, Maria Robertson, Jenica Rogers, Beccy Shipman, Lauren Smith, Edith Speller, Michael Stead, Jane Stevenson, David Streatfield, Ioannis Trohopoulos, Sarah Wachter, Suzanne Wheatley, Laura J. Wilkinson, Caroline Williams, Jo Wood, Laura Woods, and Gil Young. Without their hard work and generosity, this book would be half the length and not nearly as interesting.

I'd also like to thank my colleagues at Mimas for their support, feedback, and patience when faced with my book-obsession. Colleagues at SLA, SLA Europe and CILIP also gave valuable encouragement and advice.

Thanks to the team at Facet Publishing, especially Sarah Busby who first thought I could write a book, and gave excellent editorial input.

My Twitter network has been invaluable, offering me encouragement, information, and much needed distractions! Particular thanks to all those who responded to my plea to find out 'what's the oddest/most unusual thing you've ever done as an information professional?', especially Karen Blakeman, John Davies, Fiona Forsythe, Cathy Foster, Alan Fricker, Gary Green, Samantha Halford, James Mullan, Roland Quintaine, Katharine Schopflin, and Matthew Soare, whose examples are used in the introduction. Ned Potter (also writing his first book) was a great source of reassurance and answers to 'so how did you...?' questions.

Finally, an extra-special thank you to Jennifer Findlay, who took a big pile of panic and helped me organize it into a Proper Book.

Glossary

ALA	American Library Association
ALIA	Australian Library and Information Association
API	application programming interface
APM	Association for Project Management
ARA	Archives and Records Association
BIALL	British and Irish Association of Law Librarians
CILIP	Chartered Institute of Library and Information Professionals
CIPFA	Chartered Institute of Public Finance and Accountancy
CPD	continuing professional development
CSS	Cascading Style Sheets
EAD	Encoded Archival Description
HTML	Hyper-Text Mark-up Language
ICA	International Council on Archives
ICT	information and communications technology
IFLA	International Federation of Library Associations and Institutions
JISC	Joint Information Systems Committee
LIANZA	Library and Information Association of New Zealand Aotearoa
LIS	library and information science
LISNPN	LIS New Professionals Network
MLIS	Manchester Library and Information Service
NHS	National Health Service (UK)
OPAC	online public access catalogue
RDF	Resource Description Framework
SAA	Society of American Archivists
SIG	special interest group
SLA	Special Libraries Association
URL	uniform resource locater
XML	eXtensible Markup Language

GLOSSARY

Introduction

Being a new professional isn't always easy. With the range of roles available to information professionals becoming ever more diverse, the variety of required skills and knowledge is also growing. New professionals often find themselves in a role where they are expected to acquire and use new skills rapidly. In a time when budgets are being reduced, it is unlikely that all of these learning and development needs will be satisfied by formal, workplace-provided training, and staff are increasingly expected to be responsible for their own training and development.

This toolkit is designed to help you through this transition – from settling in to your first professional role to managing your career development. Packed with case studies from new and experienced professionals, the toolkit will give you new perspectives on library and information science (LIS) work, and guide you towards the resources and information you need to help you grow professionally.

This book is aimed primarily at newly qualified librarians and archivists who are in their first professional roles. Students, trainees and those interested in a career in the information professions will also find it useful, especially if they wish to prepare themselves for what might be expected of them in their first professional role and tailor their professional development accordingly. Established professionals may also find useful information or exercises, especially if they are moving into a new role, or coming back to the profession after a career break.

Building on the experiences of both new and established professionals, this book contains contributions not only from the UK and the USA, but also Canada, the Netherlands, Greece and Australia, and from a wide variety of sectors, including academic, public and law libraries; archives and special collections; and specialist information providers in a number of environments.

There is practical advice about how to get your library or archive service online, tips on digital preservation and project planning, and information about external funding sources and how to apply to them. Learn how to carry out a skills audit to find out what you need to learn and what training you need, then discover how to make the most of your formal and informal learning, and apply it in the workplace.

You will learn how to identify and communicate with your stakeholders, how to find and apply their value terms, and how to promote your service to your stakeholders on a shoestring, along with resources for learning about copyright and intellectual property legislation, information about professional ethics, and ways to educate users about copyright. Exercises and suggestions for further reading allow you to direct your own learning and investigate topics at your own pace. The toolkit will give you an excellent grounding for sustainable professional and personal development.

But it can't cover everything. Life in the information professions is full of the unexpected. These are some of the things the toolkit won't teach you to do:

- make pirate hats
- hold a horse while a potential donor of archives examines its leg
- pose next to a silver cigar box in the shape of Broadcasting House – for the scale
- film a glass of gin and tonic glowing in the dark
- try to source an (empty) 25lb shell casing
- pick apples for a cider festival
- go from one part of a campus to another two miles away on a camel
- book a Scalextric track for a client event
- find articles on the change in sound as a replacement hip joint is banged home ('ding ding ding donk', apparently…)
- find someone somewhere to live after they arrived in the country with no accommodation organized
- strap pillows to yourself and dress up as Father Christmas.

These are all real-life examples from my peer network. The toolkit won't be able to help you with these – but it might help you find someone who can, and leave you feeling a bit more prepared to deal with whatever your career may bring.

See the website *⊘* **(http://lisnewprofs.com)** for lots of extra content – case studies, links if we decide to add these, information about contributors, and an exclusive behind the scenes 'making of' blog.

CHAPTER 1
Project management

Introduction

It is likely that one of the first things you do in a new professional role is to get involved with project management. Perhaps your workplace is running a project your managers would like you to get involved with, or someone has asked you to manage a small-scale project. You might be specifically employed to do project work – there are frequently project-based roles in library and information science (LIS), which may appeal especially to early career professionals. These roles frequently have short-term contracts (of a year or less), and allow you to gain experience in different areas of LIS work. There may also be the chance to turn a project position into a permanent role with your employer. Your project involvement might be:

- managing a project that you are undertaking
- working as one of a team on a project someone else is managing
- managing a project that a team is working on.

These projects might be formal or informal, work-based or external. Allan (2004, 6) classifies projects into the following categories:

- strategic or operational
- simple or complex
- local or distributed
- having 'hard' or 'soft' outcomes
- fixed or changing the environment.

Whatever the type of project, they will all have certain things in common.

What is a project?

A project is a task, which has the following characteristics:

- *start and end dates*: so it is completed within a certain time span, defined in advance
- *measurable goals and outcomes*: what the project is to achieve
- *a budget:* with an allocation of resources, including money, time and staff.

The success of a project is measured by these characteristics: a successful project is one that is completed on time, within budget, and achieves its goals.

Project work frequently requires you to collaborate across departments and disciplines. While projects might just involve library or archive staff, it is more likely that they will also require the involvement of other departments, such as finance, information technology (IT) and human resources. The ability to liaise with staff from different departments is a core skill required for project work.

Although projects can be large and complex, they can also be small-scale and relatively simple. These are some examples of possible LIS projects:

- implementing radio frequency identification (RFID)
- moving stock and services to a new room or building
- digitizing a collection
- designing and building a website
- undertaking a retrospective cataloguing conversion project (moving paper-based catalogues onto an electronic collection-management system)
- designing an induction programme for new students or staff
- purchasing a new collection management system.

Finding project work

Positions for people to work on or manage projects are often advertised through recruitment agents or on mailing lists. Sometimes it is spelled out that the job involves project work; other times you may need to follow the clues in the job description, as in the example in Figure 1.1.

Figure 1.1 is a good example of a typical LIS job advert for a project position. Note that although the activity is called a programme rather than a project, it shows all the characteristics of a project: it has a fixed duration (the interview date is Friday 26 August 2011; it is a fixed term post up to 31 March

Dear All

Please find attached details of an exciting vacancy at Tate Archive, Tate Britain, London. Details of how to apply online are given below.

Post: Archive Cataloguer
Reference: TG0050
Band: Specialist
Salary: £22,900 per annum
Contract: Fixed term to 31 March 2012
Location: Tate Britain, Millbank, London SW1P 4RG

Tate Archive is a major national resource comprising the Archive of British Art since 1900 and Tate's institutional records. The opening of the Hyman Kreitman Reading Rooms in 2002 and the launch of our catalogue online has created excellent access to Tate staff, academic researchers and the public.

We have embarked on an ambitious programme to completely catalogue our 800 collections with just 22% of the total remaining to be listed. To help us achieve this aim, we are seeking an enthusiastic archive cataloguer to join the team of six in a fixed term post up to 31 March 2012.

You will be responsible for sorting and cataloguing the papers of the art critic David Sylvester, and other selected collections, according to ISAD(G) and in-house standards, entering records onto CALM and generating lists for public access. You will also participate in the delivery of services to researchers.

You will hold a postgraduate diploma or MA in archive administration or equivalent experience. You will also have experience of archive cataloguing and familiarity with ISAD(G). A high level of accuracy and good IT skills are essential.

For more information and to apply using our online system, please visit www.tate.org.uk/about/workingattate

Closing date: Friday 19 August 2011
Interviews: Friday 26 August 2011

Figure 1.1 *Sample job description for a post at Tate Archive*

2012), measurable goals and outcomes ('completely catalogue our 800 collections with just 22% of the total remaining to be listed'), and a fixed level of resources (team of six). This advertisement was posted on the Archives-NRA (National Register of Archives) mailing list in August 2011, and is reproduced by permission of TATE.

Why projects?

Defining something as a project allows you to make changes and developments in a structured way. Project management tools and strategies can help to maximize staff and stakeholder buy-in, and measure, record and report on outcomes.

What skills does project management involve?

Project management fits well with the traditional LIS skill set, as it is heavily based on managing information, time and resources. Project management is a transferable skill, and can help you find employment in non-traditional or non-LIS sectors, as this case study from Annette Earl, a change facilitator, shows.

✒ How to . . .
Get started with project work

I began my professional career as a public and school librarian, before taking on the role of project manager within the medical higher education environment. The primary remit of my role is to help develop and deliver new postgraduate courses for doctors and dentists, as well as devise and oversee the processes and procedures that accompany this. The work is multidisciplinary and requires me to work across sectors and teams within the organization, and to form constructive, positive relationships with external partners.

Project management requires a good understanding of how things work at both the strategic and operational level, and many of the skills I had acquired as a librarian were quickly utilized within the project management environment. For example, the need to source, collate and organize large amounts of information and disseminate to a variety of users was something I had previous experience of. Project management is essentially the process by which a number of outcomes are achieved based on working within set criteria. Accuracy and relevance of information are crucial to the successful outcome of a project; an information professional is easily able to translate their skill set to do this.

These are some suggestions to help get you started.

Learn the project management language

It is always possible to become more professional, and adopting the terminology of a discipline is one way of doing so. Learning the specific terms used in project management demonstrates an active understanding of the professional area in which you are working and allows you to communicate in a common language with those outside your immediate professional environment.

A great place to start to understand what project management is, how it works and how you can apply it to your own situation is the Association for Project Management's (APM's) book *Starting Out in Project Management* by Ruth Murray-Webster and Peter Simon (2006). This is a seminal text and is worth investing in for the glossary alone.

Attend conferences and events outside your normal scope

A conference about knowledge management or library services will almost certainly contain some emphasis on project management but may be packaged differently from those you are familiar with. Look at conferences outside your specific sector and you may be surprised at how many relevant events there are. They need not be expensive; Project Challenge runs twice a year, is free and runs sessions relevant to all those working in the information profession. Details can be found at www.projectchallenge.co.uk.

Self-study your way to project management

While project management has its own formal training structure and career path, it is not always desirable or necessary to learn about project management through expensive training courses. There are a number of online resources available to help you achieve a thorough and comprehensive understanding of project management, if you are willing to spend a little time and energy on adopting a self-study approach. There are numerous websites, organizations and publications dedicated to project management.

Read

I have mentioned it already but I cannot recommend it highly enough! The text by Ruth Murray-Webster and Peter Simon, *Starting Out in Project Management*, really should be the first port of call for any aspiring project manager, and is an excellent reference book covering all the basic tenets of project management.

Know

Any of the following websites provide a useful entry point to project management as a professional discipline:

- Association for Project Management (APM), www.apm.org.uk
- Project Management Institute (PMI; UK Chapter), www.pmi.org.uk
- Project Manager Today, www.pmtoday.co.uk.

Supplement

It is helpful to supplement the professional organizations' websites by visiting those that provide a more practical basis for your learning. These are some of the best:

- Business Balls, www.businessballs.com
- Mindtools, www.mindtools.com
- the Open University's Openlearn, which offers a number of free modules specifically relating to project management, http://openlearn.open.ac.uk.

Do!

- Many of those reading this book are likely to be using project management in some way – it is important to make this visible and tangible to managers and colleagues if it is to be recognized:
- When writing reports, use project management terminology; this immediately adds credibility and professionalism to the work you already do.
- Many of the foundations and principles of project management that are taught on project management courses can be learned through self-study; use the information freely available on corporate and professional organization websites to develop and enhance your project management knowledge.
- Mind map the processes, activities and tasks that make up your current role. Now overlay the basic project management process; see, you are probably already a project manager!

Since becoming a project manager I have acquired and developed a number of transferable skills. Perhaps the most obvious and tangible benefit has been the acquisition of professional qualifications such as the APM Introductory Certificate to Project Management and PRINCE2 and change management qualifications. I have learned the language of project management, which has enabled me to converse with colleagues in a clearer and more helpful manner than I had in the past, especially with those from a different professional background.

I have also been able to gain a different perspective on the value of information, and how its needs and meaning can alter according to audience and purpose, which I believe has made me a better information professional. I have found it reassuring to discover that there is a formal process for my natural way of thinking and I strongly believe that the information profession and project management profession are complementary partners to achieving organizational objectives. The most successful people are those who recognize the importance and natural overlap of both.

Methodologies and tools

Annette has given us a general introduction to project management, and how your information professional skills can translate to those of project management. There are a number of tools and methodologies available to help with project management, and this section gives a brief introduction to some of them. Always keep in mind the scope and resources of the project and the aims of the organization when choosing a tool.

Formal training

PRINCE2

If you are planning to do a lot of project work, you might consider PRINCE2 training. PRINCE2 is an internationally recognized standard, used extensively in the UK public sector. It sometimes is listed as a required or desired skill for those applying for (usually high-level) project management positions.

There are two levels of PRINCE2 qualification: Foundation and Practitioner. Training can cost from £500 to £1500, and requires the commitment to attend a multi-day course, or complete an online self-study course. New professionals who are only undertaking small amounts of project management and have to pay their own course fees might find it difficult to justify paying for a PRINCE2 qualification. If your job requires a lot of project management, your organization may pay for training.

Other training

As well as the general training providers mentioned by Annette in the case study above, a number of LIS training providers provide introductory courses to project management, with an emphasis on the information and cultural heritage sector.

In the UK, ASLIB runs a one-day project management course, which looks at planning and implementing library and information projects. See www.aslib.com/training/courses/course.htm?eventid=19.

In the USA, the Society of American Archivists runs a course on project management for archivists. See www2.archivists.org/prof-education/course-catalog/tst-project-management-for-archivists.

Professional organizations may run project management training from time to time. This may be subject to demand, so if you can't find a course in your area, it might be worth contacting relevant organizations to express an interest. Larger organizations such as universities might run internal training courses on subjects such as project management. These are likely to be general introductions, and may not be tailored to the LIS environment.

It is also worth looking for online courses. IFLA have Project Management and Planning as part of module 3 of their Building Strong Library Associations course, available through their online learning platform at www.ifla.org/en/bsla/learning-platform. The Georgia Library Association Carterette Series of webinars are freely available for download at http://gla.georgialibraries.org/mediawiki/index.php/Carterette_Series_Webinars_Archive; they include an introduction to project management as well as other great topics including digital rights management, podcasting and transliteracy.

Tools

You may already be familiar with some of the tools of project management – others, you might not have come across. Here is a brief introduction to some of the most commonly used tools.

Software

There are a number of software packages available to help you manage projects. Products such as Microsoft Project can be costly, and may only be available to you if your organization has a licence. You may prefer to use an open source, Software as a Service (SaaS) or freeware product. Wikipedia has a useful page comparing features of many different software packages, which may help you find a package that suits your needs and budget. See http://en.wikipedia.org/wiki/Comparison_of_project_management_software.

Remember that a package that is suitable for a large-scale project may not be as suitable for a smaller project, and that learning to use each set of software will require you to invest time and effort.

Mind maps

Mind mapping can be a useful tool to help you start planning a project. It allows you to move away from a linear approach, and capture all the tasks and potential difficulties associated with a project.

There is mind mapping software available, but this isn't necessary – mind maps can be low-tech, requiring just a pen and paper.

The mind mapping website www.mind-mapping.co.uk/mind-maps-examples.htm has some useful examples. Figure 1.2 shows a hand-drawn mind map by Lyndsay Rees-Jones of Real Time Release.

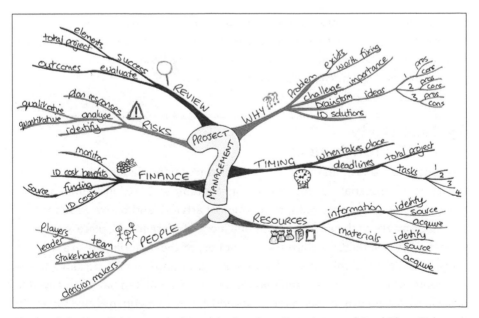

Figure 1.2 *Hand-drawn mind map by Lyndsay Rees-Jones of Real Time Release,* *http://real-time-release.co.uk*

	week 1	week 2	week 3	week 4	week 5	week 6
Choose project team	▓					
Communicate with users	▓	▓	▓	▓	▓	▓
Enter changes into catalogue		▓				
Print new barcodes		▓				
Print new spine labels		▓				
Relabel Bay 1			▓			
Relabel Bay 2				▓		
Relabel Bay 3					▓	
Check shelving and labelling						▓

Figure 1.3 *Example of a Gantt chart*

Gantt charts

Gantt charts allow you to express time-critical activities visually, and to plan workloads. Activities are often expressed as elements of a bar chart, with tasks on the y axis and duration on the x axis, such as in the example of a reclassification project shown in Figure 1.3.

A similar process is critical path analysis, which involves finding the key elements of a project by mapping out dependencies, durations and earliest or latest start or finish times.

Although these tools can be useful, you don't need formal project management training to run a successful project. Follow Hannah Green, archivist at Seven Stories, as she talks about the challenges of running a project that is very much in the international eye.

📁 Case study
The Blyton Project

The estate of Gillian Baverstock, Enid Blyton's elder daughter, put a large collection of material up for auction in September 2010, including original typescripts for numerous books, some original artwork and books. Seven Stories was made aware of the auction about one month before it took place – we knew we definitely wanted to acquire some, if not all, of the material. We are working towards building a collection of national significance, which documents the development of modern children's literature, and Enid Blyton has an undisputed place in such a collection. Her name also consistently came up in visitor surveys as the person visitors would most like to see an exhibition about, so we knew there would be a great deal of public interest in her material.

We knew that external funding would be required to support the acquisition of this material. Because of the short notice, we had little time to apply for funding, so the project bid was put together very quickly and without knowing exactly what material we might end up acquiring from the auction! The lack of records of any previous sales of original typescript by Blyton at auction made it very difficult for us to estimate the likely sale value of the typescripts – relatively little of Blyton's draft material has survived, so there was no point of reference for previous sales of similar material. We were very aware that there would be a lot of interest from Blyton collectors which might also drive the price up at auction. This meant we didn't really know how far any funding we might be able to raise would actually stretch at the auction. Funding applications to the V&A Museum and the Museums, Libraries and Archives Council purchase fund and the Heritage Lottery Fund were successful – these bids were not only for funding to purchase material, but also covered costs of repackaging and preservation, and a programme of public events and activities making the Enid Blyton material accessible to the public. The funding bids included a strong element of online engagement, proposing a cataloguing blog, and developing access to the original material online via the Seven Stories website.

After the successful funding bid, Seven Stories was able to secure at auction typescripts for 13 of Blyton's novels, along with some short stories; some personal books and papers belonging to Gillian Baverstock, including her childhood diary; merchandise and other ephemeral material relating to Blyton's most popular series; and some printed books. Overall management of implementation of the project lay with the collection director, with the main workload split between the archivist and the events co-ordinator. The archivist had primary responsibility for managing the cataloguing and digital element of the project, while the events co-ordinator had responsibility for public events and access.

Some elements of the project were extremely straightforward – cataloguing took place relatively quickly, and it was very easy to set up a cataloguing blog on WordPress (http://blytonsevenstories.wordpress.com) to disseminate information about cataloguing and repackaging as it was going on. This blog was promoted via relevant mailing lists, and through the Enid Blyton Society website, tapping into existing online communities of Blyton fans rather than trying to generate new audiences. It was also promoted via Seven Stories' presence on Twitter and Facebook, with Twitter proving a particularly successful method of driving visitors to the blog. The blog was undeniably successful but had a significant impact on workload, as keeping the audience engaged and regularly visiting the blog required new posts at least twice a week.

Other elements of the project proved more challenging. Plans to make material available online had to be significantly revised to accommodate the concerns of the copyright holders. Our project proposal outlined a desire to make full manuscripts available online, and this could have been relatively easily achieved through Flickr. However, the rights holders refused permission to make full works available online, and raised significant concerns about the security of images made available via Flickr. Consequently, we have only been able to make single images from each typescript available via our website, in the catalogue and on a page dedicated to the Enid Blyton archive.

Despite such challenges, the project did have several very positive, unexpected outcomes. The discovery of the typescript for an unpublished novel by Blyton, *Mr Tumpy's Caravan*, was publicized through the cataloguing blog. After the BBC picked up on the story, it spread very quickly both nationally and internationally, creating a huge amount of publicity for Seven Stories and the Blyton archive. Further, significant donations of material have also been made to the archive by Sophie Smallwood, Blyton's younger daughter since we acquired the typescripts at auction. These subsequent donations, along with the material originally acquired at auction, will form the core of an exhibition dedicated to the work of Enid Blyton. The most exciting, and unexpected, outcome was the establishment of a new £¾m fund to benefit the work of Seven Stories, founded thanks to the Enid Blyton Trust for Children. Its Trustees decided to wind up the Enid Blyton Trust for Children and donate its assets to set up a permanent fund to support the work of Seven Stories.

Conclusion

Hannah's case study highlights many important aspects of project management:

- *time constraints:* the funding bid was put together in less than a month
- *team responsibilities:* the workload was split between three team members, each with responsibility for a certain area
- *impact on workload:* greater than expected, due to public interest in the blog
- *unexpected challenges:* because of copyright concerns original plans for digitization had to be shelved.
- *the whole team can benefit from project management techniques:* Hannah wasn't the project manager – she was a project team member – but she's

learned enough to write this case study, and obviously feels highly involved with the project.

In *Project Management* Barbara Allan talks about not needing to use complex project management tools for simple problems: '[It] is rather like taking a sledgehammer to crack a nut. The time spent using the methods would be better spent working on the project' (2004, 7). Whatever project management tools you choose to use should be suitable to the project at hand – balance the benefits of proper planning with the time and resources available, and the risk factor of the project. Getting into the mindset of choosing the appropriate project management tools for simple projects will help you when it comes to bigger projects. You don't need to carry out a Gantt chart or a critical path analysis for everything, but think about planning your time and resources, and prioritizing and delegating tasks where required.

You will never be able to plan for all the challenges you might face, but having a plan in place, with allowances for slippage, will make it easier to deal with challenges when they arise. Planning and delivering successful projects will improve your productivity and time management skills, benefiting you in all areas of your career.

References and further reading

Alcock, J. (2011) Productivity for Librarians, *Joeyanne Libraryanne: librarianship in the modern age*, www.joeyanne.co.uk/2011/11/01/productivity-for-librarians-ili2011.

Allan, B. (2004) *Project Management: tools and techniques for today's ILS professional*, Facet Publishing.

Allen, D. (2001) *Getting Things Done: how to achieve stress-free productivity*, Piatkus.

Berkun, S. (2008) *Making Things Happen: mastering project management*, O'Reilly.

Cervone, H. F. (2008) Good Project Managers are 'Cluefull' Rather Than Clueless, *OCLC Systems and Services*, **24**, 199.

German, L. (2009) No One Plans to Fail, They Fail to Plan: the importance of structured project planning, *Technicalities*, **29** (3), 1, 7–9.

Meg, B. and Robyn, P. (2008) Diversification . . . Where Libraries, Riffraff and Crusty Demons Meet!, *Electronic Library*, **26** (5), 662–72.

Murray-Webster, R. and Simon, P. (2006) *Starting Out in Project Management: a study guide for the APM Introductory Certificate in Project Management*, APM Publishing, 2nd edn.

Revels, I. (2010) Managing Digital Projects, *American Libraries*, **41** (4), 48.

➡ Over to you . . .

Think about a project you have been involved in. Did you use a project management technique? How might doing so have helped?

Choose a project management technique, and write a short plan (c 300 words) of how you might apply it to a project you are involved in. This can be any work or study related project – writing your dissertation definitely counts! Think about:

- time spent planning vs time saved in execution; a simple, low-risk project will require a less detailed strategy
- the nature of the project: how many people are involved? What sort of flexibility is there?

CHAPTER 2
Teaching, training and communicating

Introduction

At some point your role as an information professional will almost certainly involve some form of teaching or training, such as:

- teaching users in large groups (e.g. as inductions)
- teaching users in groups, with hands-on (e.g. information literacy or database training)
- teaching users one to one
- training fellow professionals (e.g. at a workshop, training day or conference)
- training colleagues (e.g. training new staff, passing along information from a training course or conference)
- delivering presentations to users, stakeholders, colleagues or professional peers.

Even if you don't – or think you don't – have to do any of these things, learning the principles of teaching and training will help you to communicate effectively, and become more confident when communicating with others.

Effective communication

Most roles will cite communication as a core skill. For communication to be fully effective, it needs to fulfil a need for both parties: the communicator must impart the information they intended to; and the recipient must feel a benefit from receiving this information.

It takes skill to craft a message that is clear, concise and relevant. This can be much easier in one-to-one communication than in group communication. With one-to-one contact you can tailor your communication specifically to the person you are communicating with: use their preferred vocabulary, meet their needs, and fall within their frame of reference.

With large numbers of people it can be a little harder. It helps if you can address coherent groups – groups that are likely to have the same communication need and receive the same communication benefit. You can start to do this by dividing your potential audience into sections, and deciding how you can most effectively communicate with each section (see Chapter 4 for more about identifying and engaging with stakeholders).

Effective communication can help you to show value and encourage use by using the value terms your communicatees recognize.

Teaching and training

The information professions have traditionally been seen as professions for introverts. In a panel at the 2011 Special Libraries Association (SLA) Conference in Philadelphia, Stephen Abram outed himself as an extrovert, and admitted that it made him unusual in his chosen profession. He suggested that the proportion of extroverts to introverts (approximately 75:25) in the population as a whole is reversed in librarianship and related professions.

Being an introvert doesn't mean that you won't be a good teacher or trainer. Introverts are known for doing well in one-on-one situations, but also for performing well at the centre of attention, such as leading group discussions and delivering presentations; see Rauch (2003) and Zack (2010) for further discussion of this point.

There is no doubt that being the focus of attention can be disconcerting, especially when you are trying to impart important information, and want to do the best you can for your subject and listeners. There is nothing wrong with being nervous! Even experienced professionals will still get stage fright – the key is to find ways to conquer your nerves and deliver your material well.

Lisa Jeskins, Promotions and Outreach Officer for Library and Archival Services, Mimas, and founder of Lisa Jenkins Training (http://lisjenkinstraining. com), gives some tips on how to prepare yourself to deliver great training.

⚒ How to . . .
Run training sessions

As a new professional, preparing for your first induction or training session can be a daunting task. Preparation and planning are vital for making yourself as comfortable and confident as possible.

Preparing yourself

These are some ways to prepare yourself:

- *Observe:* Watch another colleague perform similar training. Observe what they do and how the users respond to them. How did they deal with any difficulties? Have they any advice for you? You can pick up tips this way and steal ideas! Choose someone who enjoys training and who you think is good.
- *Prepare your presentation in advance:* Make sure it isn't too text heavy with confusing fonts or excessive use of colour. Always spell check and ask someone else to proofread all your materials (whether created in PowerPoint or Prezi, or simple handouts) as it is difficult to spot errors in your own work.
- *Check:* Ensure links work and double check again on the morning of the presentation. If you are scared that the technology will fail, prepare screenshots of any database demonstrations you are including. It is more effective to perform a live demonstration but it can be reassuring to have back-up. You can click anywhere on the slide to move on but if you click on the search button, you can make it appear as though you are searching live.
- *Print out your handouts in plenty of time:* If you leave printing until the morning of the training, something will go wrong. If you have devised exercises for users to do, go through them step by step and then get someone else to go through them as if they were the trainee, to see if they work. This is vital when working with technology because as a professional user you can see things very differently from a first-time user, and often miss steps.
- *Rehearse:* Going over a presentation in your head isn't enough; you will find that once you start speaking, it doesn't quite come out the way you had imagined. So as silly as it might make you feel, you need to practise out loud. I practise in front of a mirror so I can see if I'm looking down at my notes all the time, or if I'm engaging with the audience. It is also a good idea to practise in front of a colleague – they can give you feedback, and you get experience of presenting in front of someone. Go and see the room you are training in, and practise in it if you can.
- *Practise your demonstrations and make sure your examples work:* As you begin training, it is best not to ask your audience for keywords as it can shake your confidence if you keep getting zero results. Typing in front of an audience is nerve-wracking, so don't worry if you make typing errors.
- *Anticipate:* Have you thought about worst case scenarios? It can be useful to write a 'what could go wrong check list' and come up with ideas about what

you will do if these situations occur. Before you go into a training session, check that the internet and databases are working. Keep an eye out for any scheduled maintenance of databases and websites you may be using.

Prepare for your audience

You can ensure you are prepared for your audience in a variety of ways:

- What do you know about the students and what can you find out beforehand? This is particularly important as training is most effective when it is relevant and timely, so where you can, tailor any examples to them. If you are training college or university students, try to create your training around their assignment, or try to be subject specific. Tailor your slides to them. Don't leave last year's date on the PowerPoint or click through five or six slides saying 'Oh, these don't apply to you.'
- Is it possible to include a knowledge or expectation check? If you ask people what they know already or what they are expecting from the course, you can adjust your training accordingly which can lead to higher levels of satisfaction.
- Always do a 'so what?' check. What are the benefits of the training not the features? This will help people see the relevance of your training.
- Make your presentation as audience friendly as possible. Ensure your PowerPoint (or other software) uses a variety of visual styles as this taps into your audience's different learning styles, for example: bullet points for mathematical intelligence; images for visual or artistic intelligence; and playing sounds or music (if appropriate) to help those with musical intelligence.
- Include the goals or outcomes of your training in your presentation. It helps to manage expectations. Check your training to ensure it matches the outcomes.
- Include a variety of exercises that appeal to different learning styles and help make the session more interesting and interactive. Can you do any hands-on activities? Could you include group discussion?
- Add reflection into your session. Getting people to reflect on what they have learnt is a useful tool to embed learning. It can even be added into your evaluation. Ask 'What will you take away?'
- Evaluation is essential. It will allow you to celebrate success if you have done well and to improve for next time. Some organizations use a peer review

system to improve training, where colleagues sit in on each other's sessions and give feedback. If your institution doesn't do this there is no reason why you can't set this up informally.

Further qualifications

If you enjoy teaching and training, you could think about taking formal training or studying for a qualification. This would give you a grounding in pedagogy, can help to make you more confident, and provide a better experience for your users. If you are working in an academic environment, obtaining a teaching qualification could be a great way to raise your profile with the academic staff: not only do they appreciate the value of a teaching qualification, you may also find that you are learning alongside new lecturers. This will give you the opportunity to learn more about the teachers at your institution, and to build personal ties.

You could undertake a formal qualification, such as the Postgraduate Certificate in Higher Education (PGCHE) or the Postgraduate Certificate in Further Education (PGCFE) in the UK, or a certificate from the National Board for Professional Teaching Standards (NBPTS) in the USA.

Formal qualifications can be expensive. Your workplace may contribute towards your fees, especially if teaching expertise is required by your role. If formal qualifications don't meet your needs, look out for training opportunities – these may include courses run by your professional organization, tailored specifically to the needs of the information professional as teacher. You can also learn a lot from the community and the available literature. The Librarians as Teachers Network (http://latnetwork.spruz.com) and Teacher Librarian journal (www.teacherlibrarian.com) are useful resources.

What is it actually like to train to teach while working as a librarian? Two librarians give us some insights in the case studies below.

💼 Case study
Postgraduate Certificate in Adult Learning and Professional Development

Teaching staff and students is a considerable part of Lynne Meehan's job as a subject librarian at University College London Library. She enjoys teaching, but had never had any formal training or knowledge of teaching theory. Encouraged by the actions of her peers on Twitter, and the establishment of the Librarians as Teachers Network, Lynne decided to study for a Postgraduate Certificate in Adult Learning and Professional Development, with the aim of enhancing her students' learning.

Lynne has found her peer networks to be a huge support, and has learned a lot from being around a group of people who are enthusiastic about teaching. She hopes she is raising awareness in the wider university environment of the amount of teaching carried out by librarians.

The course hasn't always been easy, but Lynne believes she is getting a benefit proportional to the effort she's putting in. She said, 'What I have learned on my course will stay with me throughout my professional life.'

    2   **Read Lynne's full story on the website (http://lisnewprofs.com/pgcalpd).**

Case study
Fellow of the Higher Education Academy

Edith Speller is Systems and User Education Librarian for the Jerwood Library of the Performing Arts at Trinity Laban Conservatoire of Music and Dance. There she helps staff and students make the most of the library's resources through training, marketing and managing effective systems. She has recently become a fellow of the Higher Education Academy (HEA), an independent UK organization which provides professional recognition to academics and others involved in teaching and learning support. The HEA provides support and advice to individuals and organizations, and organizes events and conferences to disseminate best practice. Edith tells us about her involvement with the HEA.

How has it benefited you in the workplace?

As a librarian who has taken a lead role in developing information skills classes for students and staff for several years, my institution agreed I was qualified to apply for fellowship status. My institution runs regular two-day seminars for staff applying for HEA recognition; these involve staff considering their work in each area of practice, then discussing their work in small groups and finally sharing their ideas and thoughts with the whole group, assisted by a facilitator. Attending such seminars gave me plenty of food for thought: as well as helping me to prepare my application, the discussions encouraged me to reflect on my current practice and compare it with work done by teaching staff across the institution. It also provided an opportunity to network with colleagues.

Being a fellow of the HEA demonstrates that I have a professional and reflective approach to teaching and am committed to improving and developing the library's information skills sessions in partnership with academics and using evidence gained from best practice elsewhere. Purely attending the in-house seminars (with another librarian) helped to raise our profile with academic colleagues, as not all of them were aware of the level of teaching and support provided by librarians. Becoming a fellow allows use of the postnominals FHEA (AHEA for associate membership). Using these in written communications with teaching staff is a small but effective way of enhancing the status of library staff in the institution. I believe that academic colleagues will become more aware of the teaching capabilities of library staff as more library staff achieve associate and fellowship status.

How has it benefited your personal and professional development?

Putting together my FHEA application has given me space to reflect on my practice, both when directly teaching students and providing individual support or supporting study generally as part of the library staff team. It has encouraged me to delve further into the literature on learning styles, supporting learning and varying teaching techniques and in the process has given me further ideas to improve the service we provide. Gathering positive feedback from referees and independent validation from the HEA itself is very valuable for boosting confidence and affirming good practice, and I would recommend HEA accreditation to all eligible library and information professionals.

Read Edith's full story on the website (http://lisnewprofs.com/fhea).

Getting your users involved with learning

Once you have started to get to grips with teaching and training, you might like to start thinking about innovative ways to get your users involved with learning. Games can be a very effective way to encourage learning while keeping users engaged – this can be particularly useful for dry subjects such as library inductions. One example of this is the pilot Lemon Tree Project at the University of Huddersfield, which allows users to earn points for interacting with library resources (www2.hud.ac.uk/tali/support/proj11_lemon.php).

But using games to engage your users can be tricky! Rosie Jones, Learning Commons Development Manager, John Rylands University Library, University of

Manchester, shares some of the challenges she faced when running an alternate reality game for learning.

📁 Case study
A brief introduction to alternate reality games and learning

Alternate reality games are an emerging game form, which combine a variety of media in the real world and online. They typically rely on viral marketing to promote them, which is often fundamental to the game play. A narrative is unfolded over time as players solve challenges and release more plotline. 'White space' is intentionally left within the game to allow players to incorporate content based on their responses to actions, analysis and speculation. It is not usually clear that alternate reality games are a game and so the narrative presents a fully realized world: any phone number, e-mail address or website mentioned actually works. The game takes place in real time and is usually not re-playable. Characters function like real people, not game pieces, respond authentically, and are controlled by real people, not by computer artificial intelligence.

The ARGOSI project

Alternate Reality Games for Orientation, Socialisation and Induction (ARGOSI; http://argosi.playthinklearn.net) was a Joint Information Systems Committee (JISC)-funded project that aimed to produce an integrated gaming environment for induction, while meeting serious learning outcomes, assisting in creating social networks, improving student confidence when navigating the campus and city and allowing students to actually have fun with induction. There was an overarching storyline, which allowed major challenges to be released at various regular plot points. Underneath this main storyline were customizable sub plots, which allowed the incorporation of learning outcome sets – in this case, Manchester Metropolitan University's InfoSkills Level 1 learning outcomes.

The main narrative for Viola Quest centred on the mystery of Viola Procter, a first year student who had a puzzle to solve. She set up a blog to do this, which was discovered by librarian Percy Root. Percy set up a website to help Viola in her quest and also to set some puzzles of his own. Percy's puzzles were the customizable sub plot of this main narrative, which offered a mechanism for delivering the library learning outcomes. The quest started when Viola discovered a strange letter in her grandma's attic. The letter talked about a great secret, which was hidden in a map, divided into six pieces and given to members of a secret society. With the letter she also found a map piece – this was used as the entry point to the game.

The challenges which scattered the storyline and sub plot occurred both online and offline. Although some could be completed individually, working as a group often made them easier and some required collaboration to be completed. The challenges had varying degrees of difficulty: it was felt that making all the challenges too easy or too difficult would put users off. The challenges offered a range of ways for the user to provide evidence of completion.

Measuring success and addressing non-use

Alternate reality games are typically niche, but those who become keen players tend to have high levels of engagement. This was certainly the case with those involved with ARGOSI: those students who played became extremely addicted, contributing to forums and competing to complete challenges first. However, take up of the game was low overall and only 5–10% of those who signed up became keen players. While this is fairly typical of an entertainment alternate reality game, it is an issue when persuading senior management that it is worth investing time and money in a game.

One of the factors that may have had an impact on take up was its promotion. In the ARGOSI project viral marketing was used to promote the game (which is typically how alternate reality games are marketed) but many students did not understand what to do with the initial promotional postcard. The postcard was one of the initial map pieces and simply promoted the web address for the game, providing no clear guidance on what the nature, purpose or benefits of the game were. It became clear that students needed better indicators of how it would help with their studies, especially as the game was launched at what was already a very busy time of the year for them: Freshers' Week, when students were already being bombarded with lots of new information. The game stood little chance of standing out among the other postcards and leaflets students were receiving.

The game struggled to make some of the drier library learning outcomes fun. Trying to make an awareness of referencing or knowledge of university services locations fun was extremely difficult at times. Targeting the challenges at the right level was also problematic: the easier puzzles were much more accessible but far too easy for some, the more challenging ones left many floundering. The challenges that involved offline work such as navigation of the city were seldom completed, which disappointed members of the project team, who believed this would get the students orientating themselves in the city. The time taken to support the game was also underestimated, the project team was extremely small and already very busy at time of launch.

Despite these issues, there is definitely exciting potential in using alternate reality games in education. They:

- allow users to learn in a gaming environment, providing challenges, context and purpose while motivating them with the mystery
- facilitate collaboration and support active learning
- are low-tech, but encourage users to engage with a range of technologies
- can support digital literacy
- use actual reality, which can enable things like orientation to a city, and links to organizations such as tourist information, major landmarks
- can offer wider student support, directly linked to subject curricula and assessment and cover a longer time frame
- could have a role to play in pre-entry and transition periods for new students.

Tips for new professionals wanting to get involved with games-based learning

- Find someone in your organization who is either already engaging or thinks creatively about learning and make yourself known to them. I met my project manager because she taught me a unit on educational gaming on the postgraduate certificate in academic practice.
- Get involved with the Games and Learning special interest group for the Association for Learning Technology (www.alt.ac.uk/get-involved/special-interest-groups/glsig). This group is interested in the design, use and evaluation of games in practice, and the academic study of games and player communities and their potential contributions to learning.
- Don't just look at education; look at games that engage you, work out what motivates you to play and think about how you can incorporate that into your teaching.
- Follow some of the keen bloggers in this area, in particular Dr Nicola Whitton (http://playthinklearn.net) and Alex Moseley (http://moerg.wordpress.com).

Rosie's case study has shown that it can be difficult to anticipate how and where your users will engage. While game-based learning can be an excellent added extra to appeal to certain sections of your audience, it won't engage everyone, and is best used as an extra channel rather than replacing traditional teaching.

One of the advantages to game-based learning is that it forces you to re-assess how your users learn, and think about how you can teach them in innovative and inspiring ways. You might decide to incorporate aspects of game-based learning in your teaching and training – perhaps have small, in-class games that can reinforce the key points of a training session or presentation.

There is one group who will always welcome the inclusion of games: children. Working with a young audience will require many of the same skills as an adult audience, but applied in slightly different ways. Would you find a group of toddlers to be your most challenging audience yet? Would you believe they can also be your most rewarding? Linsey Chrisman, Children's and Youth Librarian at the London Borough of Barnet, tells us how and why to successfully work with children.

📁 Case study
Rhymetime for everyone!

In the past decade one of the areas where public libraries have been most successful is in providing services for children, particularly those under age five. Issues of children's books have increased despite the decline in adult book issues, and events for under-fives are bringing lots of people into libraries. Although many library authorities have now diversified their offerings, it all started with Rhymetime (sometimes also called Bounce and Rhyme or Baby Bounce), which started to appear in the UK in the 1990s and has proved so popular that it is now difficult to find a British public library branch that does not hold Rhymetime sessions.

Everybody does it a bit differently, but essentially Rhymetime is about parents and carers singing nursery rhymes accompanied with motions with their babies on their laps. For example, when we sing 'Head, shoulders, knees and toes', parents touch their babies' head, shoulders, knees and toes. This makes it a multi-sensory experience, and more engaging for babies. Most sessions last half an hour, and are led by a library staff member.

Before I started working in public libraries, I would not have guessed that this was a public service that people were crying out for. But people love Rhymetime. At my branch, customers regularly queue outside the door before opening time to get in, and we frequently have to turn some away from full sessions. It is simple, social, and babies love it.

There is a big difference developmentally between babies, toddlers and older pre-school children of age four or five. Many public libraries now cater for these differences by offering different sessions for different age groups. Toddlers want to be active rather than sitting in a lap, and can develop their motor skills by doing motions themselves, like marching to 'The grand old Duke of York'. Choose rhymes with big motions so that toddlers can 'get their wiggles out'. Toddlers can also listen to short, simple, interactive stories. Choose ones where they can join in with animal noises, actions or a repetitive phrase.

In sessions for four or five year olds, you can make things like collages and masks, read and act out stories and predict what is going to happen next, and tell rhymes. The Early Years Foundation Stage, the Department for Education's curriculum for children under five, emphasizes the importance of child-led activities. Rather than activities being prescribed by adults, children should be given opportunities to be creative, and play in ways that are meaningful to them. For example, instead of giving children a colouring in sheet, you could provide Play-Doh and invite them to make whatever they wanted in response to a story. It is acceptable for some activities to be more directed, but there should be a balance.

Why do we do it?

Singing nursery rhymes with children promotes the development of language. Hearing rhyming sounds helps babies to develop an awareness of which sounds are alike and which are different. Interaction with carers is also key to babies' development, and Rhymetime encourages this and provides a clear model for it. When parents learn the rhymes and motions, they can repeat them at home as well and continue the learning experience.

The social aspect of events helps prevent parents from feeling isolated at what can be a difficult time, and build connections with other families. They are an excellent opportunity to bring people into libraries who haven't been inside one since they were children, or have never used them. Popular events are an opportunity to foster a 'library habit' in families, and grow the library users of tomorrow.

Children's events are one of the only occasions in public libraries where you have a relatively large group of users listening to you at the same time. They are an invaluable opportunity to promote library events and services, membership, borrowing and information resources relevant to young families. If people hear relevant information from the session leader, it promotes the library as a good source of information and encourages them to use the library fully. Just don't try to promote everything in the same session – one brief message at the beginning and one at the end is enough, otherwise people will get restless and switch off.

Although at first glance the hokey cokey may seem far removed from the skills of an information professional, when you lead a session like Rhymetime you are facilitating learning, promoting reading, marketing services and connecting people with relevant information sources.

Practical tips

The logistical side of events requires planning and attention. Think about where you will ask parents to put buggies and how you will arrange chairs or cushions. Announce where the nearest fire exit is, and ensure that the route is clear of obstructions.

If you have well attended sessions for under-fives in your library, it should not be the responsibility of one member of staff to manage them. Another member of staff (or two) should be on hand to direct buggy parking, answer queries, and if necessary tell people when the session is full. Have a maximum number of attendees in mind, depending on your space. Overcrowded sessions can pose a health and safety risk and are generally no fun for anyone involved.

If you can, use a large puppet or doll on your lap to model the actions that go with the rhymes. This makes it easier for parents to see how to do the actions and involve their babies. Keep up the pace – gaps between rhymes will encourage chatting. If adults are chatting during the rhymes, make eye contact and remind them that their babies love to hear their voices. Smile a lot, and tell everyone how pleased you are to see them at the library.

It is perfectly alright for events for the youngest children (babies and toddlers) to be substantially the same from week to week, and nice to introduce a new rhyme, or sing seasonal rhymes occasionally. But young children love repetition and it helps them learn, so you shouldn't change things too frequently. It is a good idea for the opening rhyme and the closing rhyme to remain the same every week.

To involve books in Rhymetime, you can have a 'book break' for five minutes in the middle where you walk round with a crate of board books and everyone chooses a book. This will encourage parents to share books with their babies and borrow as well.

Help! I can't sing or entertain people

Rhymetime, and all services for under-fives, are not about singing. Nobody cares if you have a terrible singing voice, and neither should you. People are not there to hear you sing, they're there to sing to and play with their babies, to participate in a fun, communal experience, and to meet other families.

It is also not about performing. Sessions are meant to be fun and engaging, but you are not a children's entertainer. You are there to facilitate parents interacting with their children and promote literacy, language skills and the library. Don't worry about making mistakes; these sessions are just an opportunity to have a laugh with the parents.

Finally, I have genuinely never done a session for under-fives and not felt happier afterwards than I did beforehand. Singing and moving as a group is a great mood lifter. Don't miss a chance to get involved.

Resources

The website www.booktrust.org.uk/events/bookstart-rhymetimes has good, detailed training resources on Rhymetime, including rhyme lists and lyrics. The Booktrust website (www.booktrust.org.uk) is also a good source of book reviews.

To watch Rhymetime videos, search 'Nii Parkes bookstart' on YouTube.

For planning events for three and four year olds, the series 'Little Books with Big Ideas' edited by Sally Featherstone and published by Featherstone Education is a great resource. Each book is on a different topic, for example messy play or mark-making, and they are full of practical ideas.

Presenting to professional peers

Presenting to professional peers requires slightly different strategies from teaching or training users. Your peers are more likely to be familiar with the principles behind your work, and may already have strong views on your subject matter. Don't let this worry you – they're also more likely to be engaged and willing to listen than a group of overloaded freshers at an induction! Don't worry about questions, either – the old librarian adage 'I don't know – but I'll find out!' applies here, as well as at the reference desk.

Many information professionals are excellent presenters, informing, engaging and amusing their audience. How do you produce a presentation that will stand out from the crowd? Bronagh McCrudden was voted winner of the best paper for her presentation at the 2010 New Professionals Conference, organized by the Career Development Group of the Chartered Institute of Library and Information Professionals (CILIP).

✎ How to . . .
Make your first presentation a winning one

The challenge

As a newly qualified professional, I remember feeling that the library profession was a rigidly hierarchical world. In a job that offered me little room for development, I found it difficult to find ways to progress my career. I submitted a proposal for the New Professionals Conference 2010 because it offered me an opportunity to gain skills and find my voice as a new professional. With my limited experience, however, I struggled with the question of how to get a proposal accepted, and (subsequently) write a paper that would generate interest.

The solutions

These were my solutions:

- *Writing what I knew:* I realized that my perspective is my unique selling point. Although I had little professional experience when I wrote my paper, I did know about volunteering (I had done my fair share of it) and had noticed that, with the rise of the Conservative Party's Big Society idea, volunteering in libraries was becoming a hot topic in the UK. I decided to write my proposal about unpaid work in the information profession.
- *Writing on the edge of my topic:* Though initially I struggled to find a topic that no one had explored before, I discovered I didn't need to: by thinking of a popular idea (for example volunteering in libraries) and connecting it to other interesting ideas (in my case, feminism, 'grindhopping' and labour relations), I was able to create something unique. I created surprise and entertainment in that intersection of my topic and the seemingly unrelated ideas.

- *Writing like a copywriter:* I wrote my title first. I see the title as being the writer's promise to the audience; its job is to communicate the benefit that will be delivered to the members of the audience in exchange for their time. This is how I linked my title to the theme of the New Professionals Conference, 'Proving Your Worth in Challenging Times', and crafted it to spark interest. My title was 'Would you Work for Free? Unpaid Work and How to Make it Count'. In the first part of my title, 'Would you Work for Free?', I proposed a challenge and asked a question with which I hoped new professionals could empathize. I also chose to be deliberately provocative by using the words 'work for free' rather than 'volunteer'. In the second part of my title, 'Unpaid Work and How to Make it Count', I suggested I had a practical solution by using 'how to'; and I related the title back to the theme of worth, money and value through the words 'make it count'. After creating a hook with my title, I worked carefully on structuring the presentation so the audience would want to hear the first point of the presentation, then the next, and the next.
- *Writing like a screenwriter:* Storytelling is a good way of capturing attention. I decided to use stories as the basis of my presentation, and gathered them by conducting interviews with volunteering librarians. I read widely about issues surrounding volunteering in libraries. As I wrote my paper, I also crafted an idea of what I wanted my presentation to look like. My view is that you should work on the slides and narrative together, allowing one to feed into the other. Creative Commons on Flickr provided a goldmine of images that gave my slides a distinctive and consistent look (I used vintage advertising).
- *Finding my voice and preparing it:* To brush up on my breath control, projection and improvisation, I attended a course in verbal communication at a local arts centre in the weeks in the run up to the conference. I read blogs and books on public speaking. As the time for my presentation drew closer, it wasn't possible to quell the sense of panic rising in me. However, I feel the verbal communication classes helped me to realize a 'style' and boost my confidence. My nerves were also controlled by belief in my material. There is a school of thought that if you know your talk too well, it can end up sounding dead. However, lots of practice helped me to own my talk, giving me more control over how the audience would respond to it.

Once my conference proposal had been accepted, I believe the key to my success with this presentation lay in lots of research, practice, a bit of self-talk – and ultimately having the chutzpah to execute my idea boldly.

The benefits

Presenting was challenging and time-consuming, but highly rewarding. A number of opportunities have opened up to me since then. And I have a new found sense of confidence in voicing my opinions about professional matters.

Bronagh's presentation was indeed effective, and you can see her slides and script online at http://tinyurl.com/mccrudden.

Posting your slides and script online can be very useful – it can allow users to pursue points (especially if you have links or references on your slides), refer to and quote your presentation, and open it up to a wider audience than the event attendees.

Writing

Of course, communicating isn't all about face-to-face communication and presenting. You will also need to communicate in writing. This might take the form of:

- reports from projects or events
- reviews of resources
- results of research
- newsletters
- blog posts
- how-to training guides.

The same principles apply as for verbal communication: know your audience, and tailor your communication to them. In Chapter 3 we will look in more detail at how to choose the most appropriate method for communicating with your stakeholders.

Many people find it difficult to start writing. Staring at a blank piece of paper or document is almost guaranteed to produce a mental block, and many people feel pressured to produce something great straight away. One way to deal with this is the concept of 'draft zero' – a draft that only you see, and which can be very rough. The main aim is to get over the psychological block by simply getting some words on paper. Once this is done, you should then find it easier to refine and redraft your writing.

As well as writing that you have to undertake for work, you might want to consider writing for the professional press. This is a great way to communicate to a wide audience. It is also good experience, promotes you and your service, and looks great on your CV. But how do you do it? Here is Jo Alcock, an evidence-based researcher at Evidence Base, Birmingham City University, and ALA Emerging Leader, with some tips.

✦ How to . . .
Write for publication

Why should I publish?

Writing for publication is a very rewarding process – not only does it give you a sense of pride, but it also enables you to share your views, knowledge or experiences more widely than you would ordinarily be able to. Many people start writing as part of their professional development, and any items you have published are valuable pieces of evidence for a professional development portfolio.

Where do I start?

You might already have some ideas of what you would like to write about, in which case you will need to start looking for places to publish. If you don't yet have an idea of a topic, have a look at some of the recent issues in publications and the biblioblogosphere (library blogs) to see if anything inspires you. Maybe you have an interest outside the profession – is there any way you could bring your knowledge from that into your writing?

Either way, my advice is to start writing a blog. It doesn't have to be a public blog (although there are many advantages to this and I would strongly recommend it to open up opportunities to publish), but just getting into the habit of writing about professional issues is a useful start. Write about what you are passionate about – your passion will show in your writing and make it far more compelling.

What types of publication can I write for?

Once you have your topic, think about the type of publication you want to write for – this will affect the style and format of your writing. Do you want to publish an article in a newsletter reporting on an event you attended? Do you want to write a practical article to share something you have been working on? Do you want to write a peer reviewed article in an academic journal? These will each involve a very different writing process so it's good to decide this early on.

There are certain publications that welcome contributions from new professionals. In the UK these include your regional CILIP newsletter, your regional CILIP career development newsletter, and the national career development publication, Impact. For American Library Association (ALA) members there is the newsletter Footnotes for the New Members' Round Table.

Don't let that limit you though – there is no reason you can't publish in any LIS publication (or further afield).

How do I find opportunities to get published?

Sometimes journals have special issues based on a certain subject. Look out for these which are often announced on mailing lists or to special interest groups.

Sometimes opportunities arise from previous activities – if you wrote a blog post or presented about a topic, an editor might contact you to see if you would be interested in publishing on this topic, or a potential collaborator may get in touch asking if you would like to contribute to a joint publication.

How do I decide which publication to submit to?

The best advice I received about choosing where to submit to was to consider the ones you read yourself. Why do you choose to read them? Is it because the style of writing and the topics interest you most? They are likely to be the ones that will be most interested in your writing too!

Have a look at the publication's website – many have guidance for authors. This will give an idea of the topics considered for publication, the format and style of submission and the recommended length. Read the guidance offered, and if you are unsure whether or not your paper would be suitable, contact the editor to discuss it.

Conclusion

All of the case studies in this chapter have a common message: to communicate effectively, you must know your audience. You need to find out what is important to them, and express your message in language that will resonate with their value terms. You will need to take the different needs of various sectors of your audience into account, too – do they have preferred communication methods? Different learning styles?

You also need to assess the impact of your communications – whether by feedback sheets from a training session, comments on a blog post, citations of an article you have written, or tweets from the audience in your presentation. Once you have measured your success, make sure you do something with the knowledge! There are always improvements you can make.

In the next two chapters we will look in more detail at how to identify your stakeholders and their priorities, and get your messages across successfully. We'll also think about some ways to measure success and assess your impact.

References and further reading

Communicating

Rauch, J. (2003) Caring for your introvert, *Atlantic Magazine* (March), www.theatlantic.com/magazine/archive/2003/03/caring-for-your-introvert/2696.

Sheldrick Ross, C. and Dewdney, P. (1998) *Communicating Professionally*, 2nd edn, Neal-Schuman.

Zack, D. (2010) *Networking for People Who Hate Networking: a field guide for introverts, the overwhelmed, and the underconnected*, Berrett-Koehler.

Teaching and training

Bewick, L. and Corrall, S. (2010) Developing Librarians as Teachers: a study of their pedagogical knowledge, *Journal of Librarianship and Information Science*, **42**, 97–110, http://lis.sagepub.com/content/42/2/97.abstract.

Carnevale, R. and Chambers, C. et al. (2006) Rock & Rhyme: development and implementation of an early childhood development program at the state library of Tasmania, *ALIA New Librarians' Symposium*, Sydney, http://conferences.alia.org.au/newlibrarian2006/programme_files/carnevale_chambers_zylstra_paper.pdf.

Cragg, E. (2011) Ideas for Library Inductions, *Digitalist*, www.digitalist.info/2011/06/17/ideas-for-library-inductions.

Gustavson, A., Hisle, D. and Whitehurst, A. (2011) Laying the Information Literacy Foundation: a multiple-media solution, *Library Hi-Tech*, **29** (4).

Hogan, K. (2011) Training One-on-one at Cassels Brock, ILTA KM, the International Legal Technology Association knowledge management blog, http://km.iltanet.org/2011/06/15/training-one-on-one-at-cassels-brock.

Paul, L. (2006) Librarian as Lecturer: how information literacy is paving the way for librarians to be integrated into student's learning with advantages for both the student and your career, *ALIA New Librarians' Symposium*, Sydney, http://conferences.alia.org.au/newlibrarian2006/programme_files/paul_paper.pdf.

Potter, N. (2011) Student Induction, Libraries, Prezi, and Interactive Maps, The Wikiman, blog, http://thewikiman.org/blog/?p=1796.

Presenting

Bradley, P. (2010) Giving a Talk in Public?, Phil Bradley's weblog, http://philbradley.typepad.com/phil_bradleys_weblog/2010/07/giving-a-talk-in-public.html.

Ruddock, B. (2011) Presenting, Bethan's information professional blog, http://bethaninfoprof.wordpress.com/2011/05/16/presenting.

Yelton, A. (2011) Three More Things I Know About Public Speaking, Across Divided Networks, http://andromedayelton.com/2011/11/three-more-things-i-know-about-public-speaking.

Yelton, A. (2011) The Two Most Important Things I Know About Public Speaking, Across Divided Networks, http://andromedayelton.com/2011/10/the-two-most-important-things-i-know-about-public-speaking.

Writing

Arnopp, J. (2011) The Magic of Draft Zero, Int. Jason Arnott's Brain – Day/Night, http://jasonarnopp.blogspot.com/2011/08/magic-of-draft-zero.html?m=1.

Brewerton, A. (2010) Writing for the Professional Press: skills for today's information professional, *SCONUL Focus*, **50**, 37–42, www.sconul.ac.uk/publications/newsletter/50/12.pdf.

Gordon, R. S. (2004) *The Librarian's Guide to Writing for Publication*, Scarecrow Press.

LIS Publications Wiki, http://slisapps.sjsu.edu/wikis/faculty/putnam/index.php/Main_Page.

This wiki gathers information about publications that LIS professionals might want to write for – whether they want to reach their colleagues or their communities.

StEvelin (2011) Lose 500 Words Instantly!, Succentorship Without Sneers, http://saintevelin.blogspot.com/2011/10/lose-500-words-instantly.html.

Woods, L. (2009) WPB: words per brew, Organising Chaos, http://woodsiegirl.wordpress.com/2009/05/23/wpb-words-per-brew.

➡ Over to you . . .

Think about a situation where you have to do some training or communicating. Consider:

- Who are your audience? What do they know and care about?
- What are you trying to communicate to them? What is your key message?
- Can you include elements to cater to different learning styles?
- How can you follow up – get feedback and assess the impact of the communication or training?

Write a short plan for your training or communication (around 400 words), including audience characteristics, desired learning or communication outcomes, proposed communication methods (and why), and follow-up or impact measurement.

After delivering the training or communication, look at your plan again. Did you follow your plan? Did it help you communicate more effectively?

CHAPTER 3

Meeting your users' needs and measuring success

Introduction

Meeting users' needs has always been central to the library and information profession. It is no coincidence that user needs are at the heart of one of the LIS community's unofficial mottoes, Ranganathan's (1931) five laws of library science:

1 Books are for use.
2 Every reader his book.
3 Every book its reader.
4 Save the time of the reader.
5 The library is a growing organism.

They have stayed at the heart of every reimagining and reinterpretation since. 'Books' may have been replaced with 'media' or 'information' and 'reader' with 'user', but the key principles of connecting the user with the right information, in the right way, and at the right time have remained.

While the format of information has definitely changed, the principles behind its provision haven't. You can think of good information provision as being like providing a well balanced meal. It must look appetising (be presentable), be delivered when the user is hungry (be timely), taste good (meet users' wants) and be nutritionally balanced (meet users' needs).

One of the big challenges for information professionals is to distinguish between users' wants and users' needs. We all know that half of the art of a good reference interview is to get past what users think they want to what they actually need. Unfortunately, not all interactions and services come with a chance to talk in detail to your users about their wants and needs. So how do you find out whether you are providing the services your users really need?

One of the first things to do is to find out who your users are. How easily you can do this will depend on your organization – a firm's internal law library will probably have a much better defined user group than a public library, for instance. But no matter how well you think you know your users, it is always worth an occasional stakeholder scan. You might find users and non-users in unexpected places (see Chapter 4 for more about working with stakeholders).

To communicate effectively with your users you need to understand them, their culture and their vocabulary. Understand the words they use and how they use them – you might already be doing something they say they want; you are just not telling them about it in the right way. We covered the general need for and principles of effective communication in Chapter 2. Now Amy Affelt, Director of Database Research at Compass Lexecon and Chair of the SLA Public Relations Advisory Council, tells us how the Special Libraries Association (SLA) has been helping members develop themselves and communicate effectively with their stakeholders.

📁 Case study
The Alignment Project of the Special Libraries Association

The industry landscape for information professionals has changed dramatically since the founding of the SLA in 1909. The evolution of the Internet and the discovery of revolutionary new technologies have created significant challenges for individuals working in information provider roles in organizations. The SLA seized the opportunity to assist its members in this new environment by commissioning the Alignment Project (www.sla.org/content/SLA/alignment/portal/index.html) to determine how information professionals could best hone their skill sets to align with their employing organization's overall goals, missions and strategies.

Aims

The SLA Alignment Project sought to help information professionals answer questions such as:

- What is the future role of the information professional in the workplace?
- How can information professionals align their skills, knowledge and expertise

with the goals of employers?
- How can information professionals best communicate the value of their work and the impact that they have on their organizations?

The project focused on identifying tactics that can be used to align strategically with organization strategy, including:

- developing vocabulary to explain what information professionals do and the variety of services they can offer
- quantifying the deliverables, value and intelligence they provide
- cultivating the unique skill set and specialized knowledge that are hallmarks of the information profession.

Method

SLA contracted consulting firms Fleishman-Hilliard and Outsell Inc. to collect extensive data from a range of corporate executives in information-intensive organizations. Their views, attitudes and key priorities for information services were compiled using surveys, interviews and 'dial testing' focus groups (sessions in which participants turn a dial to indicate a reaction to a statement or concept). The data were then used to develop a framework within which information professionals can deliver strategic results that positively affect their organization's bottom line.

Future Ready

When Cindy Romaine became SLA President in 2011, she set a theme for the year: 'Future Ready'. She described Future Ready as an attitude – one of being adaptable, flexible and confident in displaying the key skills that employers need, as determined by the SLA Alignment Project. Future Ready is a strategic shift toward adding value to the information product to surprise and delight users and stakeholders.

Whether a new LIS graduate seeking a first professional position, or a seasoned practitioner hoping to keep their current job or find a new one, it is imperative that information professionals apply the findings of the SLA Alignment Project research to not only their everyday work but also their careers as a whole.

But how to do this? It was out of that question that the SLA Future Ready Toolkit was born. The Toolkit took the rich data gleaned from the Alignment Project and translated it into real value-added tools that could be used by SLA members.

The Future Ready Toolkit is 'alignment in action' – a set of ready-to-use tools and tried and true best practices that translate the alignment research into tangible tips and advice that can be implemented immediately. It addresses each point uncovered by the alignment research by analysing the challenge presented and then offers a toolkit solution that explains how information professionals can turn that challenge into an opportunity using their innate expertise. What follows is a discussion of a few of the most important tools in the SLA Future Ready Toolkit.

The Toolkit
Tool 1 Dictionary of future ready terms

Sometimes, when conversing with stakeholders information professionals inadvertently construct barriers between themselves and those who can benefit from their services, by failing to speak a common language. The SLA Alignment Project determined that certain 'Future Ready terms' resonated well with senior leaders in organizations. The Dictionary of Future Ready Terms defines a key vocabulary that information professionals can use when describing what they do and its importance to their organizations. For example, 'knowledge', 'intelligence', 'value' and 'analysis' resonated well with C-suite level executives (chief executive officers, chief information officers, chief financial officers and so on) in organizations. The Dictionary of Future Ready Terms incorporates these words into descriptive phrases, which can be used when writing job descriptions or explanations of the roles of information professionals in organizations.

Tool 2 Examples of value-added deliverables

Cindy Shamel, author of this tool, describes value-added deliverables as 'delivering a meal ready to eat as opposed to a grocery sack full of ingredients'. The Alignment Project determined that users look to information professionals to save them time and money by analysing the information found and delivering the most relevant, on-point information, at the point of need and in the format most desired. This tool explains the differences between information and knowledge and offers downloadable and customizable templates for creating value-added reports.

Tool 3 Writing a mission and vision statement

Management guru Peter Drucker advocated that to be effective, an organizational mission statement must be short enough to fit on a t-shirt, but must define the organization's or work group's contributions to its overarching goals. The Alignment Project determined that stakeholders look to information professionals for three mission-critical contributions:

- unique knowledge regarding available information sources and how they can best be used in each organization's unique setting
- assurance that the organization's information professionals are aware of the newest and truest sources of information and are making that information available to the organization
- best practices in the most efficient use of information resources.

The mission and vision tool helps information professionals write mission statements that identify how these contributions will be made to best serve the organization's needs. It features a list of questions for practitioners when brainstorming to help focus on how these contributions will be made. It is unique as it focuses on keeping missions and visions broad enough for future tweaking in the ever evolving information landscape.

Tool 4 Marketing and branding

The marketing and branding tool helps users create marketing materials that reflect the language and priorities of stakeholders, as determined by the alignment project research. Relevance, timeliness and accuracy of information were seen as much more important than the format and packaging. Therefore, the marketing and branding tool focuses on ways to emphasize the product rather than the research process that produced it. Content of information and how it can meet intelligence needs were seen as most important; this tool emphasizes promoting uniqueness of content as well as reinforcing one's identity and building awareness of how the information centre can make life easier for its users.

Finally, in addition to all of the qualities identified by the alignment research, two of the most important skills that information professionals need to face the challenges of the 21st-century workplace are listening and curiosity. If information professionals are curious enough to ask users about their work, and they listen carefully enough to understand stakeholders' pain points, they will be able to create information work products that exactly meet the needs of these stakeholders.

Evaluating users' needs

Amy has given us some useful tools to help align ourselves with users' needs, and talk to them using the right vocabulary (we'll come back to vocabulary and value terms in Chapter 4). But no matter how much you align yourself, you still need to ask your users what they need, and measure the extent to which you are successful in providing them with this. You won't get anywhere by providing the services you think your users need.

You might find it useful to get into the mindset of constant evaluation. At the Online Information Conference 2010, Mary Ellen Bates suggested making feedback a part of your work cycle – solicit feedback at the point of delivery, and don't consider a project complete until you have received (and acted on!) feedback. Get your users into the habit of talking to you, and they are more likely to be open about what they need, and whether you are delivering it.

When thinking about measuring your success, you need to consider what you are actually trying to measure. Is it use of the service as a whole or of a set of resources? Satisfaction with the service? The extent to which the service meets users' needs and expectations? Impact on the user? Value for money or return on investment?

David Streatfield of Information Management Associates introduces us to the principles of evaluating the impact of your services, and how this might differ from traditional performance measurement.

✔ How to . . .
Evaluate the impact of your library

One thing we can be sure of is that library and information work will evolve and change over the coming years as we confront new economic challenges and respond to fresh opportunities offered by advances in information and communications technologies (ICTs). The advent of 'new managerialism' in the public sector, with its heavy emphasis on accountability and target setting, combined with advances in ICT applications resulting in library service innovation, has already led library service managers to start looking beyond the monitoring of service efficiency to assess how changes in service delivery are affecting users. Traditional service efficiency performance measurement based on 'busy-ness' statistics has served libraries of all kinds well in the past, but most library service managers are now faced with the challenge of showing how effective their services are from a user perspective, both to enhance those services and as part of the strategy for long-term survival.

But why should new professionals be concerned about impact evaluation? Becoming an effective professional is fundamentally about learning from experience and developing practice as situations change. Focusing on the effects of what you are doing on the people for whom you are providing services should give you the basis for modifying and enhancing your practice. Libraries of all kinds are at an interesting stage in disentangling their approaches to evaluation; there is a growing body of good practice in the LIS field but few firmly established approaches. This offers an ideal opportunity for young and keen professionals to combine personal, professional and organizational development by getting involved in evaluating service impact.

To clarify terms used here, we define impact as 'any effect of the service (or of an event or initiative) on an individual or group'. This effect may be positive or negative, intended or accidental, and may affect users, LIS staff and senior managers (or other people). We are looking for changes in people brought about by developments in the service.

Impact evaluation requires a shift in perception and a change in practice. Until recently, most library service development plans were essentially activity plans, based on continuation or expansion of existing services and occasionally making a new departure in service provision. Traditional performance indicators and targets worked well in this context, with process indicators ensuring that the stipulated activities were undertaken and output indicators measuring the level of service use. Impact evaluation requires a more strategic focus on effectiveness, combined with a wider repertoire of evidence-gathering methods. If we want to know how our services are affecting and changing service users, we need to ask why we are providing these services – what are our objectives in deploying resources in a particular way? For this reason, our impact evaluation workshops encourage participants to generate specific and time-limited objectives (usually, what can be achieved within one, two or three years) for each key element of service provision to users. If we are not clear about what we are trying to achieve by providing a specific service, how can we tell whether we are succeeding?

The next step in the process is to decide what will tell us whether each objective is being met or not – to decide which impact indicators we want to use. Since our focus is on change, it is likely that each indicator will illuminate part of this picture, such as change in:

- behaviour (doing things differently)
- competence (doing things better)
- levels of knowledge

- attitudes (for example confidence of users when engaging with information; the view of LIS staff held by others).

Once we have decided on our performance indicators, the challenge is to collect evidence by using appropriate methods, which are usually variations on observing, asking questions through surveys (including e-surveys), structured interviews or focus groups, case studies and stories about the effects of using the library services on people's lives, or inferring that change has happened by looking at the output from activities (such as student references in assignments after a library session on citation). This is the other main area of reorientation for library service managers. How do we persuade staff that collecting social science research evidence is appropriate? And how can we convince senior managers or politicians that impact evidence provides a better picture of the effects of library services than the regular aggregation of statistics which they are probably accustomed to receive? This is where impact evaluation takes on an educational role. It is important to ensure that reporting the results of impact evaluation should focus on the key findings and proposals for action. Impact evaluation requires substantial work in designing the process, agreeing objectives, choosing impact indicators and especially gathering the evidence. The temptation is to report all this work to show how much you have done. This temptation should be strongly resisted! Senior managers and politicians will not be impressed by quantity.

The relationship between traditional performance measurement and impact evaluation and the key steps in addressing both forms of evaluation are shown in Figure 3.1.

This contribution is not an argument against traditional performance measurement – if the data are chosen well they will tell us whether the service is performing efficiently. Impact evaluation is an addition to the evaluation repertoire, which (if the impact indicators are well chosen to test whether the objectives are being met) should tell the new

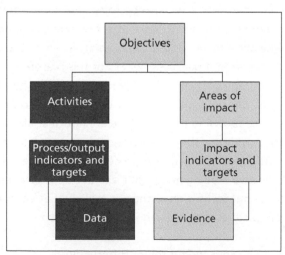

Figure 3.1 *The relationship between traditional performance measurement and impact evaluation*

professional and the service management team whether the service is being effective in helping to change peoples' lives (changing people's lives is the focus of the Global Libraries Initiative of the Bill and Melinda Gates Foundation, which is making public access ICT available through public libraries in a number of countries). It should also help the new professional to reassess professional practice continually and review potential areas for service development.

As David mentions, impact measurement may require a mixture of tools and methods to be effective and persuasive. You might answer questions about use with quantitative data; other questions will require either qualitative data, or a mixture of quantitative and qualitative data. A mixed approach allows you to combine the hard quantitative data (which can be expressed as charts, infographics and so on) with the soft qualitative data, which can be richer, and expressed as narrative.

There are a number of tools you can use for researching user needs and satisfaction, including generic research tools such as surveys and LIS-specific implementations of these tools.

Encouraging user participation

To find out what your users think, you need to encourage them to participate in your information gathering. This becomes easier if, rather than just asking for their time and input, you make it clear how they are going to benefit from taking part. I've classed these benefits and rewards into three categories: tangible, intellectual and future or deferred:

- *Tangible benefits:* A tangible reward is one which the user can immediately benefit from. This might be a voucher or entry to a prize draw on completing a survey, or coffee and biscuits for attending a focus group. You could offer institution-specific incentives, such as a fine waiver or a free use of a paid-for service (DVD loan, inter-library loan). Remember to tailor your reward to your target audience – for instance, free photocopying or printing is more likely to appeal to students than to institution or company staff. A tangible reward is likely to have the most immediate impact on user participation levels, and will probably appeal to a wide cross-section of users.
- *Intellectual benefits:* An intellectual benefit is where the user gains knowledge or satisfaction from taking part in the evaluation. A possible

scenario for this is participation in focus groups or trials, where the users are among the first to try and give their opinion on a new system. The user might feel valued because their opinion has been asked, be interested to hear the thoughts of others, or be genuinely interested in the research or outcomes for their own sake. This type of benefit is more likely to motivate those who are highly interested in the service to begin with – frequent users and user-advocates.

- *Future benefits:* A deferred benefit, which can be tangible or intellectual. This could be improved resources for the user, or a new library service from which they will benefit. It is important to make this future benefit clear; for instance, if a survey about which e-reader users favour is intended to inform the library's decision to support that e-reader, or purchase some for in-library use, make this clear to the users. A future tangible benefit is likely to be less appealing than an immediate tangible benefit, but probably more appealing than any kind of intellectual benefit. A future intellectual benefit will appeal only to the most dedicated.

These benefits should be clear to users at the point at which you ask them to take part in your assessment. Lay them out clearly: don't expect users to infer what the benefits will be, especially if they are future or intellectual. Try to be specific – saying 'this survey will help us decide whether to open at weekends' is much more persuasive than 'this survey will help inform the future of the service'.

Tools

Surveys

Surveys are perhaps the most commonly used method of data collection. They are a great way to collect quantitative data, and can also be used to collect qualitative data, but one of the drawbacks of surveys is due to their popularity: survey fatigue. Users may encounter surveys several times a day. Local government websites in the UK, for instance, will often ask you to complete a survey every time you access the site. The average person may encounter several requests to complete a survey per day, which makes them much less likely to complete your survey.

There are a number of factors which are likely to make a person even less inclined to respond to your survey:

- lack of tangible benefit or reward
- poor survey design
- poor survey distribution.

Keep in mind the vocabulary your users use and value. Phrasing your questions using this vocabulary will help ensure that users answer the questions you think you are asking.

Even a purely quantitative survey should have space for users to comment. This can help to bring out opinions and motives, and provides a blank canvas for users to mention their thoughts on the service in general. You may find you get comments that are entirely unrelated to the actual content of the survey, but which nevertheless provide important feedback. A comment space also gives users the opportunity to tell you if your survey design is broken, questions irrelevant, terminology not fully explained – all of which will help you design better surveys in the future.

LIS-specific tools

The SCONUL Satisfaction Survey

The UK-based Society of College, National and University Libraries (SCONUL) provides a number of assessment templates. These are usually available to members only, but guest access may be granted to others.

The SCONUL Satisfaction Survey (http://vamp.diglib.shrivenham. cranfield.ac.uk/performance/quality/sconul-satisfaction-survey) is designed to measure the satisfaction levels of service users, and cover five key sectors: demographics, activity, satisfaction with key services and facilities, the importance of key services and facilities, and overall satisfaction levels (SCONUL, 2011a).

Last updated in 2005, there are two possible surveys – one for converged services (where the library service forms a single department with another service, most often IT) and one for more traditional single services.

SCONUL Annual Library Statistics

These statistics have been collected from members since 1987, and a report is produced annually based on the findings. Previous reports are available only to members (or for purchase), but the questions are open to browse with a demo account (SCONUL, 2011b). The questionnaire can be accessed at http://vamp.diglib.shrivenham.cranfield.ac.uk/statistics/sconul-statistical-questionnaire.

A number of libraries have shared their experiences of using SCONUL statistics. See http://vamp.diglib.shrivenham.cranfield.ac.uk/statistics/sconul-annual-library-statistics/experience.

In the USA, similar data are collected by the National Centre for Education Studies, http://nces.ed.gov/surveys/libraries/academic.asp bi-annually, and previous surveys are available for download from the website http://nces.ed.gov/surveys/libraries/aca_questdefs.asp. Data from these surveys are used to inform a comparison tool (http://nces.ed.gov/surveys/libraries/compare), which allows users to compare academic libraries on various criteria, including number of branch libraries, number of e-books held, and whether the library supports virtual reference services. You can also see detailed statistics for each library service.

LibQUAL+

LibQUAL+ is a web-based survey tool that boasts users from around the world: 2010 participants included the University of Western Australia, Bibliothèque nationale universitaire de Strasbourg, Royal College of Surgeons in Ireland and the European Parliament.

Run as part of the Association for Research Libraries Statistics and assessment Program, LibQUAL+ describes itself as '22 items and a box', with the 22 items measuring perceptions of Affect of Service, Information Control, and Library as Place, and 'the box' being for open-ended user comments. LibQUAL reports that 40% of users make comments in 'the box' (LibQUAL+, 2011). There is now also a 'lite' version, designed to encourage participation by reducing the number of questions answered by each respondent (http://libqual.org/about/about_lq/LQ_lite).

Participation in LibQUAL+ can be costly, with registration from $3200, and payable extras.

The National Archives self-assessment

The UK National Archives runs a self-assessment programme for local archive services. Started in 2007, the programme 'enables authorities to judge the adequacy of their archive service, measured against the public task of such services, as expressed in the Standard for Record Repositories and the

Framework of Standards' (Archives, 2010).

Results from the previous surveys and questionnaire and guidance notes for current assessment can be downloaded from the website www.nationalarchives.gov.uk/information-management/our-services/self-assessment-results.htm.

The assessment combines qualitative and quantitative data, to come up with a quantitative 'measurement' of the archive's performance in five key areas: governance and resources; documentation of collections; access, preservation and conservation; and buildings, security, and environment.

Figure 3.2 presents an example question and answer from the 2010 survey to illustrate this mixture of quantitative and qualitative information.

Another resource for archive services is the Archives and Records

---

Question
Using the data that is available to you about the use of your online services (web pages, catalogue, databases etc.), indicate how levels of use of these services changed between 2008/9 and 2009/10. Please outline what your online service consists of, whether this is still in active development and comment on changes to the scale of the service that may account for the change noted.

Options
(a) Usage increased by more than 100%
(b) Usage increased by 50–100%
(c) Usage increased by 20–50%
(d) Usage increased by less than 20%
(e) Usage decreased by less than 20%
(f) Usage decreased by more than 20%
(g) Information not available

Answer
(b)

Feedback
Our online service includes our information web pages, guidance on popular types of research, our online catalogue, a number of genealogical databases, and about 7000 downloadable images in our 'Borset Digital History' collection. We are actively adding to the databases and image collection, but the catalogue is largely complete and other resources are largely static. We count page-views for web pages, user sessions in the online catalogue, and downloads of images. Across all these categories, traffic increased by an average of 74%.

Figure 3.2 *Sample question and answer from the UK National Archives survey in 2010*

Association (ARA) Archive Visitor Survey (www.archives.org.uk/latest-news/2011-archive-visitor-survey-published.html), organized by the Public Services Quality Group, and run by the Chartered Institute of Public Finance and Accountancy (CIPFA). The results of the 2011 survey were used to create a benchmarking tool, which includes the questions asked, and is available for download from the ARA website, www.archives.org.uk/images/documents/news/2011surveybenchmarkingtool.xls.

CIPFA also administers the Home Delivery Survey and Plus, Children's Plus and ePlus for UK public libraries; see www.cipfasocialresearch.net/libraries. These are designed to solicit feedback from library users. Plus is aimed at all library users; Children's Plus is designed specifically for children and teenagers; and ePlus aims to capture information from users of online and ICT services.

Using your figures

You will naturally generate and collect many figures in the course of your business. Most library and information services will keep some kind of statistics about number of visitors, loans and enquiries, ranging from five-bar gates to sophisticated reporting systems. If you use an automated library or archive management system you should be able to extract detailed statistics.

Make the most of the data you collect. Circulation data is particularly valuable. Privacy laws, and what you are allowed to do with these personal data, vary from country to country, but you should be able to map the usage of certain classes of items to certain classes of users. At the very least, circulation data can provide you with a good insight into the strengths and weaknesses of your collection, and help to inform your collection development policy.

If your service uses internal billing to charge other departments in your organization, these figures can also be valuable. Look at where most of your work is coming from – is there a particular department that makes a lot of use of a particular service? Could you ask staff in that department to be internal champions or advocates for you? Is there a department that doesn't use your services at all? Would it be helped by them? Use this to inform and direct your marketing strategy.

Can you be creative with how you use your figures? Do you have any other information you could combine them with, to help prove benefits? The University of Huddersfield have been particularly innovative in how they've been using their circulation data. They've been leading on the JISC-funded Library Impact Data Project, which looks at anonymized circulation data from eight university libraries. These data are then correlated against anonymized final grade data, and the project has discovered that 'there is [a] statistically significant relationship between both book loans and e-resources use and student attainment' (Library Impact Data Project, 2011).

While this is a very encouraging correlation, the project team warns that it is not proof of a causal relationship, and is eager to address questions that have arisen during the project, and continue working on the key project aim: 'to seek to engage low/non users of library resources and to raise student achievement by increasing the use of library resources' (Library Impact Data Project, 2011). Though the results of the project are significant for the library and information community, the focus of the project has always been on user needs. See the Library Impact Data Project blog for more information about the project: http://library.hud.ac.uk/blogs/projects/lidp.

Measuring success internally

Reviewing your service doesn't always need to directly involve the user. It is also important to internally audit processes and expectations. Pantry and Griffiths suggest considering the following questions:

- What is the core business of the information service?
- How is it doing?
- Why are particular jobs in the service done, need they be continued, and can the need for any of them be avoided?
- How are jobs carried out, why are they done in a particular way, and can a better way be found?
- Why are jobs carried out when they are? Can a better time be found?
- Where are jobs performed? Why there? Can a better place be found?
- Who does this job? Why is it done by this person? Is there someone else within the organization or outside who can do this job?
- Are the staff able to deliver the service or products – what training will be needed?

Where the question has been asked with the word 'can', ask it again with the word 'should' (Pantry and Griffiths, 2009, 10).

This process of questioning can be called an information audit, and these are questions which new professionals, especially those who are new to their role, are well placed to answer. You bring a fresh point of view to a workplace, and might be asked to review current procedures and processes.

Even if you are not asked these questions, you should be asking them of yourself. Doing so will help you to better understand your workplace and organizational culture, and you will be placed to offer suggestions about improvements to the service.

Although new professionals might be trepidatious about offering suggestions for changes, most managers are keen to hear from staff. You should follow procedure to communicate with the appropriate person. If you are not sure who that is, or are nervous about approaching them, you should speak to your line manager, mentor or buddy. Show that you have carefully considered the question. Don't just say 'I think this should change' without offering a solution. You don't have to get the right solution first time, but show you have considered alternatives.

Conclusion

Library and information professionals have long been committed to meeting their users' needs, but haven't always been as successful as they might be about communicating this. The profession needs to use the right language and communication methods to ensure that we are meeting the needs that users really have (not the ones that we think they have), and that we are correctly communicating the value of the work we do.

In Chapter 4 we will look in more detail at working with stakeholders, and getting the message about you and your service out to your users.

References and further reading

Affelt, A. (2009) Aligning the Information Centre to create the future, *Information Outlook*, **13** (4), 33–8.

Affelt, A. et al. (2011) *SLA Future Ready Toolkit*, www.sla.org/content/resources/toolkit/index.cfm (membership required).

British Library (2004) *Measuring Our Value*, www.bl.uk/pdf/measuring.pdf.

Carter, S. and Ambrosi, T. (2011) How to Build a Desk Statistics Tracker in Less than an Hour Using Forms in Google Docs, *Computers in Libraries*, **31**, www.infotoday.com/cilmag/oct11/Carter_Ambrosi.shtml.

Crawford, J. et al. (2006) *The Culture of Evaluation in Library and Information Services*,

Chandos Publishing.

Diane, K. C. (2005) Resource Review: conducting an information audit, *Information Management Journal*, **39** (2), 68.

Elliott, D. S. et al. (2006) *Measuring Your Library's Value: how to do a cost-benefit analysis for your public library*, ALA Editions.

Latham, J. (2008) A New Twist to Information Audits, *Information Outlook*, **12** (6), 78.

LibQUAL+ (2011) *General FAQs*, http://libqual.org/about/about_lq/general_faq.

Library Impact Data Project (2011) The Final Blog Post, Library Impact Data Project, http://library.hud.ac.uk/blogs/projects/lidp/2011/07/21/the-final-blog-post/.

Mandy, W. (2001) A Guide to Information Audits, *Information World Review*, 175, 66.

Pantry, S. and Griffiths, P. (2009) *How to Give your Users the LIS services they want*, Facet Publishing.

Ranganathan, S. R. (1931) *The Five Laws of Library Science*, Madras Library Association.

Rebecca, J. and Bonnie, B. (2004) Information Audits: building a critical process, *Searcher*, **12** (1), 50.

Romaine, C. et al. (2009) Strategic Alignment: positioning our brand for the future, *Information Outlook*, **13** (1), 10–15.

Roswitha, P. (2007) Benchmarking With Quality Indicators: national projects, *Performance Measurement and Metrics*, **8**, 41, http://dx.doi.org/10.1108/14678040710748076.

Saunders, E. S. (2008) The LibQUAL+ Phenomenon: who judges quality?, *Reference & User Services Quarterly*, **47** (1), 21–4, http://rusa.metapress.com/content/l8514l42158uw348.

St Clair, G. (1997) Matching Information to Needs, *Information World Review*, **123**, 20.

Stone, G. et al. (2011) Looking for the Link between Library Usage and Student Attainment, *Ariadne*, **67**, www.ariadne.ac.uk/issue67/stone-et-al.

Susan, S. D. and Lynn, B. (2000) In Search of the Information Audit: essential tool or cumbersome process?, *Library Journal*, **125** (4), 48.

Ulla de, S. (2004) Hunches and Lunches: using the information audit to understand information culture, *Searcher*, **12** (4), 57.

Welch, J. M. et al. (2011) Archives, Accessibility, and Advocacy: a case study of strategies for creating and maintaining relevance, *Journal of the Medical Library Association*, **99** (1).

West, C. (2004) A Survey of Surveys, *SCONUL Newsletter*, **31**, 18–22, www.sconul.ac.uk/publications/newsletter/31/7.pdf.

Zamora, G. and Lachance, J. (2009) *Positioning SLA for the Future: alignment initiative results and recommendations*, SLA Leadership Summit Savannah, Georgia.

Resources

Archives, T. N. (2010) *Self-Assessment*, www.nationalarchives.gov.uk/information-management/our-services/self-assessment.htm.

Bates, M. E. (2011) The True Value of Information, free webinar, www.factiva.com/campaigns/2011/15767/?from=webinar_viral_iqfactiva29sep2011 www.brighttalk.com/webcast/6693/34027.

Journal Usage Statistics Portal, http://jusp.mimas.ac.uk.

Library Impact Data Project (2011) *Library Impact Data Toolkit*, http://eprints.hud.ac.uk/11571.

SCONUL (2011a) *SCONUL Satisfaction Survey*, http://vamp.diglib.shrivenham.cranfield.ac.uk/quality/sconul-satisfaction-survey.

SCONUL (2011b) *SCONUL Statistical Questionnaire: questionnaire guidance*, http://vamp.diglib.shrivenham.cranfield.ac.uk/statistics/sconul-statistical-questionnaire/questionnaire-guidance.

➡ Over to you . . .

1. Look at a written example of how you or your organization communicates with users. Consider the form of the communication and the vocabulary. Is it appropriate? Have you used any LIS jargon that might confuse your users? Mark every word that might be confusing or ambiguous. How might you rephrase it? What impact could that have?

2. Think about the statistics you gather as part of your normal business. Could you use these to prove value and measure success? Are you missing any important statistics? If so, could you start gathering them?

   Are there any barriers to using these statistics? Think about collection and analysis methods, time and effort required, and data storage and protection.

CHAPTER 4
Marketing your service and engaging stakeholders

Introduction

As an information professional you may find that marketing doesn't come naturally to you. Unfortunately, just having a great service isn't enough. If you don't let people know about the benefits that your service can offer, you are not doing all you can to provide them with the service they need.

Marketing isn't a dirty word, or an extra that sits on top of your services. It is an integral part of meeting your users' needs – as the CILIP code of professional conduct states, members should 'Ensure that information users are aware of the scope and remit of the service being provided' (CILIP, 2004).

A key point about marketing, particularly of information services, is that it needs to be benefit-led. While this might sound obvious, much library and archive marketing has traditionally been feature-led – 'we have [x number] books! And [x number] databases! Come visit!'. These types of marketing message will only resonate with those who are naturally inclined to be excited by large numbers of books or databases – other information professionals.

What marketing should be doing is informing your users (and non-users and lapsed users) of what you can do to make their life better. Rather than telling them how many books you have, tell them that you can find them something new and exciting to read. Don't state that you have many original historical documents available – shout about how you can help them to find unique sources to produce unique research. Don't send out a bland e-mail telling staff that the electronic library is now available from their desktop; lead by asking, 'Want to save time on your research?'

If people don't know why they should use you, they won't, and will therefore not get the benefits of all the carefully curated information resources you have purchased for them. It could be argued that lack of proper promotion of library and information resources will have a detrimental effect on the quality of information that your users will receive – either driving them to Google, or leading them to pay for information which they could have got free from the library. Increased visibility will increase usage, and is the best possible way to stop accusations of irrelevance and prove your value.

What is marketing?

Marketing comes in a number of different forms. You might be more comfortable with the term advocacy – marketing can sound intrusive and overbearing, advocacy is gentler and more relaxed. Call it what you will, it's all about communicating your value to your users, and it should come into every interaction.

You might think of marketing as running a poster campaign, creating a new slogan, or actively accosting people to tell them about your brand. It can be all of those things – and there are many guides to doing such things well and cheaply – but marketing is also about building a relationship with your users. Your main tool in this is your point of interaction – make it a great one, and people may forget. But make it a bad interaction, and people will not only remember – they will tell others. Being thoroughly professional in all your activities is one of the best ways you can advocate for and market your service.

Plan your marketing

Effective marketing relies on knowing what your users value. Without knowing which benefits they are looking for, how can you promote those benefits to them? The principles we looked at in chapters 2 and 3 apply just as much to marketing and promotions as to any other form of communication. Choose the right channels and vocabulary to engage your audience. Dempsey describes this as 'true marketing', saying, 'at the core of true marketing is a commitment to really understanding your users (and non-users)' (2010).

To do this, you will need to identify your stakeholders – those people who are involved or interested in some way in what you do and the service you provide, who are affected by what you do and who would be affected if you didn't do what you do. They include users, non-users (who could benefit from your services), funders, those in the management structure – anyone who might impact or be impacted by your services. How do you identify and communicate with such a disparate group? Michael Stead, Information and Digital Services Manager at Wigan Leisure and Culture Trust, describes how and why to identify and communicate with your stakeholders.

Case study
Stakeholders: identifying and working with the people who care about what you do

What are stakeholders?

Broadly, stakeholders are the people with an interest in the services your organization provides. This is a bit vague, so let's break it down a little:

- funders
- delivery partners and partner organizations
- senior managers of your service
- other departments within your organization
- politicians (for local authority services)
- senior academics (for services in higher education).

Each of these groups has an interest in what you do and how you do it. Other departments within your organization may perceive the risk of reputational damage if your service is substandard; politicians and academics might base their professional reputations and continued employment in those roles on their ability to ensure that your service meets certain criteria. The delivery of any service is increasingly dependent on working with partners, either internally – with the university's computing services department, for example – or with other public service delivery agencies such as charities and children's centres.

There is one stakeholder group whose importance is much greater: the users of your service. Without them, there is no service. You have no job. The archive has no holdings, the library has neither books nor digital services. While the other stakeholder groups may be more vocal, or may have more perceived power within the hierarchy of your organization, working with and for your users is paramount. To paraphrase the great Bryan Adams: everything you do, you do it for them.

Why are they important?

The visible stakeholders on the periphery of your user communities – the politicians, partners and academics, for example – have an interest in what you do and how you do it. Each of them has something they want from you, something that will address their own agenda. The term agenda is used here not in a way to imply suspicion or Machiavellian strategizing: those big stakeholders are rightly interested in the things they are interested in, some of which will include you, and some of which they might perhaps want to include you in.

Addressing these agendas, which are likely to have some overlap with those of your own organization, makes you visible and demonstrates your relevance. This perceived relevance is vital, given that the future funding of library, information and archive services will increasingly rely on novel revenue streams and partnership-based financing and delivery. Make all the friends you can: you never know when those relationships will be needed.

How can you identify stakeholders in your workplace?

The stakeholders relevant to your workplace will vary, depending on the nature of your work and the context within which your service sits. If you are lucky, you might find an existing stakeholder engagement strategy, which neatly identifies all of them and addresses their needs. If not, you will need to be a little more creative.

The categories listed above should give you a head-start. To make them more specific to your service, you will need to talk through the issue with your colleagues and managers. Even if there is no existing, formal stakeholder engagement strategy, it is very likely that there are some established contacts and procedures. Build on them.

How can you effectively communicate with them?

You will need to modify your communication techniques, even going so far as to change the type of language you use, for each group.

Some stakeholders – such as politicians – will have relatively little time to consider issues related to your service because of the broad nature of their political portfolio, or the time taken up by each of the many areas with which they have involvement. Councillors in particular have many demands on their time – from constituents, committees and often their own day jobs – so they tend to appreciate concise, clear messages with minimal jargon. Managing relationships with politicians is a discipline you will have to learn; it tends to be the preserve of more senior managers. For now, your approach might be to express an interest with your managers in this kind of stakeholder engagement, and see what you can learn.

Senior managers are relatively easy: you already know what they want, and they speak your language. They want your service to be successful, to meet and even exceed its objectives.

Delivery partners, like your senior managers, should have clearly defined objectives, which will provide you with your way in. If your organization already works with them, you will be able to build on that work. Again, as with your senior managers, you already know (or should have access to knowledge of) what they want.

How can you work effectively with them?

A few simple steps should be considered. Mix and match them: not everything will work for every group, and you will most probably come up with your own ideas in addition to these suggestions:

- Share what you do with colleagues and in your wider professional network.
- Talk to existing committees, 'friends of' groups and so on.
- Give and take: potential delivery partners, in particular, will want something demonstrable in return.
- Be prepared to put a lot of work in.
- Talk to people at every opportunity.
- Prepare your 'elevator pitch' – your two-minute hard-sell – so you are ready to evangelize your stakeholders when the opportunity arises.

The holy grail: engaging with the disengaged

If there were a simple solution to this issue, somebody would have found it and made their fortune from it. Unfortunately, the only solution that works consistently is the application of hard work.

As with your stakeholder engagement strategy, this daunting task – engaging with everyone who could possibly have even the slightest hitherto unexpressed interest in what you do – becomes simpler when broken down. Think about the people who you think should use your service, yet apparently do not. Your starter for ten:

- lapsed users
- specific demographic groups (teens, freshers, new parents, new staff)
- random strangers.

Lapsed users are people who used to use your service but, for some reason, no longer do. You have plenty of information about them: you know their names, you have their contact details, and you know – particularly if they used to borrow books from you – what their interests are. Data Protection Act permitting (make sure you take some local advice on issues like this), a quick e-mail to lapsed users reminding them of your excellent services might be a relatively cheap win.

You will be able to identify plenty of fairly narrowly defined groups of people with whom your service ought to engage. Chances are that a route to each of them exists already, possibly via another organization that already works with them, or an existing process within your broader working context, which might allow you access to them. For public libraries, the difficulty of maintaining the sustained interest of teenagers causes considerable anxiety. Other organizations – schools, career services, youth centres – might give you a way in, provided your services can match the target audience's expectations. If you can secure a slot for your services in the induction programme for new staff, you have an opportunity to pitch them to a receptive audience. There is always the risk that the timing, while it works for the people organizing the programme, might not work for you or the recipients, but establishing relationships with the organizers could reap benefits later.

Random strangers are the most challenging group. You could spend your days buttonholing people on the street, trying to convince them to use your service, but that way lies a citation for assault. Plan your approach carefully: be clear about what your objectives are, which will probably mean returning to the idea of identifying discrete groups within your potential user community.

Working with stakeholders can often be challenging, but it is also rewarding. Getting it right means that you are closer to providing a service that best meets your users' needs. It is unreasonable to expect that you will learn how to be perfect at all of it, all at once, but you will have opportunities to acquire the necessary skills by working with your colleagues and managers. As a new professional, you need to plan for the future management, planning and delivery of your services; the skills required to work with stakeholders will become even more essential as the landscape you work within changes.

As Michael says, you need to think about how, where and when to communicate with your stakeholders: your work needs to be tailored to them and how they would usually interact with you. All communications with stakeholders are part of marketing your service – they get an impression of you, your capabilities and competence, every time they interact with you. A lot of marketing comes down to making the most of your interactions.

Quick-response marketing

Once you have identified who your stakeholders are, you are ready to do some marketing. Your marketing initiative might be a general promotional exercise, in response to a specific event, or prompted by a particular set of circumstances. The more targeted your marketing is, the more effective you might find it to be.

It is pleasing to have lots of time to plan out your marketing strategy, but marketing is like any project, and sometimes you need to move quickly. Alison Circle, Marketing Director for Columbus Metropolitan Library (CML), Ohio, tells us about a situation that called for quick-response marketing.

Case study
Creating customer-friendly e-reader experiences

The problem

There is no question that the popularity of e-readers hit an all-time high during the 2010 holiday season. CML was suddenly called on to explain the e-book and e-reader marketplace to customers and support them in their move to e-books. Amazon now reports that e-reader sales top hardcover and paperback sales. Libraries must be agile, adaptive and creative to continue relevance in a world where a recent study by OCLC shows that 75% of people associate the library with books on shelves (De Rosa et al., 2010).

The e-reader explosion has dramatically altered the way customers interact with the library and reading. It also impacts library staff as more and more customers ask for detailed assistance in downloading content. Many library staff are still attached to paper books; now they are expected to be technical experts as customers come to the library looking for recommendations on which e-reader to purchase, and assistance as they wade through the technical complications of downloading books to variable devices.

In early December 2010 staff at CML realized we had to act quickly to respond to developments in the marketplace. We had three weeks to demonstrate:

- existing e-reader content
- which content is available and on which type of device
- that we can assist customers in selecting the e-reader that's right for them
- that our staff – who enjoy a reputation as smart experts – have the training and comfort level they need to face this new technology.

The innovation

CML developed an e-reader committee, which consisted of various departments including librarians, IT, marketing, training and development and property management. The committee was responsible for five tactics: staff training, vendor demos, designated website, public programs and stations for customers to have a hands-on experience with various devices.

To start, CML purchased five each of five different types of devices. This helped to focus our training and customer experience. Then in three short weeks we created training materials, trained front-line staff, built two pilot e-reader stations, installed the devices on the stations (including networking, securing, labelling), built a robust website and promoted the services to customers through publicity and media attention.

Importantly, to accomplish all of this in a short time required a transformation in how the library approaches our work. Historically we took a great deal of time involving a lot of people to make sure every detail was set. In this instance we worked more like a quick strike team: meeting quickly, making decisions, and getting work done. We embraced the importance of change management, and spent time understanding staff resistance to change and addressing it. When facing a fundamental change, the last thing we want is for resistance to change to have a negative impact on customers. We deliberately chose early adapters for high profile work to showcase their success to others. This is how we treated staff and customer:

- *Staff:* CML aggressively developed written documentation for each type of device. Additionally, we created kits containing each type of device and training documents to give staff intensive hands-on time with the devices. Called the 'e-reader Learning Roadmap', all staff were guided through ten activities to enhance their familiarity with e-readers. An internal blog was developed to provide 'how-to' information as well as a wiki, which gave plenty of resources, answers to frequently asked questions, and details to equip staff to answer customer questions. These training documents were scaled down and offered to the public through a designated website. Again, this was completed in three weeks.

• *Customers:* CML placed e-reader stations at two libraries as pilots. The stations were built by our property management staff using existing materials. We also purchased two laptops, securing devices and cables. We launched a multi-page e-reader website on 26 December (right after Christmas) to showcase CML as an e-reader destination. The website included product information, tutorials, opportunities to receive an e-reader newsletter, video instruction and more. We also included a page just for other libraries, which could freely use our experience and materials to provide service to their own customers.

Progress and outcomes

Our work had huge success. CML e-reader stations are now at six additional locations. We started an e-reader newsletter to share the latest information with customers and we hold monthly tweet chats (#e-readerchat) as open forums to discuss books, devices, publishers and even downloading challenges. Our circulation of e-reader content has skyrocketed. Next steps include development of programs around e-reader content, including helping customers understand the complexity around digital rights management to manage customer expectations on quantity and types of available content. It is important for customers to understand that the limits around content availability are driven by the marketplace, not by the library. Finally, we proved to ourselves that we can respond quickly to meet market demands and that we can learn new ways of getting great work done.

Alison's case study demonstrates that marketing works in the same way as any other project within an LIS organization. You need to have a plan and a target in place, manage your project effectively, have the right staff and mix of skills in your project team, measure your progress, and reflect on the outcomes. Agility is useful – the ability to respond quickly to a situation in a way that maximizes its potential for the service and your users. This will help your service to be perceived as timely and relevant.

Which channels you use for communication can make a difference to the speed at which you can react. If you are relying on a monthly newsletter to communicate with stakeholders, you are unlikely to be able to capitalize on events, news and innovation. Contrast this with LIS organizations using services such as Facebook or Twitter – who can announce to readers that they have 20 copies of the Booker Prize winner in stock within minutes of the announcement.

This applies to communication with staff, too. Using quick-response social media tools for staff training, knowledge-sharing and communication helped Columbus Metropolitan Library to be successful in their e-reader promotion.

Marketing doesn't just consist of a series of single, defined projects. This especially applies to marketing internally within your organization, where the promotion of your service can become an integral part of your day-to-day job. This can include 'guerrilla marketing' strategies, such as asking to attend departmental meetings, cornering colleagues by the kettle, making full use of your e-mail signature, and slipping flyers under office doors.

Taking this to its furthest level, we find embedded information professionals. This is an ethnographic form of information work – instead of sitting in a separate department, you will often be located within the functional team you are working with. This can help you to understand the needs of your users, and increase acceptance of your role and skills. It gives you the chance to demonstrate all of your skills – it is unlikely that an embedded librarian has ever been told that their job consists of 'just stamping books'.

It is not always an easy step to take. You will need to make an effort to integrate yourself with your new team, and you might feel isolated from professional colleagues. But you will benefit from contact with an expanded range of professionals, and the fact that you have been allowed to embed yourself and your skills within multi-disciplinary teams will often result in information professionals being highly valued in your workplace.

Reece Dano, Senior Lead Researcher at Artefact Group, a Seattle-based experience design and user research consultancy, shares his experiences of being an embedded librarian.

📁 Case study
Embedded librarianship

I'm often asked, 'What is embedded librarianship – and how can I implement it within my organization?' Because this type of role is highly dependent on context, my reply is often, 'It depends.'

If I were to sum it up, embedded librarianship requires a deep understanding of the context of the user, as well as their ultimate product or deliverable. The embedded librarian goes beyond the retrieval and delivery of information. He or she is often involved with both the initial framing of the research question and the subsequent analysis and synthesis of the retrieved information. In short, the embedded librarian's responsibilities extend into the before and after of the traditional librarian's transaction-based model.

As an information specialist embedded within a design consultancy, I am often assigned to multidisciplinary teams where we work together to solve design challenges for clients. These teams are often composed of graphic designers, industrial designers, materials specialists and ethnographic researchers. These team members have different educational backgrounds and highly specialized skills; each has a different way of looking at the world. For example, if we are to design a train station, an ethnographer must interview and understand the world of the train station's passengers. An industrial designer must learn and transfer the principles of environmental design that prevent crime to station elements. A graphic designer may need to find and analyse inspirational imagery related to transportation and green spaces. It is my job to understand each of their needs and advise and assist them with finding the resources they need to complete their job.

This is a typical workflow within the embedded model:

1. Understand the team's objectives. Meet with the team to clarify scope of the work to be done. Ask:
   - Who is the external client? What are their strengths, weaknesses, opportunities and threats?
   - What is the overall goal of the project?
   - What will the final deliverable be?
   - What are the roles of each person on the team?
   - Who are the individuals on the team who are most and least familiar with the project's domain?
2. Iteratively frame and refine the users' queries. Perform information audits to assess the organizational knowledge gaps of the internal team members and the client. Develop research questions designed to fill these knowledge gaps. This part of the workflow most resembles a traditional reference interview. Ask:
   - What are the broadly stated questions?
   - What are the presumed authoritative sources of information?
   - Are there analogous subject domains to reference?
   - Which types of delivery formats are best suited to the client?
3. Understand how the research serves the broader strategic goals of the organization. Again, audit the needs and expectations of the clients. Ask:

- What is mission of the organization? What are the interim goals?
- What does the client intend to do with the information?
- How will the retrieved information affect the current course of the client's organization?
- How broadly will the received information be disseminated within the client organization?
- Which types of resources are most trustworthy for the client?
- Who are the key stakeholders within the external client's organization who will be receiving this information?

4. Conduct the research. Routinely check in with both internal and external clients for feedback. Refine or redirect research as necessary.
5. Analyse and synthesize the information according to the preferences of the users. Present information to clients in a way that acknowledges their current strengths and weaknesses.

Step 5 of the workflow is the most important aspect of my job as an embedded librarian. My job doesn't end with the delivery of secondary research to team members. It also requires me to translate the queries' findings into a deliverable that speaks to the needs and preferences of each team member. Depending on the team, the format of this synthesized information can be textual, visual and even experiential. For example, does the user want to read several books on the topic? If they are a visually oriented individual, would they prefer to receive an annotated deck of inspirational images? Would a one-on-one presentation of the findings be more direct? Or would they rather visit a local museum exhibit that I've determined will answer all their questions? Being able to provide this kind of service requires an embedded librarian to have a much closer, more personal relationship with their user.

How does the embedded model raise your profile within an organization?

The embedded librarianship model raises the librarian's profile by default. Because you are working alongside your users, you have a stronger sense of their daily work objectives, the manner in which they approach their work, and nearly continuous input on how they interpret retrieved information. This allows you to be sympathetic to their needs and provide more targeted information. In turn, your users have a better understanding of how you approach your work, your methodologies and the breadth of skills it takes to deliver their requests.

Another benefit of embedded librarianship is the ability to take on greater, more flexible roles. Within the four years I've worked at my design research company I have graduated from being a supporting secondary researcher to leading and conducting large-scale primary research projects. This has arisen from my willingness to deeply understand my users' processes and, subsequently, work alongside them in a hybrid role.

What should you consider before implementing this model?

There are many things to consider, but the main challenges are those related to stakeholder identification, individual needs assessments and workflow management.

Who are your existing champions? Find non-librarian individuals within your organization who have a strong understanding of what you provide. Have them help you articulate your offering to other stakeholders within the organization. Encourage them to invite you to team and stakeholder meetings so that you can observe conversations that will provide you with more situational context.

How will you conduct information audit and needs assessments? Closely serving your users requires a careful understanding of their needs. If you cannot meet your users, determine the best way to understand their information needs frequently and regularly. Face-to-face meetings are best. Be sure to interview as many stakeholders as possible, including organizational leaders.

Which tasks are you willing to give up? The demands of embedded librarianship can easily overshadow the more administrative tasks of collection development and referral. Be willing to reassign routine tasks and low-priority tasks to junior professionals or interns. Keep in mind that the embedded model takes you out of the library. Can you still call yourself a librarian when you are no longer working in a library?

Conclusion

New professionals may feel intimidated when asked to market their service, but, as this chapter's case studies have shown, marketing is not actually very far removed from the work you would expect to do as an information professional. Marketing is about connecting with your users, non-users and other stakeholders, and its aim is not to promote the service for the service's sake, but for that of the users.

Individual marketing strategies will depend on the organization and its users, but they will probably be a mix of sustained advocacy and specific marketing projects. See the further reading below for examples of some successful and innovative marketing strategies.

References and further reading

Marketing and advocacy

Abram, S. (2010) Advocacy for Libraries: in our own interest, free webcast, SirsiDynix Institute, www.sirsidynix.com/advocacy-for-libraries-in-our-own-interest-and-our-communities.

Adeloye, A. (2003) How to Market Yourself and Your Library Organization: a solo librarian's guide, *The Bottom Line*, **16**, 15.

Adeyoyin, S. O. (2005) Strategic Planning for Marketing Library Services, *Library Management*, **26** (8/9), 494.

Anderson, J. (2011) Activism, Advocacy and Professional Identity, *Johanna Bo Anderson's Blog*, http://johannaboanderson.wordpress.com/2011/08/23/activism-advocacy-and-professional-identity.

Bates, M. E. (2011) *A Marketing Plan That Works! Who are you talking to and what are you saying?*, www.batesinfo.com/store/store_files/MarketingPlan.pdf.

Brewerton, A. (2003) Inspired! Award-winning library marketing, *New Library World*, 104, 267.

CILIP (2004) *Code of Professional Practice*, www.cilip.org.uk/get-involved/policy/ethics/Pages/code.aspx.

Columbus Metropolitan Library (n.d.), Learn and Play @ CML, http://columbusmetropolitanlibrary.wordpress.com.

De Rosa, C. et al. (2010) *Perceptions of Libraries, 2010: context and community: a report to the OCLC membership*, www.oclc.org/reports/2010perceptions.htm.

Dempsey, K. (2009) *The Accidental Library Marketer*, Information Today.

Dempsey, K. (2010) The Key to Marketing Success, *Information Outlook*, **14**, 6, www.sla.org/io/2010/12/943.cfm.

Dowd, N. (2010) Bite-Sized Marketing: real solutions for overworked librarians, free webcast, SirsiDynix Institute, www.sirsidynix.com/bite-sized-marketing.

Dowd, N., Evangaliste, M. and Silberman, J. (2010) *Bite-sized Marketing: realistic solutions for the overworked librarian*, American Library Association and Facet Publishing.

Hackman, L. J. (ed.) (2011) *Many Happy Returns: advocacy and the development of archives*, Society of American Archivists.

IFLA (2011) *Interest and Influence: identifying your stakeholders (case study)*, www.ifla.org/node/5712.

James-Gilboë, L. (2010) Raising the Library Profile to Fight Budget Challenges, *Serials Librarian*, **59** (3–4), 360–9.

McLachlan, D. (2006) Your Library is a Marketing Organization, *ALIA New Librarians' Symposium, Sydney*, http://conferences.alia.org.au/newlibrarian2006/programme_files/mclachlan_paper.pdf.

Potter, N. (2012) *The Library Marketing Toolkit*, Facet Publishing.

Potter, N. and Woods, L. (2011) *Escaping the Echo-Chamber (presentation)*, http://prezi.com/if9wccvvunup/escaping-the-echo-chamber.

Sue, H. (2004) Creating User Profiles to Improve Information Quality, *Online*, **28** (3), 30.

The 'M' Word – Marketing Libraries: marketing tips and trends for libraries and non-profits, http://themwordblog.blogspot.com.

Thomas, T. (2011) Building the Brand from the Inside Out, *Feliciter*, **57**, 110, www.cla.ca/Content/NavigationMenu/Resources/Feliciter/PastIssues/2011/Vol57No3/Feliciter3_Vol_57_2011_WEB.pdf.

White, E. and Collinson, T. (2010) Exterminating Boredom: synergy and creativity in an academic library, *ALISS Quarterly*, **6** (1), 26–31, http://eprints.port.ac.uk/1508/1/Microsoft_Word_-_White_%2B_Collinson_-_Exterminating_boredom_final.pdf.

Wosh, P. J. and James, R. D. (eds) (2011) *Public Relations and Marketing for Archives*, Neal-Schuman Publishers, Inc., Society of American Archivists.

Embedded librarianship

Dano, R. and McNeely, G. (2011) Embedded Librarianship Part 1: aligning with organizational strategy to transform information into knowledge, FUMSI, http://web.fumsi.com/go/article/use/63659.

Iowa Library Association – Association of College and Research Libraries (2011) *Embedded Librarian Selected Works*, www.iowaacrl.org/content/node/314.

Robinson-Garcia, N. (2011) Embedded Librarianship Part 2: a case study from Spain FUMSI, http://web.fumsi.com/go/article/use/63962.

Robinson-Garcia, N. and Torres-Salinas, D. (2011) Librarians 'Embedded' in Research, *CILIP Update Gazette* (June), 44–6.

Shumaker, D. (n. d.) The Embedded Librarian, http://embeddedlibrarian.wordpress.com.

Shumaker, D. (2009) Who Let the Librarians Out? Embedded librarianship and the library manager, *Reference & User Services Quarterly*, 48, 239, http://rusa.metapress.com/content/lk361771rwp78790/ ?p=cb82993a8285447d9abb105dd199dd5a&pi=0.

Shumaker, D. and Talley, M. (2010) Models of Embedded Librarianship: a research summary, *Information Outlook*, 14, 26, www.sla.org/io/2010/01/802.cfm.

Siess, J. (2010) Embedded Librarianship: the next big thing?, *Searcher*, 18, 39.

➡ Over to you . . .

Stakeholders

Think about your workplace, or somewhere you have worked in the past. Do you know who your stakeholders are? Can you group them? These groupings might include different categories of users. Taking each group in turn, consider:

- What's important for them about your service? Is it that the service continues? Is it that you save them money? Is it a particular aspect of the service?
- What would be the impact on them if the service was withdrawn?
- How do you usually communicate with them? How else might you communicate with them? Does how you communicate reflect what they care about?

Embedding

Think about Reece's question, 'Can you still call yourself a librarian (archivist) when you are no longer working in a library (archive)? Is your job intimately bound up in a physical place? How important is this to your users? If you are bound up in a physical space, think about what would happen if you were told that was to be taken away. What impact would that have on how you work and on your users?

If you are not space-based – in an embedded or remote service – consider the implications if you had to move to a separate physical space which would define your functions.

Think about the stakeholders you identified earlier. For each group, think about how what they value would be affected if you were to change the physical space in which you work. Who are the most important people to keep happy?

How could you best arrange and market the new arrangements to ensure the least service disruption and highest stakeholder satisfaction?

CHAPTER 5
Using technologies

Introduction

Information professionals and technology have been linked for a long time. While it may be tempting to think that the association began with the move towards computer-cataloguing in the late 1960s, Murley (2009) mentions that one of 'the featured programs at the 1938 AALL [American Association of Law Libraries] Annual Meeting was "The Use of Microfilm in a Law Library"', and that microfilms and microfiches were still being discussed well into the 1970s.

Nearly 40 years of talking about a single technology may seem to show libraries as being slow-moving adopters. While this may be true for some, others have been at the forefront of implementing new technologies: Berners-Lee mentions how librarian Louise Addis at the Stanford Linear Accelerator encouraged the establishment of the 'first web server outside CERN' (2000, 50). There is a digital divide with our very profession: at the time when many information professionals are taking a leading part in driving new technologies, many libraries and archives still have records on paper, or locked into proprietary software.

Why this dichotomy? Although stereotypes would have you believe that information professionals are either computer-fearing luddites who would write with quills if modern feathers weren't so shoddy, or devoted technophiles who would sooner lose an arm than their smartphone, the reality is much less clear-cut. Much of the disparity comes down to resources, human as well as technical. To implement a new technology in an information environment, you need staff who can appreciate possible uses and learn how to use it, know enough to teach others to use it, and can install and maintain it. You also need a management and a user base of people who are prepared to accept change, and enough time and money to fund the project.

You can be as enthusiastic as you like, but if your organization is tied into Internet Explorer 6, or can't afford to replace its obsolete computers, you are unlikely to be able to implement whizzy technical solutions.

The move towards automation

A major technological change in libraries was the move to cataloguing on computers. The movement started in the 1960s when the Council on Library Resources funded a study of 'the possible methods of converting the information on Library of Congress catalogue cards to machine readable form for the purpose of printing bibliographical products by computer', followed by a pilot machine-readable cataloguing (MARC) project from 1966 to 1967 (Avram 1968).

This move was primarily a transferral of catalogue cards to computers, and didn't take advantage of many of the capabilities of computerized systems. Fast-forward to 2002, and Roy Tennant's infamous declaration 'MARC must die!' (Tennant, 2002). In October 2011, after an investigation by the Working Group on the Future of Bibliographic Control, the Library of Congress announced that 'MARC has served the library community well in the pre-web environment, but something new is now needed', and announced the development of a new bibliographic framework (Library of Congress, 2011).

In archives, the move to computerization began slightly later. The archival data encoding standard, Encoded Archival Description (EAD), was first investigated in 1993, and the first official version of the specification was launched to the community in 1998 (Library of Congress, 2006). Work on the third edition of the specification is in progress at the time of writing, with release expected in 2013 (www.loc.gov/ead/eadrevision.html; see also the site of the Society of American Archivists (SAA), www2.archivists.org/groups/technical-subcommittee-on-encoded-archival-description-ead/encoded-archival-description-ead).

While many libraries are now on their second or third generation of library management software, or looking to ditch MARC altogether and move to catalogues based on Functional Requirements for Bibliographic Data (FRBR) or linked data, some library and archive services are still producing catalogues in products such as Microsoft Word.

What skills do you need – and why?

When thinking about which technology will work best for your service, you need to be aware of the different levels of resource and involvement and to consider:

- the needs of your users
- the needs and aims of your institution or organization
- the resources available
- the needs and standards of the information community at large.

This isn't always an easy balance to achieve. One of the things your organization will almost certainly need are information professionals who are familiar and comfortable with technology. Riley-Huff and Rholes (2011) investigated whether the technology skills available in the librarian community met the technology needs of organizations (with particular emphasis on library school programmes and new professionals). They concluded: 'There are clearly still difficulties in both the acquisition of needed skill sets for certain positions and in actual hiring for some information technology positions.'

While there has been some discussion in the library community about the value of technological skills (see Riley-Huff and Rholes for a review of this), the general consensus is that technological skills have become a vital part of the information professional's skill set.

Your exact level of technological involvement will depend largely on your role and organization, but at the least you should have a theoretical appreciation of the technologies involved in information provision, and be comfortable if required to investigate new technologies.

Knowing enough to be able to help or teach users is also important. You may need to support users who are using library-provided services, such as online databases or e-books, or be first-line support for searchroom computers. If you loan items of technology, such as laptops, iPads, e-readers or MP3 players, you will need to know enough about each to provide basic support and troubleshooting.

You may (especially if you are a solo practitioner) find yourself with responsibility for the library or archive management system and public catalogue. Maintaining this might involve learning how to tinker with its innards: you might need to write customized reports, use Cascading Style Sheets (CSS) and Hyper-Text Mark-up Language (HTML) to personalize and embed the interface in your web pages, and use application programming interfaces (APIs) to use all the tools your catalogue offers.

Maintaining the library or archive website might also be part of your remit. This will most likely involve using a content management system or software such as Dreamweaver, but it helps if you are familiar with CSS and HTML.

This will help you to understand how and why bits of the website work, even if you don't have to code them directly yourself.

You may want to go further, and learn to code, or develop expertise in a particular area. In the next case study, Digital Access Librarian and ALA Emerging Leader Bohyun Kim gives you some tips about what you need to know, and how you can learn it.

⚙ How to . . .
Become a zen master of technology

Why technology?

Almost all information resources and services now reside in the realm of the web. As a result, no information professional can successfully navigate, research, curate and manage these information resources and services without the ability to use the technology attached to them.

Increasingly, job descriptions and responsibilities in all sectors include technology as a common component. In a competitive job market, technology skills also give you a strong advantage.

Technology skills for all information professionals

It goes without saying that all information professionals need to learn how to use a computer, be comfortable with surfing the web, and using common software such as Microsoft Office suite. But there are so many other technology skills useful in the library and archive setting that there isn't just one set of skills that you can pick and conquer in one fell swoop. What are the most essential and basic technology skills that information professionals should know?

These are some skills related to the computer operating system:

* knowing how to download and install programs
* being able to connect an auxiliary device to a computer such as a printer, a scanner and so on
* understanding the system settings.

These are some troubleshooting skills:

* knowing what to ask a library user who reports a technology-related

problem, whether it is a hardware or software issue
- knowing how to replicate a problem
- knowing how to research a solution on the web.

These are skills related to understanding how electronic resources work:

- understanding what a persistent URL is and being able to tell if a URL is persistent
- knowing what 'authentication' and 'proxy' mean in the library setting
- understanding how an electronic resource is set up for access – from a trial, to the link placed in different library systems such as an open public access catalogue (OPAC), electronic resources management system, OpenURL Link Resolver and the library website
- knowing how to troubleshoot remote access issues to electronic resources.

Skills related to systems include:

- knowing what different library systems do and how they work together to provide users with access to information resources, for example an integrated library system (ILS), OPAC, discovery service, OpenURL Link Resolver, electronic resources management system, digital repository system, content management system or proxy server.

These are some web skills:

- proficiency in research tools available on the web
- knowing how to properly use the WYSIWYG editor in a blog or any content management system
- understanding the difference between HTML and a Microsoft Word document
- understanding what a web browser does
- knowing how to make screen casts (video tutorials) and podcasts
- knowing how to create and edit images and video for the web
- knowing what usability is and how it applies to a library
- knowing how to write for the web
- knowing how to utilize social media such as Facebook and Twitter
- understanding the mobile devices and related technology that are applicable to a library.

More advanced technology skills

The basic technology skills listed above should serve most information professionals well in their daily work. However, depending on your area of specialization, curiosity or specific problem-solving purposes, you may want to acquire more advanced technology skills. These are examples of some of those skills:

- mark-up languages such as HTML, CSS, eXtensible Markup Language (XML) and EXtensible Stylesheet Language (XSLT)
- programming languages such as JavaScript, PHP: Hypertext Preprocessor, Python, Perl, Ruby
- JQuery and other similar JavaScript libraries
- relational databases and Structured Query Language (SQL)
- Unix
- open source content management systems (e.g. Drupal, WordPress, Joomla) installation, customization, upkeep and so on
- proprietary integrated library systems
- open source digital repository and indexing systems
- APIs and mash-ups
- semantic web and Linked Data
- web analytics and statistics
- data mining and data visualization.

This is only a random selection of skills but it will give you some idea about the diversity of technology skills utilized at today's libraries. Even the most experienced systems and web services librarians have a wish list of technology skills they would like to obtain when they can find time to spare. For these reasons, it may be best to start with the ones that you find most interesting and immediately practical to learn for your environment, and to solve your own problems at hand.

Where to start?

The most important thing about becoming comfortable with technology is not to be afraid. The more experienced you are, the more likely it is you know how much you do not know and how much there is to learn. If you are only dealing with things you already know every day, you are probably not keeping up with changes.

What can you do if you suddenly find yourself in charge of some technology-related problem that you don't understand and have no previous experience with? Research and learn. Read the help documentation and join the community of users and practitioners. Get your hands dirty and play with the technology you want to learn and practise.

Remember to set up your own learning environment. You can follow technology-oriented listservs, read technology blogs and magazines, and scan professional journals regularly. Try to keep up with the fast-changing technology landscape and be active in the community of peers who share your interests in technology.

Don't worry about not being able to learn everything. You will always have more things to learn than the time you have. Patience and persistence will pay off in the long run.

Bohyun's case study highlighted some important technological skills for information professionals, and Boyhun has blogged about the idea of 'librarians as coders' (Kim, 2011). There is another movement in the information professional world, to get coders involved in libraries – 'shambrarians', as they call themselves. (For a rather tongue-in-cheek background of the shambrarian movement, see www.shambrarian.org.)

How is a shambrarian born, and what insights can they offer us into how we should be thinking about technology? Lukas Koster, Library Systems Co-ordinator at the Library of the University of Amsterdam, tells us about his technological library life, and offers some predictions for the future of systems librarianship, Linked Data and mash-ups.

📁 Case study
I, shambrarian

I had an education oriented mainly towards humanities and social sciences, but after graduating from university I entered a retraining programme targeted at getting unemployed academics into the IT business. I worked as a systems designer and developer in institutions for higher education and scientific information for more than ten years, before I had enough of it (IT) and wanted to do something more related to my original background.

By chance I entered the library world, implementing, managing and co-ordinating library systems of all kinds, at the National Library of the Netherlands and the Library of the University of Amsterdam, where I now work as Library

Systems Co-ordinator. I have a lot of experience with administering commercial library systems, without attending library school. I belong to the species known as 'shambrarian'.

With ready made commercial and open source library systems the bulk of the work lies with implementation and configuration, accommodating the system to the specific library circumstances. Theoretically there are no technical skills required. But in real life all 'out-of-the-box' systems need more or less sophisticated tweaking to be able to fulfil all requirements, which may need technical programming skills. Until now library and information professionals did not usually possess these skills, because they never needed them.

Tasks and responsibilities have always been conveniently divided between completely different job types. Librarians and information professionals knew how to find information in the form of tangible physical objects (books, CDs, tapes and so on) available in a specific location. Systems people and developers took care of the computer stuff.

The landscape is changing. Information is not solely stored in physical containers anymore. Books and journal articles are increasingly becoming available in digital form. Not only is the content that libraries have traditionally been focused on digitally available on the web, there are lots of other readily available information sources, such as sound, images, video, maps, research and other data. Traditional library search and discovery systems ignore this wealth of valuable information.

But wasn't providing access to information the original *raison d'être* of libraries and librarians? Yes, and that's what they have been doing for a long time with the tools and skills needed to find and deliver information stored in the only information carriers that were available: physical objects such as books.

To be able to continue performing the primary role of libraries, it is essential that librarians and information professionals start learning the tools and skills required for working with all types of digital information on the web, not just physical objects. In the future libraries will somehow evolve into more or less virtual 'information access portals' relying on technology, not on systems.

Systems librarian 2.0

In the meantime, it would be a good idea for libraries and archives to start serving their users better by 'mashing up' information from all kinds of online digital sources with their current traditional content management systems. As people searching for stuff about a specific subject in library catalogues are interested in information about that subject, why not give them immediate access to relevant information on the web, besides showing them some books that might help them, for instance:

- showing production and performance data, including images and video registration, with a theatre play catalogue record
- showing a map with a travelogue catalogue record
- showing a concise biography of the author.

Pending the coming of new easy to use tools (like Yahoo Pipes), some technical and programming skills are required to make mash-ups. These skills are often still the realm of system administrators and developers, who may not have enough time to be involved in creating mash-ups, or lack the professional knowledge to decide on the type of information to use. Instead of setting up dedicated projects, mash-ups should become a normal procedure for libraries. It is time to mash up different skill sets, technical and information professional.

In the near future we will see a new type of information professional role, combining and replacing the old jobs of librarians and systems people: the systems librarian 2.0.

This will be facilitated by two parallel developments arising from web developments. If library information systems are hosted 'in the cloud' in a software-as-a-service (SaaS) environment, systems people will no longer need to spend time on routine technical system administration tasks like back-ups, updates and upgrades. Bibliographic records and other metadata will be available on the web directly from the source, thereby freeing up the time of information professionals and cataloguers to spend more time in making innovative information discovery tools.

More and more, Linked Data is being used to connect information on the web from a number of sources. This means that institutions use the Resource Description Framework (RDF), a global API format, to publish their data on the web in the form of relations between information units ('triples') using 'vocabularies' (thematic data models), and using URLs as persistent identifiers for the information units and relations. This can enable users and researchers to find new routes into data, make new connections, and see bibliographic data in new ways.

Technology for the non-technical

There are plenty of ways you can use technologies to delight, educate and inform your readers without learning to code. Lukas talked about the idea of mash-ups: taking one set of data and linking it with another set of data to produce something new. A fairly well known example of a mash-up is the UK snow map (http://uksnowmap.com). Twitter users tweeted the #uksnow hashtag, including a rough measurement of how much it was snowing (a score out of ten), and their location information. This location information (based on place name, postcode or geotag) was then used to create a map, which visually represented snow coverage.

Mash-ups are popular in the library and archive community, and there have been a number of mashed library events in the UK. These are unconference style events, usually lasting a day, which are aimed at bringing together expertise and ideas from librarians, archivists and programmers. See www.mashedlibrary.com/wiki/index.php.

Mash-ups can be very effective, but, as Lukas points out, they often require some technical expertise. If you don't feel up to doing your own mashing, there are other ways to use technology. Website ifttt (if this, then that – http://ifttt.com) allows you to create rules based on simple triggers and using common web services. No coding required! As well as being useful for personal time management and productivity, you could develop rules and recipes for your service. How about automatically e-mailing users when there is snow forecast, to tell them you won't charge fines on items due that day? Or post a message on Twitter 15 minutes before closing to remind users to save any work and get ready to leave? Automating these small courtesies could help you to provide a better service with little extra effort.

Quick response (QR) codes can also be a useful tool. They are scanable codes into which you can embed information, URLs, photographs, contact details – pretty much anything that can be expressed in data and viewed on a mobile device. There are a number of programs available that allow you to create quick response codes quickly and easily. Link shortening website bit.ly, for instance, will allow you to create quick response codes of links and track how many people use them. Once you have created the code, you can print it out or display it on screen in a suitable location. Users scan the code with their device's camera (usually a smartphone or tablet). What happens next is up to you!

For some great examples of how quick response codes are being used in the library community, check out the Library Success Wiki at www.libsuccess.org/index.php?title=QR_Codes. You might also like to try QRpedia (http://qrpedia.org), which allows you to use quick response codes to direct users to Wikipedia articles in their preferred language.

Introduction to digital preservation

With all this talk of technology, at some point you are bound to wonder about the future. Sure, all of this stuff is great now, but what about in five, ten or 50 years? Will the technologies we use now be obsolete? Will we still be able to get our data out?

These are the questions that drive digital preservation. Digital preservation enables us to be sure we will still have access to digital materials in the future. It applies to both born-digital content (such as e-mails and databases) and digitized copies of physical content.

In recent years digitizing content has been prominent in the information landscape. This has especially been the case in the archive community, where a plethora of projects have been under way to digitize archive materials. This has partly been driven by preservation needs, but also by user demand. Users increasingly expect online access to material, and archivists have been assiduous in trying to make this available. Digital surrogates allow archives (and library special collections) to reach a larger audience; to offer users the convenience of 'at-your-desk' access; and to minimize handling of fragile materials.

There are many examples of popular and successful digitization projects, including:

- the British Library newspaper archive (www.britishnewspaperarchive.co.uk)
- Library of Congress prints and photographs (www.loc.gov/pictures) and historical sound recordings at National Jukebox (www.loc.gov/jukebox)
- the British Cartoon Archive (www.cartoons.ac.uk)
- National Archives of Australia 'Faces of Australia' project (www.naa.gov.au/collection/snapshots/faces/index.aspx).

The challenges

Digitization is not without its pitfalls. The process of digitization itself can be fiddly, invasive and time-consuming, and some fragile artefacts may be unsuited to the potentially damaging processes. Time, resources and expertise are needed to run digitization programs, which often require specialist knowledge and equipment. For this reason, many archive services have contracted out their digitization programs to external providers.

One of the major challenges to digitization is copyright. You may remember that staff at the Enid Blyton project at Seven Stories (Chapter 1) had to revise their plans to digitize content and make it available online at the request of the copyright holders. It is always important to ensure that any copyright implications are discussed before starting a digitization project (we will discuss copyright in more detail in Chapter 9). If you are using an external provider for your digitization, look into their terms and conditions before proceeding – you don't want to find out you have accidentally signed away your copyright!

As many digitization projects are fixed term, new professionals might find them a good way to gain experience. You won't be expected to be an expert straightaway, but some grounding in the issues is important. Beccy Shipman, project manager of the LIFE-SHARE collaborative digitization project, gives us an introduction to working with sustainable digital preservation.

⚒ How to . . .
Preserve collections digitally

Sustainable digital preservation is about ensuring long-term access to digital content. As librarians, archivists and curators have long been custodians of physical collections, so now many are finding themselves custodians of digital collections. Digital content can suffer from bit-rot in the same way that books can rot away on a shelf if they are not kept in a suitable environment. Digital preservation is vital to ensuring that these new collections can be accessed now and in the future. There are various reasons why digital content becomes unusable and so it requires a team of people with various skills to plan for and create methodologies to ensure long-term access. Digital preservation planning should be addressed long before there is a problem.

Sustainable digital preservation begins with the creation of digital content

You can help safeguard against future problems with a number of basic strategies:

- Use non-proprietary file formats where possible.
- Save files without compression or with lossless compression.
- Create a digital preservation plan and review it regularly.

- Keep up to date with trends.
- Educate the users on how to create content.

There are a number of digital lifecycle models, for example the LIFE model (www.life.ac.uk), Digital Curation Centre (www.dcc.ac.uk) and LIFE-SHARE (http://library.leeds.ac.uk/tutorials/digitisation_toolkit), which provide more detailed strategies for addressing digital preservation from the point of creation. They also provide an overview of all activities related to digital content.

Consider the needs of all your different types of digital content and plan accordingly

Digital preservation does not just apply to digital content you create yourself. You may acquire digital content in a range of different formats:

- *data:* may include statistics, interview transcripts, fieldnotes, analysis, digital lab books
- *born digital archives:* documents, e-mails, images, audio, video, databases
- *digitized content:* images, audio, video
- *e-journals, e-books and databases:* think about how you will ensure the permanence of your purchased resources
- *websites:* think about how you will preserve regularly updated web pages
- *research and teaching outputs:* e-prints, e-theses, e-learning materials.

Diagnose the problems with your digital content: how critical is your intervention

There are a number of issues that could be affecting your digital content:

- *bit-rot:* can be caused by storage media or inappropriate file usage
- *compression:* has a high level of compression created poor quality files?
- *damaged storage media:* are files stored on a scratched CD or waterlogged flash drive?
- *software obsolescence:* think about how you will open files created using software that no longer exists
- *hardware obsolescence:* as with software, think about how you will open files without the right computer.

Find solutions to your digital preservation woes

The best approach to solving digital preservation problems is to avoid them. As mentioned above, you can take a number of steps to help this, but it may not always be possible, particularly if you did not create the digital content yourself. The following approaches can help provide long-term access to your digital content:

* *Back-up:* Absolutely vital for preservation. You can do this yourself using a range of storage devices held in different places. This may already be done by your IT department, but check what processes they have. You could also consider using cloud computing. Check the policies, as back-up means many things to different people. Are the back-up policies appropriate for the digital archive?
* *Emulate:* Use tools that imitate obsolete software (and hardware) to allow you to access files.
* *Migrate:* Transfer files from one format to another to avoid needing software that is becoming obsolete.
* *Refresh:* Regularly update files so they continue to be accessible using current software.
* *Computer archive:* Keep old versions of computers with old software to ensure you can access all your digital content. Make sure you have enough storage space!

Don't worry about the long-term future

Unlike the preservation of physical materials, it is difficult to plan for the long-term preservation of digital materials. Technologies are changing so fast that file formats, storage media and the software needed to open digital materials can be obsolete after only a few years. Digital preservation is an ongoing process, so you should plan for the next few years and then for the next few years after that, and so on. It is impossible to predict what software and hardware will be used in ten years, let alone 50. When planning digital preservation you can only really take into account the next five years or so.

You are not alone

Digital preservation is a large and complex area. There are a lot of organizations working in this area, and you may want to benefit from the solutions they have explored. Some digital preservation issues are too large in themselves to be solved by a single institution so you may need to seek out partners and collaborate. Share your stories and experiences so the entire community can learn.

Repositories

An area in which information professionals are increasingly playing a role is that of digital repositories. These are usually institutional, though sometimes subject-based, and act as an online storage and search facility for research and teaching objects. Their development has been driven by a desire for open access to research papers and data; indeed, many funding bodies such as the Wellcome Trust and the National Institutes of Health now mandate that work funded under their schemes be made available in an open access repository.

What goes into your repository will depend on your organization. If there isn't already one in place, you may need to write a collection policy, based on the needs of your institution, and any legal requirements. You are unlikely to need to actually establish an institutional repository yourself. It is more likely that your job would include persuading academics and researchers to contribute, and finding the best ways to include contribution and metadata creation into their workflow. You will probably need to advise on open access policies, and be prepared to help with questions of copyright and permissions.

It might not be your own repository you encourage researchers to submit to – there are plenty of general open-access repositories, such as Jorum (www.jorum.ac.uk) for learning objects and arXiv (http://arxiv.org) for maths and physics papers.

Conclusion

Technology, in its many forms, is saturating the information environment, and any role you take is likely to include some aspect of technological involvement. Being agile and willing to learn will help you to acquire technological skills, which you can then use to help your users, enhance your service, and further your career.

In Chapter 6, we will look in more depth at a couple of aspects of being an information professional in an online age.

References and further reading

Avram, H. D. (1968) *The MARC Pilot Project*, www.eric.ed.gov/PDFS/ED029663.pdf.

Barton, E. (2006) Adapting Open Source Software to Benefit the Library: one new librarian's experience in changing the processes of a large academic library during the first year of employment, *ALIA New Librarians' Symposium, Sydney*, http://conferences.alia.org.au/newlibrarian2006/programme_files/barton_e_paper.pdf.

Berners-Lee, T. (2000) *Weaving the Web: the original design and ultimate destiny of the World Wide web by its inventor*, Texere.

Cervone, H. F. (2010) Emerging Technology, Innovation, and the Digital Library, *OCLC Systems and Services*, **26** (4), 239–42.

Chudnov, D. (2009) What Librarians Still Don't Know About Free Software, *Computers in Libraries*, **29**, 22.

Dalziel, K. (2008) Why Every Library Science Student Should Learn Programming, Nirak.net, http://nirak.net/2008/12/why-every-library-science-student-should-learn-programming.

Dougherty, W. C. (2010) Managing Technology in Libraries: a look to the past with hope for the future, *Journal of Academic Librarianship*, **36** (6), 543–5.

Engard, N. C. (ed.) (2009) *Library Mashups: exploring new ways to deliver library data*, Facet Publishing.

Fortney, K. (2009) Comparisons of Information Technology Education in MLIS Programs, *Library Student Journal*, 4, www.librarystudentjournal.org/index.php/lsj/article/view/99/220.

Gordon, R. S. (2001) A Course in Accidental Systems Librarianship, *Computers in Libraries*, **21**, www.lisjobs.com/cilnovdec2001.pdf.

Gordon, R. S. (2003) *The Accidental Systems Librarian*, Information Today.

Kim, B. (2011) Why Not Grow Coders from the Inside of Libraries?, *Library Hat*, www.bohyunkim.net/blog/archives/1099.

Library of Congress (2006) Development of the Encoded Archival Description DTD, www.loc.gov/ead/eaddev.html.

Library of Congress (2011) A Bibliographic Framework for the Digital Age, www.loc.gov/marc/transition/news/framework-103111.html.

Little, G. (2011) We Are All Digital Humanists Now, *Journal of Academic Librarianship*, **37** (4), 352–4.

Murley, D. (2009) A Selective History of Technology in Law Libraries, *Law Library Journal*, **101** (3), 415–20.

Potter, N. (2010) Everything You Need to Know About Technology to Work in Libraries, *The Wikiman*, http://thewikiman.org/blog/?p=1168.

Quinney, K. L. et al. (2010) Bridging the Gap: self-directed staff technology training, *Information Technology & Libraries*, **29**, 205–13, www.ala.org/ala/mgrps/divs/lita/publications/ital/29/4/quinney.pdf.

Riley-Huff, D. A. and Rholes, J. M. (2011) Librarians and Technology Skill Acquisition: issues and perspectives, *Information Technology & Libraries*, **30**, 129–40, www.ala.org/lita/ital/sites/ala.org.lita.ital/files/content/30/3/pdf/rileyhuff.pdf.

Schaumann, B. (2011) QR codes – could you use them in your library?, *Extracurly*, http://extracurly.wordpress.com/2011/08/27/qr-codes-could-you-use-them-in-your-library.

Scholarly Publishing Roundtable (2010) *Report and Recommendations from the Scholarly Publishing Roundtable*, www.aau.edu/WorkArea/showcontent.aspx?id=10044.

Sheehan, K. (2011) You Know, I Know, Don't Know, *ALA TechSource*, www.alatechsource.org/blog/2011/02/you-know-i-know-dont-know.html.

Tennant, R. (2002) MARC Must Die, *Library Journal*, www.libraryjournal.com/article/CA250046.html.

Walsh, A. (2009) Quick Response Codes and Libraries, *Library Hi-Tech News*, **26** (5/6), 7–9.

Resources

Code Academy, www.codecademy.com; free, simple online tutorials teaching you the basics of coding.

Stack Overflow, http://stackoverflow.com, a question and answer site for programmers.

Digital preservation and repositories

Besek, J. M. (2003) Copyright Issues Relevant to the Creation of a Digital Archive: a Preliminary Assessment, www.clir.org/pubs/reports/pub112/contents.html.

Digital Continuity Service (UK National Archives), www.nationalarchives.gov.uk/information-management/our-services/digital-continuity.htm.

Digital Curation Centre, www.dcc.ac.uk.

Digital Preservation Coalition, www.dpconline.org.

D-Lib Magazine, www.dlib.org.

Hathi Trust, www.hathitrust.org.

Internet Archive, www.archive.org.

JISC Digital Media, www.jiscdigitalmedia.ac.uk.

JULIET – Research funders archiving mandates and guidelines, www.sherpa.ac.uk/juliet/index.php.

Open Planets Foundation, www.openplanetsfoundation.org.

OpenDOAR – worldwide Directory of Open Access Repositories, www.opendoar.org.

Portico, www.portico.org/digital-preservation.

Prometheus, The Digital Preservation Workflow Project, http://prometheus-digi.sourceforge.net.

RoMEO, publishers' copyright and archiving policies, www.sherpa.ac.uk/romeo.

SHERPA (Securing a Hybrid Environment for Research Preservation and Access), www.sherpa.ac.uk and SHERPA Search – simple full-text search of UK repositories, www.sherpa.ac.uk/romeo.

➡ Over to you . . .

Technology

1. Think about your workplace. Are there any ways you could use mash-ups or quick response codes to improve your service or engage your users?
2. Create a mash-up. Try taking data from one place, and combining it with data from another place to do something new. This can be as technical – or not! – as you like. If you don't think you have the necessary technical skills, come up with an idea, and see if you can work with someone who does.

   The Mashed Library wiki has a number of ideas to get you inspired. See www.mashedlibrary.com/wiki/index.php?title=Menu_suggestions.

Digital preservation

1. Think about the first computer program you used for work or study. Could you still open the files today? Or extract the data? What about your current files? Will you be able to open them in five years? What implications does this have for the library/archival world?
2. Write a digital preservation strategy for files associated with a current work or study project (about 500 words). Think about:

   - the types of files you need to store
   - who might need to access them
   - whether there are any security or confidentiality implications

- where you might store them – locally or remotely
- how much time and effort preservation will take
- what the implications are of losing access to this material.

CHAPTER 6
Getting and staying online

Introduction

An online presence for your service is vital, and new professionals may be expected to contribute to their workplace's web presence.

Nearly all institutions have a web presence of some kind. The advent of Web 2.0 and social media technology has made it possible to move away from static, merely informative web pages to a more interactive web presence. Moreover it has made it possible to do so quickly, easily and cheaply – without the need for experts or investment in expensive equipment. One of the things we will consider in this chapter is how library and archive services are using social media effectively.

But it is not just information about the service that users expect to find online. They want information about collections and materials – and, ideally, online access to the materials themselves. Information about collections can be made available by exposing your library or archive catalogue to Google, if the system allows, and you have the technical expertise available to do so. You could also release your data as open data, or linked open data, as mentioned by Lukas in Chapter 5.

Chapter 5 also looked at sustainable digital preservation, and talked about why it is important to ensure long-term access to materials. In this chapter we look at the principles of making your collections as online-accessible as possible, and how to facilitate access to your sustainably preserved material. First, Jane Stevenson of the Archives Hub will explain how to create archival descriptions that are web friendly, interoperable (usable by more than one system) and sustainable. Then we will look at how two library and archive services are putting these principles of openness and accessibility into practice, using social media tools.

Creating effective descriptions of archive collections for an online environment

When you think of archival finding aids, you might think of printed, or even written, handlists. Frequently stored with the materials they describe, and often on paper so old and yellow that they seem part of the archive themselves, paper handlists and printed descriptions were, for many years, the standard source for information about an archive.

The advent of the web is changing that. Many institutions still have a paper copy of the finding aid in the reading room, but these days it is just as likely to be a print-out of a pdf as an example of 'handwriting fashions of the last 100 years'. But is a pdf or Word document really any better? It might be in an electronic format – but is it a sustainable, interoperable format? Will it allow you to share your data with other systems? Jane Stevenson, manager of the Archives Hub, tells us about finding aids for the 21st century and beyond.

⚒ How to . . .
Think about sustainability and interoperability

The way people access archives is changing. Many users now rely heavily on the internet for information about archives and archive collections; this has led to changes in the way that archivists think about their catalogues: what may have been intended for researchers in your institution to consult in the reading room, in the presence of an archivist, is now expected to stand alone on a global stage. It is of vital importance that you create descriptions that are sustainable over time, interoperable with other systems and suitable for the online environment.

To be sustainable, the descriptions (or finding aids) that you create about your collections must be accessible in the long term. To be interoperable, the descriptions must be flexible, and usable in a number of ways, avoiding lock-in with a particular system. Well structured data are important because the more structured your data are, the more potential there is for them to be used in different ways for different research purposes (people often talk about reuse in this context).

When talking about archive descriptions you should think about how metadata can be shared more widely and combined in different ways for different purposes. All descriptions are classed as 'descriptive metadata' because they are describing content (the actual materials). Descriptive metadata commonly provide information such as titles, names of creators, dates and extent. They can be found in any type of format, from a card catalogue to information embedded in a web page telling you who created it, when it was created and so on. Your metadata should be accessible over time and interoperable with other systems. When creating descriptions that are suitable for the online environment you need to ensure that they work with the web, and the standards that the web employs.

Why should you care?

You will have invested time and money in creating descriptions of your collections. You need to recognize the importance of this work, and ensure that it has longevity. Descriptions are the most important marketing tool you have. Without good descriptive metadata, researchers cannot discover your collections and identify items of interest. You should think of your collection descriptions as part of what you are preserving for the future, alongside the archives.

Creating descriptions that are interoperable involves facilitating use in different contexts. If your metadata are inextricably tied to one system, particularly if that system is proprietary, then you need to think about the risks involved. What would you do if the system was no longer supported? It is important to ensure that you can export your descriptions in an appropriate format. You want to avoid ending up with metadata in obsolete formats where significant work is required to transfer the metadata to a new usable format.

As well as thinking about your users, you need to consider the expectations of your stakeholders. Many institutions are embracing the use of standard data formats, and some may find it compulsory. The UK government, for instance, mandated eXtensible Markup Language (XML) as its primary means for data integration for the public sector, as part of the e-Government Interoperability Framework (e-GIF; http://en.wikipedia.org/wiki/E-GIF).

Technology and discovery

You should consider the channels available to you for disseminating your descriptions and how you can take advantage of them. We work in the context of a fast-changing online environment in which data are open and fluid, and technology enables them to be combined and reused in different ways. If you only provide a closed database system, you aren't maximizing the opportunities for reuse and enabling the kinds of inter-connections that can advance research. Think about reaching out to your users, rather than expecting them to make the effort to find your website and your catalogues.

Cross-searching

Cross-searching is becoming more effective, with systems searching across diverse data sources. It is facilitated by creating good quality content that adheres to recognized standards. This can bring great advantages to researchers as:

- archives become more interconnected
- serendipity in searching is encouraged
- inter-disciplinary services are easier to develop
- archives are more fully integrated into the information landscape.

Data exchange

Data exchange is the ability to share data between systems, encouraging cross-searching. While you may keep your descriptions within a proprietary database system, it is important that they are not tied to this, and can be exported in a format that is suitable for data exchange (e.g. Encoded Archival Description (EAD); see below).

Data integration

Data integration is the ability to combine data from different sources and then provide end users with a unified view of the data. This may be done in a number of ways, such as through providing a single store of all the data, or through a unified query interface whereby information is retrieved from different databases. There have been a number of initiatives within the cultural heritage community to integrate data, but there are challenges around different semantics and different data formats.

Data aggregation

Data aggregation is a means to achieve data integration by bringing together data through services such as the Archives Hub (www.archiveshub.ac.uk), AIM25 (www.aim25.ac.uk), Copac (www.copac.ac.uk) for bibliographic resources and Culture Grid (www.culturegrid.org.uk) for museum resources. There are now European-wide initiatives: Archives Portal Network for archives (www. archivesportaleurope.eu) and Europeana for cultural heritage resources (www.europeana.eu).

These aggregators tend to take in data in a common format, such as MARC or

EAD. The use of common formats facilitates combining the data because there is a common structure. To be part of an aggregator and ensure your archives benefit from this type of cross-searching environment, you need to think about ensuring your data can be put into a suitable format.

Application programming interfaces

Application programming interfaces (APIs) are a means to open up your data to machines. We are used to the idea of a human-based interface, through a web browser, but APIs provide an interface that programmers can use to access your data. Thinking about this kind of access to data can help to change the mindset of the metadata-creating archivist or librarian. What is vital for machine-processable data is good and consistent structure. This is very different from creating something that is human-readable. The more you identify the different parts of your data effectively, the more a machine can do with the data. For example, the title, date, extent, access conditions and so on can all be identified. You can go further by identifying personal names and parts of names, such as surname, forename and dates. Remember, this is about identifying these parts of the data to machines, so there needs to be structure, through a mark-up or a database system .

Encoded Archival Description

EAD is an XML format for archival finding aids. It has been developed as a format for displaying descriptions online, and also acts as a useful format for data exchange and long-term storage. EAD is based on ISAD(G), the International Standard for Archival Description (General), and this conformance to standards is vital for interoperability to be realized.

It is difficult to plan for the long-term currency and effectiveness of your descriptions. Technologies are changing so fast that file formats, channels of communication and the very nature of the web are all changing at a rapid rate. This is why it is important to assess your position and think about the ongoing efficacy of your descriptions.

EAD provides a useful way to structure your descriptions in a way that is machine readable. XML is one of the most widely used formats for sharing structured information between computer programs and people. It is commonly used as a format for import and export, thus enabling descriptions to be migrated to different systems. It also has a large community of use, so you can benefit from the tools that are created to work with EAD.

Making the case

You may need to persuade your managers to change their way of thinking about the creation of metadata for archives. In summary:

- The creation of metadata involves a significant investment of time and resources and so you should think carefully about your cataloguing strategy.
- You should avoid lock-in with a particular system.
- You should think about opening up your data as much as you can. (The exception may be if you are in a situation where you do not want to get maximum profile and use of your archives, for example, if you are in a business archive where the materials are only used internally.)
- You should encourage the reuse of your data by ensuring they are machine readable and accessible through different channels.
- You should be aware of the importance of data exchange and avoid the silo mentality where your data are only available through your own website.

You can help safeguard against future problems with a number of basic strategies:

- Make sure that any management software you use exports descriptions in an appropriate format, so your descriptions are not inextricably locked in to your system.
- Have a collection policy that covers the descriptions as well as the archives. This ensures that you think about your descriptions as an important part of your work. You should address the need to access the descriptions over time, and consider the risks to your descriptions and how they can be mitigated.
- Understand how technology impacts on discovery.
- Ensure your cataloguers have an appreciation of the role of cataloguing in a digital world.
- Ensure that all of your descriptions have persistent identifiers. It is best to use HTTP identifiers (also known as URLs), as these are the basis of the world wide web.

Social media

Social media is all about interaction and collaboration. If Web 1.0 was the online equivalent of handing someone a business card and walking away, Web 2.0 is about starting a conversation. Conversation and interaction make you much more memorable and accessible to your users.

You can use social media technologies to help you build a relationship with your users. By enabling them to interact with you in methods and spaces of their choosing (such as Facebook, Twitter, Flickr and YouTube) you are allowing them to embed their interactions with you and your service into their normal internet lives.

Which social media tools you choose to use matters less than the mindset you bring to them. A social media strategy cannot succeed if you don't believe that interacting with your users will benefit both users and service. Take the time to actively listen to your users, and respond with as much attention as you would pay to face-to-face interactions.

The following two case studies show how an investment of staff time into social media can have substantial benefits for you and your users. We have evidence here from two very different scenarios: a large city's library and archive service with over a hundred staff, and a lone, part-time archivist in a small town in Canada. Both show how opening themselves up to interactions with users have helped them to promote their services, create and maintain interest, increase usage, increase and demonstrate the value of the collections and services, build good user relations, and provide enhanced customer service.

Ever wondered what it would be like to have social media engagement as part of your job? Sue Lawson, Service Improvement Assistant: Digital Marketing and Social Media at Manchester Library and Information Service, UK, gives us some insights into the social media life of a large library and archive service.

📁 Case study
Social media in the big city

In 2008 Manchester Library and Information Service (MLIS) decided to add a new activity to its marketing line up – social media. Part of a wider audience development programme, the project also included city centre outreach and e-mail marketing. A post was advertised and I was lucky enough to get the job.

MLIS has used several methods such as blogging, sharing photos and videos, tweets and Facebook to promote resources and activities and reach new audiences. It is cost effective, we can feature user generated content and it has helped us network with customers, publishers, authors, librarians, bloggers and developers from Manchester and beyond.

Today more than 7000 people follow MLIS on Facebook and Twitter, including Elbow's front man Guy Garvey! The Lit List blog has become an established part of the Manchester blogging scene and was featured on Visit Manchester's digital map of the city. We also publish content on Vimeo (http://vimeo.com, a video-sharing site) and Issuu (http://issuu.com; a digital publication site, frequently used for creating brochures) and have run several innovative Flickr projects.

Facebook and the Lit List

The story starts in 2008 when we launched a Facebook Page and a blog. The Lit List aimed to promote a busy calendar of library poetry and literature events that often got lost on our official website because of its clunky content management system, limited space and an overly bureaucratic permission system that meant some events never got published.

Facebook offered exciting opportunities to recycle library content in an engaging and shareable way, plus the opportunity to target specific audiences and even talk to our 'fans'. Daily updates point to the content of MLIS and other people in a mixture of news, events, videos, photos and links. Our aim is to inform, entertain and draw attention to services people may not know about.

Content is sourced from everywhere – colleagues, the Manchester City Council website, our archive photos, local news and a long list of blogs that I subscribe to in Google Reader. Some Facebook updates are pre-scheduled using Hootsuite (http://hootsuite.com; a social media dashboard), and there are lots more free social media management tools available. I check for comments about twice a day. Anyone can comment on our page and there are posting guidelines in our 'more info' section, which I use to deal with inappropriate posts or spammers.

Our Facebook presence has led to some exciting partnerships. We piloted the book widget of Random House's *A Christmas Carol* on our Facebook page and were able to give away 20 copies of *The Wonder* by Diana Evans to some lucky Facebook fans courtesy of Vintage Books. Libby Tempest, Library Cultural Services Manager, says 'The Lit List and Facebook have definitely raised the profile of our events. People ring up to book tickets before the posters have even gone up.'

Flickr

It is a bit of a cliché now but 'going where the people are' has worked for us. In June 2010 Manchester Central Library closed for a three-year refurbishment. As a keen Flickr user I knew there was an active Manchester Flickr community so it seemed the perfect place to recruit local photographers to record the library as it was before the closure. Publicized through Twitter, Flickr and local bloggers, 760 beautiful photographs of Central Library were submitted to the Get Wisdom Flickr pool.

Launched in December 2010 the Manchester Archives Plus project has recently published 5000 previously unseen archive photos on Flickr. Co-ordinated by Manchester Library's Archives Service, the Twitter account has amassed over 2000 followers and since December 2010 the Flickr images have been viewed over 650,000 times. More than 2642 photos have been tagged and 312 Flickr users have added Manchester Archives Plus as a contact.

Twitter

For speed of feedback, Twitter is pretty much unparalleled. Launching a new online reference resource (the *Guardian* and *Observer* archives), we needed to know whether or not it worked outside the Council's firewall. After tweeting a request for people to test it, a dozen Twitter users responded pretty much immediately to verify that it was working. Moreover, without any prompting from us, half of those testers went on to retweet the news.

Our Twitter followers differ in their demographic profile, tastes and interests to our Facebook users, demonstrating that diversifying our social media strategy has enabled us to reach diverse audiences.

Despite the 140 character limit Twitter can be incredibly effective. A retweet from Manchester musician Clint Boon sent 15,000 people to our Flickr gallery in one day. Twitter has opened up our archives to a whole new browsing audience, who would otherwise not visit or even be aware of the archives.

What does this mean for you?

This isn't a template for your organization. One size doesn't fit all. Take a look at your library and identify where social media could have a positive impact, transform communication, energize employees, or simply delight your customers.

If you decide to go ahead take some time to prepare a plan to convince the doubters. Be ready to share impressive social media statistics – how many people use Facebook in the world, in the UK or in your town?

Research successful case studies and identify projects in your organization areas that could benefit from social media tools. Know where to find social media policies and business plans in case you are asked to draft one. Be prepared to explain why a corporate website is no longer the best communication tool and have an amazing list of content ideas at your fingertips. What are you waiting for?

No time, no money?

Sue's case study is a great example of how a large service is using various forms of social media to reach out to, and engage with, their users. But one of the key points of social media tools is that they don't require a large input of time and money, making them perfect for services with limited resources.

In this next case study, Amanda Hill, Archivist at Deseronto Archives, and Consultant Archivist and Project Manager at Hillbraith Ltd tells us about how her small archives service is using social media to help promote the archives and provide access to materials.

📁 Case study
About Deseronto Archives

Deseronto is a small town in Eastern Ontario, Canada, with a population of under 2000, which was once an important centre for processing lumber. Deseronto Archives has one part-time member of staff who works there six hours a week with a fairly basic IT infrastructure. The Archives' holdings are principally photographs of the town and its people, many dating from the late 19th and early 20th centuries.

Getting online

With limited opening hours (and limited awareness of the service), making the photographs available online was a priority. This would make them accessible to anyone with an interest in the history of the town: local residents, people with family history connections to Deseronto, World War I history buffs (the town hosted two Royal Flying Corps pilot training camps) and lumber industry historians.

The decision was taken to digitize the collection and share the images using Flickr, which allows users to comment and annotate images and supports other functions that allow for fairly sophisticated description, such as placing images on maps and sorting them into sets. A 'pro' account is not free, but is not expensive: around £26 for two years. A grant from the town Deseronto enabled a mass-digitization effort in summer 2009, which put the majority of the Archives' photographs online at www.flickr.com/photos/deserontoarchives. The combined power of the descriptions of the materials in Flickr and indexing by search engines brings them to the attention of interested users.

To share information about activities in the Archives, a blog was established in late 2007. Initially, this used Blogger, but it was moved to WordPress in 2009 to take advantage of the static pages and ability to upload files of different types that are supported by that platform. The blog (http://deserontoarchives.wordpress.com) frequently links to the Flickr images, sometimes to explain the story behind them, at other times to ask for information about a particular photograph.

The Archives' Twitter account (http://twitter.com/DeserontoArch) was set up in January 2009 to share brief news items and as a means of interacting with local people on Twitter. At the time, there were not many other archives on Twitter, but that has changed and there is now an active professional Twitter scene for archivists.

An additional grant from the Ontario Ministry of Culture funded the staff time to create a new site in 2010 called 'About Deseronto' (http://aboutdeseronto.omeka.net). The idea behind this is to allow members of the public to upload their images and memories of the town directly (rather than having to do so through the archivist). This project also had an oral history component, allowing us to share audio files online. This site, like the blog and Twitter accounts, was free to set up.

The final piece of the social networking puzzle was the establishment of a Facebook presence for the Archives in 2011 (www.facebook.com/deseronto.archives). This has been successful in attracting an audience of mainly local residents with an interest in the town's history; it seems to be a different demographic from the Twitter followers, who seem to be predominately other archives and local businesses.

How do you manage this with so little staff time?

Setting up these sites was not too time-consuming. Properly describing photographs on Flickr does take a fair amount of time, so the initial grant to digitize the bulk of the images was very helpful. Now, uploading new images is part of the usual work of the Archives. Blog postings are regular but not frequent: averaging two per month, which is not too onerous.

What impact has using these tools had?

Photographs that were previously only available to be seen in Deseronto between 10am and 4pm on a Wednesday are now visible to internet users across the world at any time. Since the Flickr account was established in January 2008, the images have been viewed over 150,000 times. The benefit hasn't just been to the general public: the Archives have also gained, with information flowing back from knowledgeable people who have shared their expertise. Documents have been dated, names supplied and mysteries solved with the help of this wider community.

Awareness of the Archives has increased (locally and internationally), leading to new accessions of materials (some digital, some physical). The licence on the Flickr images is permissive, allowing others to embed Archives' photographs into their materials and share them even more widely, which helps to promote the collections. The Archives has been able to make use of the materials itself: exhibitions can be quickly assembled using the digital images and a self-guided tour of some of the interesting buildings in the town was put together using them. This was then made available on the blog for visitors to the town to download.

Are there any downsides?

Greater awareness of the Archives has led to an increase in the number of e-mail and telephone queries received, which could be seen as a disadvantage! There was one occasion when a blog commenter was rather too helpful, giving the name and address of the current occupants of a house, along with the fact that they attended a meeting on a certain evening of every month. This event illustrates that a certain amount of vigilance is required – which is not something that is a one day a week activity, but which does not take more than a few minutes a day overall.

Tips

Here are some tips for promoting your archives online:

- A lot will depend on your work environment – not everyone will be in a position to be able to set up a blog, Flickr, Facebook or Twitter account independently – you might need to work on getting managerial approval.
- See what works for other, related, institutions and think about how you can

adapt their approach for your own situation.

- You do need to worry about copyright for images you put online. But don't get so hung up about it that it stops you doing anything.
- Enthusiasm for your subject counts for a great deal. If you are passionate about your field, then it is always easier to come up with new blog posts about it. Although it does help if it is interesting to other people, too!
- You don't need a big budget, a huge amount of time or a lot of IT support to have a respectable online presence and a significant impact on the world outside your walls.

Social media tools

New social media sites emerge constantly and some social media tools are listed below. This is not an exhaustive list but it will give you an idea of some of the major sites in each category.

Blogging

A blog (short for weblog) consists of multiple entries (blog posts or just posts) on a website. These often contain personal reflections or comments. Blogs are usually displayed as a reverse-chronological set of posts, with the most recent first, and allow readers to comment on their content.

Blogging can allow institutions to communicate with users in a more informal setting than that of the official website or newsletters, and can contain all sorts of content, from short news items to in-depth opinion pieces.

The ability to comment on blog posts makes blogs a two-way social media tool, rather than just an information-dissemination tool. Interesting discussions can often start in the comment sections. Some institutions may feel inclined to disable comments for fear of abuse, but many feel that the benefits of having the channel of communication outweigh any potential risks. Most blogging platforms have good spam filters, which will reduce the need to monitor comments.

These are some blogging platforms:

- Blogger, www.blogger.com (one of the original blogging platforms, now part of the Google suite of products)
- Posterous, http://posterous.com (key selling point is ability to blog any content – photos, audio and video – as well as text by e-mail)

- Tumblr, www.tumblr.com (often used for photoblogs, but can be used with text as well)
- WordPress, http://wordpress.com (totally free, hosted online) and http://wordpress.org (free software, need your own hosting; more functionality).

Microblogging

Microblogging is great for pushing news out quickly, sharing links, and keeping up to date. While services like Twitter often come under fire in the media for being 'full of people talking about their breakfast', there is actually a lively and active information professional community on Twitter, and many information professionals use it for current awareness and professional networking.

These are some microblogging platforms:

- Identi.ca, https://identi.ca (runs on open source status.net software)
- Plurk, www.plurk.com
- Twitter, http://twitter.com (the best known microblogging service, with 100 million users in September 2011)
- Yammer, https://www.yammer.com (designed to provide private social networks for companies and organizations).

Networking

These sites are less specialized than some of the other categories. Networking sites combine characteristics of other types of site – for instance, you might be able to join in discussions (as in forums or blog comments), share photos, videos and other media (as in photo-sharing and video-sharing sites) and chat with your friends and contacts in real time (as with instant messaging software). The key selling point for networking sites is their number of users and their range of content.

These are some networking platforms:

- Facebook, www.facebook.com (widely called the most popular site on the internet, Facebook allows institutions and companies to create fan pages)
- Google +, https://plus.google.com (launched in 2011, Google+ or Google plus shares many of the features of Facebook and Twitter, with some

innovations, such as 'huddles' – live chat with a group of your contacts – and 'hangouts' – live video chat)

- LinkedIn, www.linkedin.com (designed for professional networking, allows you to post your CV, get recommendations, and make contacts)
- Spruz, http://spruz.com (allows you to create your own social networking site).

Photo-sharing

If your library or archive has a historic photo collection, think about sharing it online. Photo-sharing sites are very popular, and can be a great place to host images if you don't have the capacity to host them yourself.

These are some photo-sharing platforms:

- Flickr, www.flickr.com (with free and pro options)
- Photobucket, http://photobucket.com
- Picasa, http://picasa.google.com (includes a downloadable application for organizing your photos).

Video-sharing

Since the advent of YouTube in 2005, video-sharing sites have become extremely popular. Not just for live-action videos, cats in boxes, or people lipsynching, these sites often contain a lot of instructional and educational material. You could upload tutorials you have created using screen-capturing software.

These are two video-sharing platforms:

- Vimeo, http://vimeo.com (allows user-created content – no commercial videos)
- YouTube, www.youtube.com.

Social bookmarking

Information professionals have always appreciated a well curated resource list. Social bookmarking tools allow you to tag websites and share your bookmarks with others. You can build collaborative resource lists, or explore what other people have bookmarked under the same tag. You can also integrate your bookmarks into other platforms, such as blogs or virtual learning environments.

These are some social bookmarking platforms:

- Delicious, www.delicious.com (allows you to tag and share bookmarks, and see what others have bookmarked; Delicious was bought by the founders of YouTube, and became part of their company AVOS in 2011)
- Diigo, www.diigo.com (allows for highlighting and collaboration, as well as bookmarking)
- Pinboard, http://pinboard.in (also allows you to cache pages)
- Pinterest, http://pinterest.com (image-based bookmarking).

Wikis

A wiki is a website that is collaboratively edited. Editing privileges might be open to anyone, as with Wikipedia, or they might be restricted to a group or set of users. Wikis can be a great way to find and share information on the internet – while being cautious about how much you trust unverified information! They're also a useful collaboration tool, allowing users to work together virtually on a document or project. These sorts of wikis are often private, and can only be viewed or edited by a restricted group.

These are some wiki platforms:

- PBworks, http://pbworks.com (has free options for personal and educational use)
- Wetpaint, www.wetpaintcentral.com (one can easily create collaborative websites)
- Wikipedia, www.wikipedia.org (the most famous wiki, Wikipedia is a virtual encyclopedia that is open for anyone to edit).

Question and answer sites

These sites allow users to post questions, and (usually) vote on the best answers. Users don't have to post any identifying information, beyond a screen name, so they are a safe place for many people to ask questions they'd feel uncomfortable with asking elsewhere – or just wouldn't know who to ask. Getting involved in Q&A sites can be a great way to demonstrate your expertise and reach out to non-users.

These are two question and answer platforms:

- Quora, www.quora.com
- Yahoo Answers, http://answers.yahoo.com (the librarian-staffed 'Enquire' service is one of Yahoo Answers' knowledge partners).

Conclusion

In this chapter, we have heard from people in a range of institutions – an aggregated online discovery service, a large metropolitan library and archives, and a small archive service, with only six staff hours per week. Despite their differences, they share many of the same key points about getting and keeping your service online. One thing that comes through from all of the studies is the importance of having a sharing mindset. If you think about ways that people might like to use your data and materials in the future, you are much more likely to be able to open and transition your data successfully.

You need not be afraid to change, to experiment – and to fail. You don't necessarily need to have a social media policy in place before you start using these tools, but do think about what you are doing, and be prepared to justify it if asked.

Using social media can increase awareness and use of your collections and services, but you need to ensure that the benefit-flow is two-way. Service and users should both benefit from social media, especially if you are asking users to get involved with the work. You will get a lot more out of sharing if you allow others to share too! Don't be scared of setting your content free.

References and further reading
Interoperability and sustainability

Johnston, D. (2001) From Typescript Finding Aids to EAD (Encoded Archival Description): a university case study, *Journal of the Society of Archivists*, **22** (1), 39–52.

Miller, P. (2000) Interoperability: what is it and why should I want it?, *Ariadne*, **24**, (June), www.ariadne.ac.uk/issue24/interoperability/intro.html.

Spiro, L. (2009) *Archival Management Software: a report for the Council on Library and Information Resources*, www.clir.org/pubs/reports/spiro2009.html.

Stevenson, J. and Ruddock, B. (2010) Moving Towards Interoperability: experiences of the Archives Hub, *Ariadne*, **63**, (April), www.ariadne.ac.uk/issue63/stevenson-ruddock.

Resources

Discovery project, www.discovery.ac.uk.

Encoded Archival Description, www.loc.gov/ead.

ISAD(G) for archival description, www.icacds.org.uk/eng/ISAD(G).pdf.

Recommendations for online cataloguing, www.archiveshub.ac.uk/cataloguingtips.

UK Archives Discovery website, www.ukad.org (includes detailed indexing tutorial and case studies).

W3C Schools XML tutorial, www.w3schools.com/xml/default.asp.

Social media

Bain, S. (2010) Life is Tweet: social media at Orkney Library and Archive, FUMSI, http://web.fumsi.com/go/article/use/4527.

Bradley, P. (2009) Using Twitter in libraries, Phil Bradley's weblog, http://philbradley.typepad.com/phil_bradleys_weblog/2009/01/using-twitter-in-libraries.html.

Bradley, P. (2011) Which Social Network Should I be Using as a Librarian?, Phil Bradley's weblog, http://philbradley.typepad.com/phil_bradleys_weblog/2011/08/which-social-network-should-i-use-as-a-librarian.html.

Daines, J. G. III and Nimer, C. L. (2009) The Interactive Archivist: case studies in using web 2.0 to improve the archival experience, http://interactivearchivist.archivists.org.

Kosturski, K. and Skornia, F. (2011) Handheld Libraries 101: using mobile technologies in the academic library, *Computers in Libraries*, **31**, www.infotoday.com/cilmag/jul11/Kosturski_Skornia.shtml.

Ksenija, M.-O. (2009) New Work Spaces: wikis for cataloging collaborations, *Library Hi Tech News*, **26** (7), 15–20.

Mollett, A., Moran, D. and Dunleavy, P. (2011) *Using Twitter in University Research, Teaching, and Impact Activities: a guide for academics and researchers*, www2.lse.ac.uk/government/research/resgroups/LSEPublicPolicy/pdf/Twitter_Guide_Sept_2011.pdf.

Ruddock, B. (2011) Voices for the Library and Social Media, UKOLN blog, http://blogs.ukoln.ac.uk/cultural-heritage/2011/03/07/voices-for-the-library-and-social-media.

Stephens, M. (2008) Taming Technolust: ten steps for planning in a 2.0 world, *Reference & User Services Quarterly*, **47**, 314, http://rusa.metapress.com/content/t147665520516857.

Twitter (2011) One Hundred Million Voices, Twitter blog, http://blog.twitter.com/2011/09/one-hundred-million-voices.html.

Zeeman, D. et al. (2011) Assessing Innovation in Corporate and Government Libraries, *Computers in Libraries*, 31, www.infotoday.com/cilmag/jun11/Zeeman_Jones_Dysart.shtml.

➡ Over to you . . .

1. Pick three of the social media sites from the above list. For each one:
   - Find out more about the site – what is its purpose? Who runs it? What sort of content is there?
   - Look for institutions similar to yours which are using the site. How are they using it?
   - Think about how you could use the site for your workplace. Consider audience, format and content.
   - Think about what the strengths of the site are. What are its weaknesses?
2. Which of the three sites do you think would be most useful for your workplace? Why?
3. Write a business case for use of that site, based on your findings from question 1. This business case should be no more than one side of A4 paper. These are questions you might like to consider:
   - What advantages would using this site bring?
   - What disadvantages would not using the site bring?
   - Who would you be communicating with? Users, non-users, potential-users, other information professionals?
   - What risks are associated with using the site? Might it be sold to another company?
   - What expenditure would be needed to set up and maintain use of the site (include staff time)?

CHAPTER 7
Generating funding and doing more with less

Introduction

One of the phrases currently pervading the media is 'the current economic climate'. Whatever you may think about the global economic situation, recessions and economic uncertainties facing many countries are producing a straitened economy, with pressure on people and organizations at all levels to reduce spending, and 'do more with less'.

This is as true in the information environment as in any other sector. Libraries, archives and information services are facing cutbacks and closures. In 2011 many UK public libraries were under threat of closure due to reductions in council funding: at the time of writing, news and campaign website Public Libraries News reported, '433 libraries (344 buildings and 89 mobiles) currently under threat or closed/left council control since 1/4/11 out of c.4612 in the UK . . . Librarian professional body CILIP forecasts 600 libraries under threat (inc. 20% of English libraries)' (*Public Libraries News*, 2011 (statistics updated daily)).

Even if your service is under no threat of closure, you may be facing reductions in staff or funding. The corporate, legal and financial sectors, in particular, have been subject to some heavy outsourcing of their information work.

Demonstrating value

Services are also being asked to produce improved results with reduced resources. You might find this involves re-evaluating your services, or finding new ways to demonstrate your value for money or return on investment. You might be asked to put a monetary value on the services you provide, either a notional value for budgeting or a real value, which will be charged against other departments in your organization.

Just as internal charging can help you put a price on your services, a similar system can be used to help quantify your overall value, by looking at how much users would have to pay if you weren't available. A high-profile use of this principle is the British Library's report Measuring Our Value, which demonstrated that 'for every £1 of public funding the British Library receives annually, £4.40 is generated for the British economy' (British Library, 2004).

The Massachusetts Library Association produced a calculator to allow users to work out the value of the services they were getting from their public library. Users can fill out a web form (www.maine.gov/msl/services/calculator.htm) with details of number of books borrowed, time spent on library computers, and even how many reference questions they have asked, and get a dollar figure telling them how much these service would have cost them elsewhere. The code behind this calculator is available for other library and information services to adapt, and you can set your own values on certain services. Maine State Library, for instance, values each reference question at $15; the original web adaptor Chelmsford Public Library in Massachusetts values each 'reference assistance' at $7.

The ALA has a useful page of links to resources and articles about proving value and return on investment at www.ala.org/ala/research/librarystats/roi.

Finding more funding

New professionals might find the situation particularly gloomy, as it seems the jobs you have trained for are being slashed in front of your eyes. But there are alternatives. You could look for work in a non-traditional or emerging sector, such as information architecture or knowledge management, which uses your information professional skills. You could also look for new sources of funding for more traditional services. There is still funding available, though you may have to look at previously unconsidered sources, and might face stiff competition.

Raising revenue through charging for services can also help to generate funding. This might mean that internal charging becomes actual, instead of nominal, and your budget comes from payments from other departments within your organization. It might mean finding ways to monetize services – for instance, many archive services are seeing an increased interest from media companies in the wake of genealogy-based programmes such as *Who Do You Think You Are?* Where they may have previously allowed media free access to their search rooms and collections, many are now using this as an opportunity to generate revenue.

New professionals can bring an open outlook to funding, and may be able to suggest new and unexplored revenue sources or funding streams. But it is not always easy to know where to start looking, or how you go about identifying potential sources of funding.

Caroline Williams, Director of Research and Learning Resources, the University of Nottingham shares information about how, why and where you can get your hands on some extra income.

✎ How to . . .
Identify funding sources

When I was young I used to think that money was the most important thing in life. Now that I am old, I know it is.

Oscar Wilde

In these tough economic times, competition for scarce resources is growing, and to secure the budget we need to develop and enhance our existing services or start up something new we are required to seek and bid for external finance. So where do you start to look for funding? Unfortunately the answer is it depends on who you are, the nature of your organization, what you want to achieve and who you would like to work with (if anyone). This section aims to give a snapshot of types and sources of funding and some tips for applying for funding.

Types of funding

In my work in UK universities the major funders of library and information services work are JISC, research councils, trusts and foundations, and the European Union. The kinds of things these bodies fund range from setting up institutional repositories, developing open educational resources, digital literacy initiatives (all JISC), to digitalizing special collections (Wolfson Foundation) and adapting online educational materials from one country to another (EU Leonardo programme). Some funders issue calls for proposals so you need to sign up to their e-mail announcements to keep informed; others are open to applications at set times of the year; and others welcome proposals at any time. Selection processes can go through numerous rounds or stages of bidding, proposals, submissions and interviews.

Places to look for funding

The JISC website is www.jisc.ac.uk; see also www.jisc.ac.uk/fundingopportunities. aspx for funding possibilities.

These are some research council sources of funding:

* Arts and Humanities Research Council (AHRC), www.ahrc.ac.uk/FundingOpportunities/Pages/default.aspx
* Biotechnology and Biological Sciences Research Council (BBSRC), www.bbsrc.ac.uk/funding/funding-index.aspx
* Economic and Social Science Research Council (ESRC), http://www.esrc.ac.uk/funding-and-guidance/funding-opportunities
* Engineering and Physical Sciences Research Council (EPSRC), www.epsrc.ac.uk/funding/Pages/default.aspx
* Medical Research Council (MRC), www.mrc.ac.uk/Fundingopportunities/index.htm
* Natural Environment Research Council (NERC), www.nerc.ac.uk/funding
* Research Councils UK, www.rcuk.ac.uk
* Science and Technology Facilities Council (STFC), www.stfc.ac.uk/Funding+and+Grants/501.aspx

These are some European Union sources of funding:

* Europa, http://europa.eu/index_en.htm
* European Commission Cordis, http://cordis.europa.eu/home_en.html
* Framework 7 Programme, www.fp7uk.co.uk
* Leonardo website, www.leonardo.org.uk
* Singleimage, www.singleimage.co.uk/home (training and partner searches)
* UK Research Office, www.ukro.ac.uk/Pages/UKRO.aspx (research funding for universities)

These are a couple of sources of funding in the USA:

* Institute of Museum and Library Services (USA), www.imls.gov
* National Science Foundation (USA), www.nsf.gov/funding

These are some UK National Lottery sources of funding:

* BIG Lottery Fund, www.biglotteryfund.org.uk

- Heritage Lottery Fund, www.hlf.org.uk (uses money raised through the National Lottery)
- National Lottery, www.lotteryfunding.org.uk

These are some trusts and foundations that provide sources of funding:

- Andrew W. Mellon Foundation, www.mellon.org
- Endangered Archives Programme at the British Library, http://eap.bl.uk
- Esmee Fairbarn Foundation, www.esmeefairbairn.org.uk/index.html
- Foyle Foundation, www.foylefoundation.org.uk
- National Endowment for Science, Technology and the Arts (NESTA), www.nesta.org.uk
- Paul Hamlyn Foundation, www.phf.org.uk
- Wellcome Trust, www.wellcome.ac.uk/Funding/index.htm (supports different kinds of research and activities with the ultimate aim of protecting and improving human and animal health)
- Wolfson Foundation, www.wolfson.org.uk

Other sources include the Pilgrim Trust, the Sainsbury Family Charitable Trusts, the Gladys Krieble Delmas Foundation, the Mercers Company Charitable Foundation, the Goldsmiths Company and the J Paul Getty Jnr Charitable Trust.

There are a number of other sources of information about funding. Researchresearch.com is a provider of research news and funding information for the academic community. It provides researchers and research managers in all disciplines with coverage of the latest funding opportunities.

Harold Lewis's book *Bids, Tenders and Proposals* (2009) covers a wide range of information about funding sources and includes chapters on bidding for public sector contracts, tendering for the private sector, and bidding for research funding.

The UK National Archives (www.nationalarchives.gov.uk/information-management/our-services/funding-advice.htm) offers support to any organization in the UK planning projects involving archives and who are seeking funding advice. At the time of writing (autumn 2011) the National Archives (www.nationalarchives.gov.uk/information-management/our-services/cataloguing-grants-programme.htm) is administering the distribution of more than £1.5 million over five years to tackle cataloguing backlogs. Don't forget your own institution may provide special funding for new initiatives, for example grants for learning and teaching innovation, strategic development and larger-scale innovation. You may also have opportunities through some of the commercial organizations that provide services to your institutions such as system supplier competitions.

Before you start, ask yourself whether it is worth it

As a rule of thumb, we can estimate that three out of every four bids fail. If the chances of having a proposal funded are one in four, before they start potential bid writers should ask, 'Is it worth it?' The amount of time it takes to put together a good proposal is significant, and in my experience of responding to JISC calls for funding I estimate that writing, editing and costing a bid can take 100 hours of staff time.

So how do you decide whether to bid? Lewis (2009) gives an idea of the kind of criteria to consider when weighing up the potential opportunity against the costs of putting together a bid. You will need to consider skills and experience, your competitive situation, and your relationship with your strategy. If a decision is made to go ahead and put together a proposal, the next most important thing to remember is this: the bid writing process needs managing.

If yes, plan and manage the process

It may seem obvious but it is often overlooked – if you are responsible for putting together a bid you will have a deadline for submission, limited time (most likely because writing the bid will be a task to carry out on top of your 'day job'), and you will need backing and approval for the proposal from senior representatives at your organization. You will also need budget information, probably technical information, a range of skills embodied in different people in your department (and outside), and you may need partners from other institutions. Gathering information from others, gaining support, and getting feedback on drafts of the bid will all need careful planning and managing. Putting together a bid can be like managing a mini project in itself.

Advice from a colleague just starting out with bid writing: 'Allow the maximum amount of time possible to write the bid and start early. It will take longer than anticipated because you don't foresee all the issues.'

How to make a compelling case

The JISC Guide to Bidding for Grant Funding (www.jisc.ac.uk/funding

opportunities/funding_calls/2010/09/grant1110.aspx) presents a challenging list of criteria for successful bids and useful guidance on how to meet those criteria. This document offers a range of advice for successful bidding:

- Clarify project outputs and demonstrate wider benefits to the education and research community.
- Describe how the bid meets the criteria set out in the call.
- Demonstrate that an initial assessment of project risks has been undertaken.
- Provide a sound initial project plan and demonstrate robust project management arrangements.
- Demonstrate how the bid is aligned with the objectives of your college or institution.
- Document proposed dissemination, embedding and evaluation mechanisms.
- Comment on sustainability issues when project funding ceases.

To respond to this you will need to put together the jigsaw of a compelling case, the pieces of which will most likely include:

- well articulated and evidenced user need and demand
- clear aims, objectives and outputs
- a first draft overview project plan
- risk analysis
- stakeholder analysis
- a dissemination and communication plan
- a description of benefit(s) to be delivered (not just a list of project outputs)
- consideration of value for money so your budget is appropriate to the outcomes
- a list of outputs and benefits
- an account of the impact of the bid if it is successful and an evaluation process so you know whether your project has been successful
- consideration of sustainability issues – what will happen when the funding grant runs out
- the budget presented according to the requirements of the funder.

There could be more or fewer pieces of the jigsaw depending on the funder, so take time to read through call for funding carefully and take the advice of Eastwood and Norton (2010) and Lewis (2009) to use checklists all the way through the bid writing process, starting with noting all the key information from the initial call for funding.

What can go wrong?

As mentioned above, only one bid in four is likely to be successful. So why do some bids fail? In my experience, some of the things identified by bid reviewers in their feedback on bids that fail to get funding are lack of evidence of user demand, unclear aims and objectives, unclear deliverables, and lack of fit between the scope of the call and the bid proposal.

It is not possible to consider all of these points in detail. In short, I would recommend that you:

- send an e-mail to or telephone the contact at the funding agency to sound them out about whether your idea for a bid is in scope for the call for funding
- ask someone outside your immediate team and colleagues to review a draft of your bid and give you feedback on the clarity of what you are proposing to do and deliver; they will spot whether your case is clearly articulated to someone who does not know you, your work and your context
- focus on demand and evidence for it – this is not always easy especially if you are working 'ahead of the adoption curve'
- draw on user feedback, surveys, market research (interviews, focus groups and so on), strategies, widely applicable reports into behaviour and trends – anything that paints a credible picture of why your project is needed, solves a problem or improves stakeholders' situations.

Why do it?

Bid writing is hard work, resource intensive, time consuming and often doomed to failure. So why do it? Regardless of whether your proposal is successful or not, bid writing can be a rewarding and even enjoyable process. I asked a handful of colleagues what aspects of bid writing they enjoyed or found most rewarding and this is what they said:

> The prospect of being able to do something different and exciting motivates me. Finishing it is good – clicking on Send is a great feeling! Making the case – especially when you hit on something you think is a real clincher.

> I most enjoy working as a team to produce a high quality bid. Quite often the bids are completed under pressure to a definite deadline. This means

that the team have to focus on the work together and it can be extremely rewarding when the bid is completed on time to a high standard.

Researching the user need and finding evidence for the project from secondary or primary research is satisfying.

Finding the perfect partner for a project who is keen, enthusiastic and professional about putting the bid in.

And finally

If you are writing a bid for the first time, you will most likely find it useful to see other examples of successful bids. So talk to people at your institution or contacts in other organizations to try to get hold of some examples. If these are not forthcoming, speak to people in your organization who have had successful applications – ask advice and whether they would be willing to give feedback on drafts of your bid. Another useful way of building up your expertise in bid writing is to seek feedback on your application (important for both successful and unsuccessful bids) to learn lessons for next time.

Don't commit yourself to an unrealistic work or project plan or promise things that you cannot deliver within the time and funding available. Finally, put a bit of your personality into the bid and write with energy and enthusiasm.

Although it is fine to hear in the abstract that there is money available, and that you might be able to get hold of some, it can seem a bit like strategies for winning the lottery – does anyone actually ever succeed? Are those people holding the giant cheque real people, or just company shills? The amount of paperwork involved can also seem daunting, especially if you haven't applied for funding before. Is the return worth the effort you will be putting in?

Fiona Marriott from Luton Libraries shares her experience of applying successfully for £1.25 million of Big Lottery Award funding – why Luton Libraries applied for the award, the work staff did to prepare the bid, and the impact that receiving the funding has had on the library service and its users.

📁 Case study
The Big Lottery Award – Luton's experience

Luton Libraries (then part of Luton Borough Council) applied for Big Lottery funding in March 2007. The Central Library was built in 1962, and was showing its age, despite a cosmetic refurbishment in 1998. Usage of the library had changed over the decades, and accommodating new technology and the needs of different customers was becoming a problem. Younger people and families generally used the library in a social way, while older people often wanted quiet spaces to read or study.

The Big Lottery Fund was ideal for us, as there was the chance to apply for up to £2 million and have a significant impact on the way the service was run. More importantly, the grant would pay for extra staffing for the project, which would help with the management team workload.

The guidance made it clear that extensive community engagement and consultation was required, and any need had to be clearly demonstrated. We ensured that we gathered relevant demographic information and worked closely with other Luton Borough departments to pull the information together. This included providing fairly detailed costings for building improvements, costings and job descriptions for the staff we wanted to appoint, and information and references from current and potential partners.

Big Lottery Fund staff made it clear that the grant would only be given to libraries which were intent on major change, on updating library services and making them relevant for the 21st century, and we emphasized the proposed changes in our bid. This included the introduction of radio-frequency identification (RFID) self-service machines (funded by us as part of our in-kind contribution). These would free library staff from routine stamping of books, allowing them to spend more time on more complex enquiries and showing customers round the library. We also focused on 'zoning' the library, providing clear areas that would appeal to different types of customer.

The children's library was in a good position on the ground floor, but was cramped, so younger children and babies were using the same space as 11 year-olds. There was little room for activities of any kind. Part of the bid involved knocking down the walls between the children's library and the old story time room, to create a dedicated under-fives area, where babies and toddlers could crawl around without being trodden on by older children.

We also wanted to create a clearly defined area of the library for older customers, housing the large print and audio books in a bright and colourful space, away from the teenage area; this was to be run in partnership with Sight Concern, a local charity helping visually impaired people. We think the inclusion of partnership working was a particular strength for our bid.

The old reference library space was to be converted into a quiet study area, with more study tables and seats, which were always in demand, particularly at revision times. With zoning we would be able to enforce a 'no mobile phone use' rule in this area, because they could be used in other parts of the library. The existing IT suite in the lending library was to be glassed in to enable formal IT classes without disturbing other library customers. The final and most expensive part of the bid was the conversion of the top floor of the library to a suite of meeting rooms, classrooms and a café, to improve informal and formal learning facilities.

Putting the bid together

By using demographic information and statistics we were able to prove that the proportion of babies and toddlers in Luton was higher than the national average, but we were not attracting enough of their parents to the library. As low literacy is a problem in Luton, we could show (using evidence from Bookstart and the Reading Agency) that using the library would support these young families. We could also demonstrate that there would be significant demand for classes in English for speakers of other languages and adult literacy, to support our intention to host these classes in the new facilities.

We provided information gained through focus groups, attendance at existing forums and community groups, written feedback from customers and partners. We also ran an event called 'Love It, Hate It, Change It' in the shopping centre, to ask people what they would like from the new library, and what they wanted to keep.

As part of the bid we had to select and agree clear outcomes, including ongoing engagement with the community, offering volunteer opportunities and increasing participation in learning activities. Where we were unclear about any part of the bidding process, we made use of the contacts at the Big Lottery, to ensure that we were providing the right information. The bidding process involved most of the management team, and took over several months, but investing the time paid off, and we were finally awarded £1.25 million.

The library closed in December 2007 for the building work and reopened as a new library and learning centre in April 2008. Since we reopened, we have transferred the library service to Luton Cultural Services Trust and our services have continued to evolve. Although we had to provide regular updates for the Big Lottery, staff have been very supportive throughout the bidding and award process; our formal partnership came to an end in September 2011, having transformed the library beyond recognition.

As Fiona shows, the impact of the Big Lottery Funding on Luton's library services has been dramatic. But you can't always just apply for one big award and then sit on your laurels – many library and archive services apply for funding regularly, either as a necessity to supplement their base funding, or to allow them to work on specific projects.

In the next case study, we hear from Ioannis Trohopoulos and Dimitris Protopsaltou from Veria Public Library in Greece. Veria Public Library has an excellent track record of working with the community to secure funding for innovative and creative projects.

Case study
Veria Public Library: a case study in creativity and partnerships

The use of extensive external partnerships together with a creative approach to service delivery has enabled a library service to flourish in a difficult economic and cultural environment.

The economic problems in Greece are well documented. While Greece has a huge cultural heritage and some excellent museums, there is no history of public library provision. Veria is a town of about 55,000 people in the region of Central Makedonia in northern Greece. In the last 20 years the central library has developed from a quiet backwater in a couple of rooms above a garage in a small side street into a vibrant cultural hub for the community. It offers a range of innovative services, almost always based on information technology and often developed and funded through partnerships with external sources. Some general impression of the services can be gained from its website, www.libver.gr/en. Here you will find information about services such as hosting websites and offering free courses on topics such as creating digital media.

Partnership funding has been obtained in four ways. Initially the Library received European project funding. It has had at least one European project ongoing every year since 1995. International collaborations have enabled the development of new services such as ICT in mobile libraries, ICT skills classes, and the upskilling of the library staff.

The second source of funding has been Greek philanthropic foundations. The development of the creative area for children on the ground floor of the central library, known as Magic Boxes, was funded through the financial support of the Stavros Niarchos Foundation. Magic Boxes offers a completely novel environment in which children can relax and experiment. The library conceived Magic Boxes as a space for children to develop life-long skills and digital competencies. Emphasis is placed on promoting reading, creativity and digital literacy. To this end, we have developed this area where children may attend creative workshops such as robotics, 3D gaming, storytelling, painting, sculpting, theatre and music.

The third source of funding has been through collaborative co-operation with local organizations such as chambers of commerce and local authorities. A good recent example was the reaction to a reduction in funding which threatened the future of mobile library services in rural areas. When it became apparent that the library could no longer pay the salaries of the drivers of mobile libraries, it approached the mayors of local communities. Conscious that the mobile libraries provide a highly valued service to very rural communities, the mayors have supported the library by funding the drivers' salaries.

Finally, the partnership which has attracted most publicity nationally within Greece was the receipt in 2010 of the Bill and Melinda Gates Foundation Access to Learning Award (ATLA), worth one million dollars – a significant amount of money, which will allow the library to further develop its ICT-based services. Moreover, the library will implement further the idea of creating experience spaces (Magic Boxes) in other areas of the building.

ATLA 'recognizes the innovative efforts of public libraries or similar organizations outside the United States to connect people to information through free access to computers and the Internet' (www.gatesfoundation.org/ATLA/Pages/access-to-learning-award-overview.aspx). It is one award from a foundation, the guiding principle of which is that every life is equal (www.gatesfoundation.org/about/Pages/overview.aspx). An application was made for this award partly because it offered international recognition for years of creative work, but most importantly because it offered a significant amount of money with which to further develop services.

Writing a bid for external funding, whatever the size of the award, is time consuming. The ATLA award offered a larger reward than any of the library's other applications, and applying required drawing on the library's extensive experience of writing bids. Developing the bid involved carefully following the foundation's guidelines, writing many drafts of the bid and involving numerous people in the bid's development. The other ingredient in the success of this bid was persistence.

The successful bid in 2010 was the third bid for this award, the two previous bids having been short listed but not ultimately selected.

We don't think that there is anything revolutionary in our approach to bid writing; we recognize that it is hard work and any bid should go through many iterations, involving several people. It is important to really understand what the funders are seeking to achieve and ensure that any proposal meets their intentions and their specific requirements even if these seem eccentric. Interacting with the funding agency and cultivating a working relationship with the body can have benefits. Persistence is crucial – we applied to the Gates Foundation three times.

Other lessons that can be learned from the Veria experience are:

- to be ambitious but realistic
- to look for novel sources of funding (no Greek library had received EU funding when we first applied)
- to listen to the users and develop services which they value
- to serve the unserved; taking mobile libraries into rural areas was the first service brought to some of these communities
- to pay attention to good publicity and marketing.

Over the years, but particularly since the Gates award, the library has been featured in many national newspapers and magazines and at the time of writing this piece is about to be the subject of a feature programme on national television. Not only does this bring the library to the attention of its community and help develop a feel good factor but it also allows funding agencies to see that their support is making a difference.

Thanks to Dick Hartley for his help with this case study.

Conclusion

From these case studies we can learn that being successful in obtaining funding requires a number of attributes:

- *Creativity:* You need this in the projects you bid for and where you look for funding.
- *Persistence:* If you think the funding is right for you, don't be put off by a failure – apply again when you are able to. If you can get feedback from your unsuccessful applications, it will give you a greater chance of success next time.

- *Bravery:* It can seem daunting to apply for large sums of money. If it helps, remember that you are not asking for it for yourself – you are asking for it on behalf of your users. They deserve what this money can offer – go out there and get it for them!
- *Attention to detail:* You need the patience and attentiveness to ensure you have met all the funding criteria. A bid can be automatically rejected if a box is left unfilled.
- *Ambition:* The cliché 'you've got to be in it to win it' applies perfectly here. Although there is no point spending valuable staff time on funding applications for which you don't meet the criteria, there is also no point in not applying for funding you are eligible for because you think it sounds too prestigious, or that there will be too much competition, and you don't stand a chance. Be willing to take that chance, and you might find it pays off. And if it doesn't? It is still great experience for future applications.

Managing well in tough financial times is not just about finding alternative funding sources; it involves doing more with what you have. In many ways, this is the theme of this whole book – doing more with less experience, less time, less money. In the next chapter, we will look at managing budgets, and how to make the most of what money you do have.

References and further reading

British Library (2004) *Measuring our Value*, www.bl.uk/pdf/measuring.pdf.

Carpenter, J. (2008) *Library Project Funding: a guide to planning and writing proposals*, Chandos Publishing.

Eastwood, M. and Norton, M. (2010) *Writing Better Fundraising Applications*, 4th edn, Directory of Social Change.

Harper, R. and Corrall, S. (2011) Effects of the Economic Downturn on Academic Libraries in the UK: positions and projections in mid-2009, *New Review of Academic Librarianship*, **17** (1), 96–128.

Landau, H. B. (2010) *Winning Library Grants: a game plan*, ALA Editions.

Lewis, H. (2009) *Bids, Tenders and Proposals: winning business through best practice*, 3rd edn, Kogan Page.

Okojie, V. (2010) Innovative Financing for University Libraries in Sub-Saharan Africa, *Library Management*, **31** (6), 404–19.

Public Libraries News (2011) Historically, the "good guys" were not the ones

throwing away books, *Public Libraries News*, www.publiclibrariesnews.com/
2011/11/historically-good-guys-were-not-ones.html.

Smallwood, C. (2011) *The Frugal Librarian: thriving in tough economic times*, ALA
Editions.

Taylor, C. (2010) Thinking out of the Box: fundraising during economic downturns,
Serials Librarian, 59 (3–4), 370–83.

Van Hooland, S. et al. (2011) Opportunities and Risks for Libraries in Applying for
European Funding, *The Electronic Library*, **29** (1), 90–104.

➡ Over to you . . .

Find out the names and requirements of two funding bodies in your area. Which
would you be most likely to apply to for funds?

Write a business case of around 500 words for applying or not applying to this
funding body for a specific project. Think about:

- how well you fit their requirements
- whether you can meet the deadlines
- how much work would be involved
- what the consequences would be of getting the funding – would you need
  more staff?; is there a time limit on the spending of the money?
- what the consequences are of not getting the funding: would it have an
  impact on day-to-day service delivery?

CHAPTER 8
Managing money, budgets and negotiating

Introduction

At some point in your career you are going to have to talk money. Even if you never plan to be in a position with budget handling responsibilities, there are many other situations where you will find yourself involved with finance. You might be running a conference or event, and need to decide on charges, sponsorship packages, deal with speaker expenses, and negotiate deals with nearby hotels. Many job adverts now describe salary as 'according to experience' or 'negotiable', so you will need to be prepared to negotiate for the wage you want. You may be responsible for buying or maintaining subscriptions to services, handling fine or photocopying payments, or deciding how much to charge for commercial photography.

Depending on the organization you work for, you might have to bid internally for your funding, and make a case for all your expenditures. This is known as zero-sum budgeting, when you cannot rely on automatically receiving any money. Even if your department is a core item in the organizational budget, and is guaranteed some funds, you may find that your budget is being cut, and you are asked to find substantial savings. It is impossible to justify expenditure or identify areas where you can economize if you don't have a good understanding of your budget, and well organized documentation.

Budgets

Managing money is an important skill in all management positions. In library and information work, even if you don't run a team or a department, you will often have some financial responsibility, such as an acquisitions budget for your area. If you are a solo practitioner you might have the budget of the whole library to run.

Managing budgets and money is also a large part of project management, and showing that your organization is financially capable is important for getting external funding – no one is going to give you money if they think you are likely to mishandle it. A well managed library budget can also 'give a professional image to the library and help raise its profile amongst stakeholders' (Horsfield, 2010).

Therefore a knowledge of budgets and how they work is vital for any development work you would like to do in your service – even if you won't have control of the money yourself at the end, you will need to know enough to put in a good, feasible proposal.

It can be difficult to get experience working with budgets and finance. One way to get experience could be to volunteer as treasurer for a group or organization. Most groups will give you a chance to shadow their existing treasurer for a while to get the hang of what's involved before they hand over the books.

The library budget

There are some specific things you will need to think about for the library budget. Does it make more sense to subscribe to a journal or database individually, or as part of a bundle? Could you get a better deal as part of a consortium? What time of year are your journal renewals due? Do your journal subscriptions include back files? Have you budgeted for the VAT on your e-books? What is the real cost per download of your fixed-rate subscriptions? How much will it cost to repair your stock if it gets damaged?

These are all questions you need to answer to get the most out of your money. In the second part of this chapter we will look at negotiating, and how being part of a consortium can help save you money. First, Laura J. Wilkinson, Librarian at St Hugh's College, University of Oxford, gives us an introduction to managing a library budget.

⚑ How to . . .
Manage your budget

What is a budget?

A budget is a plan or allocation for an organization's funds, and is usually drawn up annually. At the end of a financial year, actual expenditure may be compared with the annual budget and used to measure performance.

Budgets can give authority to department heads or other managers to spend money for a particular purpose.

Preparing a budget

It is useful to have the previous year's figures available for comparison, then add a percentage to allow for inflation (the annual percentage change in the consumer price index is often used as a measure of inflation).

If the previous year's figures are not readily available in your library, try asking your finance department or senior manager for these records. If you cannot obtain the figures, ask your manager or financial supervisor for a year in which to collect this basic information before you are asked to estimate a budget and stick to it.

These are examples of costs to include:

- books
- periodicals
- library materials such as trolleys, kick stools
- marketing and promotion
- annual licences and subscriptions to services, for example photocopiers, security systems (such as RFID), library management systems, disaster recovery expenses, closed circuit TV systems
- staff salaries and payroll expenses
- miscellaneous items.

Find out if you have to take account of the costs of energy bills, telephones, maintenance and repair of buildings and interiors (often a capital expense), consumables (such as toner, paper and office supplies) and insurance.

A note about staff costs in your budget: staff costs include salaries and overtime or hourly paid work, as well as other payroll expenses such as the employer's contributions to a pension fund or similar scheme. Ask your personnel department to help you calculate the total staff costs for your team, as it will be higher than simply adding up everyone's annual pay.

Having used these retrospective guidelines to help build your basic budget, you should next consider any new expenses you may incur in the year to come and factor them in.

Types of expenditures and other things to consider

A capital expenditure is one that creates some benefit in the future (beyond the taxable year), and is unusually incurred when an organization spends money to buy fixed assets or to enhance an existing fixed asset, for example investing in a library security system.

An operating expenditure is an ongoing cost for running a product, organization or system. See the examples in the list above.

If you are preparing a budget for an expensive new project such as the installation of a security system, it is likely to be considered a capital expenditure as it will continue to benefit the library into the future, beyond the year in which it is paid for.

When researching the systems and costs for such a project, invite a number of different companies to tender for the work, so you can compare options and prices. The quoted cost is often negotiable, and it's worth asking the company if it would accept a lower price for the work if your budget won't quite stretch to the amount they have quoted.

In your budget proposal for a project which involves significant financial outlay, spell out the benefits of the project and try to allay any questions, fears or additional expenses associated with it. This will show that you have thoroughly considered all these aspects, and make it easier for the people deciding whether to authorize your proposal to approve it.

Find out if your organization is part of a purchasing consortium, as this may give you access to discounted rates for goods and services. If you work in an academic library, encourage academics to deposit in your library a copy of anything they've published – this helps to raise the profile of your organization as a research institution by showcasing academics' work, and gives your library free copies of what may otherwise be expensive items.

These are some other items you should consider:

- *Exchange rates:* If you purchase goods or services that are paid for in a currency other than your local currency, factor in an amount to allow for a less favourable exchange rate. This is particularly important for subscriptions for electronic resources, which are often paid in US dollars or euros and, because the amount is often high to start with, a small variation in exchange rates can add hundreds of pounds to the amount you pay.
- *Value-added tax:* Check that your figures take account of VAT (or other local taxes where applicable). The current VAT rate of 20% can push your final costs up considerably.

- *Acquisitions tracking:* Find out if your library management system has a function that allows you to enter the details of new books as they are added to your system. This will enable you to run reports showing the total costs of new books added during a certain period, and may allow you to split funds by subject area, or view totals by book supplier. If this is not possible, keeping track of this data using a spreadsheet is a good alternative.
- *Timings of large invoices:* Large invoices (often for electronic resources) often follow an annual cycle, which allows you to predict when this unusually big expense is due. You can then allocate a larger proportion of your annual budget to that month to allow for this (see monitoring a budget below).

Monitoring a budget

Once a budget is set, record actual expenses, compare actual results with the budget and if necessary take action to control spending.

This monitoring cycle can be easier to manage when done each month, rather than considering the year as a whole. To do this, divide the annual budget into allocations for each month. These allocations need not be equal, so if you can predict times of the year when there are more invoices to be paid than usual, allocate more funds to that period.

Then compare the actual spend with your allocation each month, as this will help keep you on track for the year. If you are overspent one month, you will be able to consider taking action to reduce your spending in the following month, and therefore bring your budget back on target.

Although your financial supervisor may not require this level of detail, it can be useful to create funds or sub-budgets for specific subjects or other subdivisions that are relevant to your library. This will allow you to track spending in more detail and may reveal areas of low spend, which may need closer attention to keep the collection current.

What skills do you need to manage a budget?

Attention to detail and basic numeracy are important. Using spreadsheets for tracking budgets will make your job a lot easier, and it is worth investing time and attending training courses to learn how to use spreadsheets effectively.

What challenges might you face?

Organizations vary considerably in their level of financial accountability from first-tier managers and in the systems they use for recording spending. Try to find out what is expected of you to ensure you can meet your organization's expectations (it may be sufficient just to stay within budget each year). You may decide to go beyond this and develop your own report as an end-of-year financial summary, and this will be a great help to you for future budget planning and as a record for your library, not to mention your professional pride.

Some workplaces use professional software such as Oracle Financials for approving invoices for payment. Alternatively, you may have a finance department that handles payments for you, and all you have to do is initial the invoice as an authorization. If you do the latter, keep a record of all invoices you have authorized.

What tools are there to help?

Because the arrangements for financial record-keeping can vary so much from one workplace to another, the best place to start is asking colleagues what they do. Having established a dialogue with them, they may be willing for you to shadow them so you can learn how they record spending, construct reports and prepare for budgeting meetings.

If your workplace uses specific software or methodologies for financial work, attend training to help you understand how these systems work.

Laura has given us a good introduction to the principles of managing a library budget, and these can be applied to any kind of financial planning you might need to do. But there is another aspect to budget management: making sure that you get the most out of your money.

Negotiating

Just as in a bazaar, if you want to get the best deal on your information resources, you have to be prepared to haggle. For many vendors, the only information on their pricing page is a prompt, 'Contact us for a quote'. These quotes may depend on proposed usage, number of licences, number of sites, number of full-time equivalent students and so on. Once you have received your quote, you will have nothing to compare it with – you don't know if you got the same deal as the library down the road, a better deal, or a much worse one. You might find you have to put in sealed bids for a service, where the vendor effectively asks what you are willing to pay.

You often have no way of knowing what other people have paid for the same or equivalent services unless you ask. This is where your network can come in. While other purchasers may have been asked not to publicize the price they paid, they may well be willing to disclose it in a private conversation. Even if you can't mention your knowledge to the vendor, it can give you an edge in negotiating, and help you to decide whether the deal is right for you. Vendors aren't out to con you, but they do have a responsibility to maximize their profits.

Taking this one step further are consortia. These are groups of institutions that band together to purchase goods and services. Consortia may find it easier to negotiate a better deal – after all, they have more bargaining power, as the vendor now risks losing several customers instead of just one. If you are a member of a consortium you don't have to do the negotiating with the vendors yourself!

Michael Stead, Information and Digital Services Manager at Wigan Leisure and Culture Trust, tells us about the importance of working together to get the most out of your money.

📁 Case study
Consortia and negotiating

What are consortia?

Consortia, in the library and archive domains and elsewhere, draw together a number of organizations, usually sharing a common geographical or functional relationship. Corporate drivers – and common sense – call for the best possible use to be made of resources that fund these services, and a consortial approach to negotiating contracts and purchasing goods and services can offer savings.

An example of a geographically based consortium is a stock purchasing group, which includes public libraries in the north west of England and Yorkshire. This group negotiates a discount on the cost of books provided to its members by their main suppliers. The consortium includes more than 20 public library authorities, which provide services to millions of people. The membership has a geographical basis: apart from this literal common ground, the communities served by the participating authorities range from Manchester's urban centres to the more rural areas of North Yorkshire and Cumbria. Drawing together these services, which have considerable combined spending power, allows the residents of each of these communities to benefit from library services whose stock budgets can be stretched by this consortial approach.

Consortia are not always formed strictly geographically. Some share a theme – perhaps shared back-end systems – in which case the members may be more closely tied in their approach to the work involved in running the consortium because of the nature of their shared characteristics.

Activities they undertake

Broadly, consortia do some or all of:

- contract negotiation
- training
- supply or service management.

Contract negotiation, often through a tendering process, is a big job. The managers of the consortium will need to balance their members' different needs, ensuring that everybody gets a good deal.

Consortia often arrange shared training for their members, perhaps at a single central venue, and often from the companies that supply services to them. If the supplier has a single point of contact for organizing these activities, and the members are all able to release staff for training at once, it can often be a cost-effective way of maintaining the skill levels and current awareness of staff.

As with organizing training, having a single, central point through which contracts, services or suppliers are managed can be beneficial.

Involvement in consortia

Your senior managers will be involved with the decision to join a consortium, particularly if it concerns areas such as stock purchase, which will require contracts for millions of pounds of expenditure over a number of years. Typically, a consortium will have nominated contacts; getting in touch with them will be the first step to further involvement.

If your employer is a participant in one or more consortia, it might be worthwhile to find out whether you can contribute to their work. You might start by finding out from your colleagues and managers which of these groups your employer has joined, and who your designated contact is. It could be appropriate for you to attend a meeting as an observer first, before you seek to take on more regular and contributory involvement having discussed it with your manager.

Involvement with these groups is a great way for you to expand your experience at little expense to your employer, and to provide input as a new professional to the decision-making process. You will meet fellow professionals from outside your current employment, allowing you to build up your contacts, and you will learn how to manage and contribute to large, relatively high-level meetings.

Involvement with the business carried out by a consortium will allow you to learn about some of the challenges involved in management. Given that the focus of much consortium work is on contracts, tenders and negotiation, and that the future of many archive and library services of different types is and will continue to be contingent on funding and related negotiations, this skill set becomes more important all the time.

The coming together of a number of different services under the umbrella of a consortium is a ready-made forum for sharing expertise. A consortium with a single focus – perhaps on online services – will manage the negotiation of supply contracts to ensure the best possible price for each participant, and will also act as a central hub for sharing information and running training sessions. The consortium will encourage its suppliers to run training sessions, and its members to participate. Involvement with a group like this will be very valuable as you build your professional networks.

Why is negotiating important?

As discussed earlier, the drive to elicit the best possible outcome from the use of your budget is a significant motivating factor in the consortial approach to the acquisition of goods and services by member organizations. It might be a while before you are required to conduct negotiations at that higher, more strategic level (or it might not!), but the principles are relevant to you and your current position.

If you are reading this book, you are most likely a new professional. It is probably safe also to assume that your reading of this book indicates a desire to progress in your profession. You will need to negotiate with your manager in setting things like personal performance targets; you should want these to stretch you, and so should your manager, but you should also ensure they are realistic and achievable.

Negotiation strategies for new professionals

There is one simple rule when beginning negotiation. It doesn't guarantee success, but will make your life easier: prepare.

Enter a negotiation knowing not only what you want the outcome to be, but why you want it to be that way. 'Because it's cool' is not an acceptable reason: think instead about how your idea fits with or enhances established corporate aims. Think about how it makes your unique collections more accessible, how it increases use of your resources, and how you can evidence these bold statements by using comparator data from other organizations.

Where can you learn more?

Start by asking around. Your colleagues and managers will be able to tell you which consortia your organization is involved with, and who your representatives are. Your enthusiasm for acquiring knowledge and skills, and for learning about your colleagues' work, is one of your greatest assets: use it to talk to those representatives and discuss with them and your managers why you would like to be involved. It helps if you have an established professional interest in the area of operations which the consortium in question covers, but you will most probably be able to find one that fits with your favourite aspects of the library, information and archive professions.

Conclusion

Being able to understand the principles behind finances and budget handling will be useful in many aspects of your information work, and can help you to express your worth to your users and stakeholders. Managing your money well will enable you to offer the best service possible, and you will gain skills that will make you more valuable and employable in the future.

Working with consortia will benefit your service, but also your personal and professional development, by allowing you to gain new skills and contacts. We'll come back to the importance of professional networks in Chapter 11.

References and further reading

Atrill, P. and McLaney, E. (2010) *Accounting and Finance for Non-Specialists with MyAccountingLab*, 7th edn, Financial Times and Prentice Hall.

Brookson, S. (2000) *Managing Budgets*, Dorling Kindersley.

Carey, M., Knowles, C. and Towers-Clark, J. (2011) *Accounting: a Smart Approach*, Oxford University Press.

Horsfield, K. (2010) *Making Ends Meet: planning and managing the primary school library budget*, School Library Association.

Novak, D., Paulos, A. and St. Clair, G. (2011) Data-Driven Budget Reductions: a case study, *The Bottom Line: managing library finances*, **24** (1): 24–34.

Weir, R. O. (2010) Trimming the Library Materials Budget: communication and preparation as key elements, *Serials Review*, **36**, 147–51.

Resources

Campbell R. Harvey's Hypertextual Finance Glossary, www.duke.edu/~charvey/Classes/wpg/bfglosb.htm (a very comprehensive glossary).

Glossary of financial terms and ratios, from Business Balls, www.businessballs.com/finance.htm (a basic glossary, suitable for beginners).

Information on financial planning and accounts from Business Link, www.businesslink.gov.uk/bdotg/action/layer?r.l1=1073858790&r.s=tl&topicId=107 3858944.

Journal Usage Statistics Portal, www.jusp.mimas.ac.uk (allows you to track journal usage across multiple providers, and work out the cost per transaction of your subscriptions).

Consortia and shared resources

Kohl, D. F. and T. Sanville (2006) More Bang for the Buck: increasing the effectiveness of library expenditures through cooperation, *Library Trends*, **54** (3), 394.

Scigliano, M. (2010) Measuring the Use of Networked Electronic Journals in an Academic Library Consortium: moving beyond MINES for Libraries (registered) in Ontario Scholars Portal, *Serials Review*, **36** (2), 72–8.

➡ Over to you . . .

See the Appendix, or download the Excel budget file from the **website** *e̸* **(http://lisnewprofs.com/budgetspreadsheet/)**. The different tabs contain templates to complete, and examples of what they look like when partially completed. Thanks to Laura J. Wilkinson for the spreadsheet.

1. Either complete this with totals for your service, or look at the example
   expenditure. Imagine that this represents your expenditure for 2012, and
   that you have been told to make a 10% budget cut for 2013. Where would
   you make these cuts?
       You might find it helps to break down books and periodicals, and think
   about the costs of various delivery models and formats such as VAT on e-books,
   swapping electronic access for hard copy collection and de-duplication, and
   using a document supply service rather than maintaining subscriptions.
2. Think about the stakeholders you identified in Chapter 4. How would each
   group be affected by these cuts? Is there a group whose needs you need to
   prioritize? Is there a way you could move some costs onto stakeholder
   groups?

CHAPTER 9
Information ethics and copyright

Introduction

Adhering to a set of common ethical standards and values is part of what defines a profession, and is as important for information professionals as it is for doctors or lawyers. When you become a member of a professional body, you agree to abide by the ethical practices of that body, and may be subject to disciplinary proceedings if you are found to have not done so. Non-members should not take this as permission to disregard ethics! Acting with integrity should be a vital part of every professional's conduct, whether they have committed to adhere to a particular code of conduct or not.

As Sturges (2003) points out, the UK didn't have an official ethical code for library and information professionals until 1983, and was again without one in the early 2000s, following the formation of CILIP from the merger of the Library Association and the Institute of Information Scientists: 'The evidence suggests that if a code has any function at all in Britain, it is not to provide a set of rules against which the conduct of delinquent members can be judged. Rather it is to set out principles that will help the membership as a whole to structure their professional conduct' (2003).

Frank Boles of the Society of American Archivists (SAA) makes a similar point: 'In the end, the Code of Ethics is for our members to use – and perhaps place in their own work environments – rather than for the Society to enforce' (2009). While this may be true in most cases, there is a recognized need for recourse in cases of breach of ethical codes, and most professional organizations have a system in place to deal with them. It may be argued that being seen to censure those who fail to uphold the ethical and moral standards of the profession is a key component of upholding professionalism in the public eye.

It is likely that most practitioners will never come into contact with official disciplinary proceedings, or serious breaches of the ethical code, but they will come into contact with ethical dilemmas, and this is where the guidelines and communities of discussion come in. Guidelines by themselves are very useful things to have, but it can be difficult to apply them in practice. For instance, the American Library Association's (ALA's) principle 'We respect intellectual property rights and advocate balance between the interests of information users and rights holders' (2008) doesn't tell you much about how to calm down the angry user who has been photocopying and storing every edition of a journal for a number of years, and doesn't intend to stop now.

Experience is vital in interpreting abstract and general codes into guidance for day-to-day practice, so new professionals in particular may find the practical application of ethical codes problematic. It is not possible to prepare yourself for all the ethical decisions you are likely to face, but it is a good idea to start thinking about some of the common situations. Read up on case studies (see 'References and further reading' and 'Resources' below), and use your professional networks. Most information professionals are happy to discuss issues in the abstract, and most professional bodies have someone you can talk to in confidence. If you have to deal with the issue on the spot, it's perfectly OK to discuss it with professional colleagues in retrospect (anonymously if necessary), to see what they would have done in the same situation, and whether you might have handled it differently given further knowledge or more time to think.

Information ethics

Ethics should inform areas of professional practice, not just dealings with users. You may have seen news stories about the autobiographies of prominent political figures (such as Tony Blair and George W. Bush) being used for political comment, by being placed in various sections of bookshops such as 'True Crime'. This highlights the need for ethical practice within the library in cataloguing and classification. David McMenemy, of the Department of Computer and Information Sciences, University of Strathclyde, gives us an introduction to ethical practice, and discusses areas where these questions may arise.

✦ How to . . .
Be ethical when working with information

For any profession, having an ethical framework to guide those practising it is a vital component of professional status. The sociologist M. S. Larson claimed that for a profession to exist, several key components have to be in place: a professional association, a body of knowledge, institutionalized training, licensing of the qualifications, university control and a code of ethics (Larson, 1977). Clearly, as it qualifies in all categories, LIS fits Larson's criteria for a profession.

However, while being a professional brings with it important responsibilities to the employer, it also brings responsibilities for the wider profession and society. It is in these potentially conflicting responsibilities that many ethical dilemmas lie.

What are information ethics?

Library and information ethics are grounded in the realities of the day-to-day life for a library and information professional. In the selection, organization and supply of information resources to users information professionals can come up against a range of ethical issues. To illustrate this let us consider potential ethical situations in different categories.

Selection

With selection of materials come ethical pressures to ensure that no bias or prejudice is shown in the selection. Foskett famously debated that a librarian's creed should be no politics, no religion, no morals (1962). However the title of the paper hid the real argument he was making: that a library and information professional must have all politics, all religions and all morals in mind when selecting materials, all the better to leave no idea or viewpoint unaired. In so doing they may need to justify why they have made available materials that many in society may deem to be offensive.

Organization

How material is organized and classified presents a world view to users of the library and information service. Even a classification system as ubiquitous as Dewey Decimal Classification offers potential offence to many people by how it presents the topic of religion; for instance Christianity takes up six of the seven divisions devoted to world religions. This places one religion above others, and may well insult users.

Gorman (2000) has also stressed that organization of materials should be rational in its logic for a user to understand, and in how that knowledge is represented as part of the collected work of mankind. It would be unethical, for instance, for someone of a particular belief to classify an item incorrectly because they do not agree with the viewpoint aired.

Supply

Equity of access to resources is a vital human right, and one that all library and information professionals should strive to maintain. Clearly in non-public settings this may not be a major aspect of the job, but ensuring users have access to what they need to function, as a citizen, employee, customer or scholar, is equally important.

Library and information professionals also have a legal and ethical duty to ensure their users do not abuse intellectual property. Putting aside ethical reasons for one moment, the liability of an organization that does not practise this way is considerable. Rights holders do not tread carefully where they are aware of an organization breaching their intellectual property, and the sums of money paid by organizations found to have breached intellectual property is deliberately designed to deter others from being relaxed.

How do you recognize an ethical dilemma, and what sort of situations might you face?

Ethical dilemmas are best identified via a sound knowledge of the appropriate ethical code for your profession; in the UK this is CILIP's Code of Professional Practice for practising library and information professionals (CILIP, 2004). Clearly some ethical dilemmas may be more obvious than others – a patron asking you to purchase offensive or illegal materials, photocopy a copyrighted piece, or supply personal details on a user would all be obvious breaches of ethics, and you would need no guide to inform you they were wrong.

Some dilemmas may not be so obvious, however; take the safeguarding of intellectual property rights. Licences for electronic resources can be complex, expensive and frustrating for library and information professionals. If they pose such obstacles to those who understand them, imagine the obstacles they pose for a layperson. Ensuring users understand these licences and are encouraged to adhere to them is an important part of ethical and legal practice.

Another example is that in 2011 a trawl of UK newspapers found seven cases reported where a member of the public had accessed inappropriate materials using a public library computer. Every one of these cases presented an ethical dilemma for the library service, with the press demanding a statement explaining why the user was able to access objectionable material. Such a scenario requires a well thought out rationale explaining why the internet service is important, and how the organization defines acceptable use. Equally the information service may have decided that a form of internet filtering has to be applied to ensure concerns of stakeholders are addressed – again this presents an ethical dilemma that must be rationalized and justified.

Where can you find support and guidance?

Like any other aspect of professional practice, the best way to understand ethical issues is to make the study of them an important part of your continuing professional development. This is much more straightforward than it used to be, as in recent years a wealth of materials have been made available on the topic.

All CILIP members must adhere to the Code of Professional Practice, and the site to support this is an excellent first port of call, featuring the document itself and background information on ethical issues. Several useful books are also listed in the further reading section below.

Copyright

One of the most common ethical issues you are likely to face is the question of copyright and intellectual property rights. It is an ever-evolving area, and one where it can be difficult to balance our duty to uphold copyright and intellectual property law, and our duty to provide our users with the information they need. It can be frustrating for users, who don't understand why you can't allow them access to or copies of particular content; and it can be frustrating for information professionals, who want to help users as much as possible.

The ubiquity of technology in libraries and archives can add to the complexity of monitoring copyright violations. It may be possible to check whether a user is photocopying a whole book; it may be virtually impossible to detect if they are scanning the same book using their smartphone. Libraries may find themselves liable for online copyright violations performed by people using library computers. Under the current UK Digital Economy Act, for instance, reports of copyright infringement can lead to action against the owner of the IP address, with no investigation of whether the owner committed or was aware of the infringement. There is currently confusion over what this could mean for libraries and other providers of public computers (Holland, 2010).

There is no one easy way to ensure that none of your users are violating copyright, but there are things you can do to educate them and encourage compliance. Emily Goodhand, Copyright and Compliance Officer at the University of Reading, gives new professionals some advice for dealing with copyright and intellectual property issues.

🔧 How to . . .
Start out in copyright

You are likely to come up against copyright as an information professional. Whatever area you specialize in, sooner or later you will hear the dreaded word. But does it really have to be as scary as all that? Here is a quick guide to getting you started in copyright, from one information professional to another.

Getting a feel for the subject

As with anything, it is useful to do some research and find out more about what copyright is all about. Here are some tips on where to start:

- *Read your national Copyright Act:* These are usually available online nowadays. Head for the section which says defences, permitted acts, exceptions or limitations, and find out where libraries and archives are mentioned. What can and can't you do according to the Act? Are there any caveats that stand out?
- *Establish yourself in a community:* Very often you can be a lone worker on copyright issues, and it is incredibly difficult to work in a vacuum. Try to find other people in your position. Subscribe to e-mail lists, or ask your professional body. Check websites of other organizations similar to yours – there is usually a copyright notice and, if you are lucky, an e-mail address of someone to contact. Don't be afraid to send them an e-mail – if they have been in a similar role for longer than you they should be more established and may well be glad to give you advice.
- *Go to training events:* Yes, budgets are tight in this day and age, but you can still find out what is on offer. That way, you can choose a couple of affordable, relevant courses on copyright and make a case for attending. You will only need to go to one or two of these courses before you find that you

are well versed enough in the basics of the law to have a better idea of how to apply it. And don't just look at the ones you have to travel to. Nowadays more and more courses are being run as webinars over the internet. And some are inexpensive, or even free!

- *Subscribe to relevant publications:* These could be in the form of journals, magazines or free e-mail digests from legal organizations. Keep the focus on intellectual property, as that is the category into which copyright falls.
- *Network!:* Go to as many seminars, conferences and events as you can justify, and talk to as many people as possible while you are there. Set yourself up on professional online networks such as LinkedIn and Twitter; search for people or groups who talk about copyright and intellectual property; and follow lawyers and other librarians, or anyone with 'copyright' in their name. You will quickly find that this solves the problem of working in a vacuum as you become settled in a little online copyright community. Note of caution though: this does take time, as you have to build a network for yourself.

Create a culture of compliance

The vital thing to remember as an information professional is that you are bridging the gap between rights holders and users. And although copyright should be taken seriously, you should not define yourself in the role of copyright cop. Rather than trying to police everything, put your energy into ensuring that your organization's infrastructure promotes compliance. Check to see whether your institution has a copyright policy; if it doesn't, write one. An institutional copyright policy should include:

- a statement that users are responsible for copyright compliance
- an outline of the responsibilities that the organization has to encourage compliance
- a section on how infringements are handled (disciplinary procedures, for example); then if infringements arise, you have a mechanism by which you can handle them.

The best way to handle infringements is by good relationship management. Remember: most copyright infringements happen perfectly innocently, with the infringer often unaware that they have done something wrong. Always respond to a complaint and apologize; state that there are measures in place to deal with copyright infringement and that the offending article has been removed or the situation has been rectified. Ignorance of the law is no defence, but an apology goes a long way to lessening the severity of the charge.

Finally, if you discover a lot of similar infringements, you have to ask yourself why they have occurred. If a lot of people in the organization are infringing copyright in a particular way, is a licence available to allow this activity to continue in a compliant manner? Learn to spot patterns and identify areas of further training and/or the need for a licence.

Living with licences

You will need to be more vigilant about compliance when there is a licence agreement in place. Blanket licences can be purchased to extend the provisions of the law and account for the type of activity with copyright material that your organization is involved in. Pay close attention to the details in licence agreements (yes this means reading the small print), find out what can and can't be done with content, and try to negotiate if the licence is too restrictive. Archivists may have to draw up licence agreements with depositors to enable further access and use of original works; try to make sure that non-commercial uses such as copying for research and study are covered, as well as the ability to exhibit works.

Educate your users!

The best thing you can do as an information professional is to take steps to educate your users about copyright. Don't tell them everything in one go – it is always better to tailor copyright education to the areas that are most relevant to them. Identify areas of high and low risk of copyright infringement to the institution and target high risk areas first. Table 9.1 lists the advantages and

Table 9.1 *Pros and cons of different types of user education*

Format of user education	Advantages	Disadvantages
Training sessions	Face-to-face contact	Only reaches a limited number of people
Leaflets and guidance	Potentially reaches everyone	Not everyone reads it
Online modules and short tests	Reaches everyone	Not everyone does it unless made compulsory
Frequently asked questions	Solves basic copyright queries	Not good for complex queries

disadvantages of different types of user education.

Here are some tips:

- Keep it positive! People tend to associate copyright with negatives, so focus on what can they do as opposed to what can't they do.
- Don't underplay the seriousness though – try to throw in a couple of real-life examples of the result of copyright infringement so that they don't adopt a laissez-faire attitude.
- Make it fun and keep it real! It is unlikely you will ever get 100% compliance.
- Be approachable – you want users to come to you to talk about copyright issues, not avoid you.

Many new professionals might feel unprepared to deal with some of the more esoteric issues of copyright and intellectual property. It is one thing to be able to remember the usual term of copyright expiry for printed works, but what do you do if someone asks for a copy of an unpublished manuscript? What about that box of old photographs – can you digitize them and sell copies to raise some much needed funds? Tim Padfield, Information Policy Consultant in the Information Policy and Services Directorate at the UK National Archives, introduces us to the principles of dealing with copyright issues with archival materials.

🔧 How to . . .
Deal with copyright in archives

As an aspiring archivist or records manager, it might not have occurred to you that copyright, of all subjects, can be interesting or even enjoyable. As it happens it can be both: the basic concept is fairly simple, while the detailed application is intellectually stimulating and involves real problems for people. Even if you do not accept this, though, it is important that you understand something of copyright, and know where to look to find out more when necessary.

Why is copyright important to an archivist or records manager? Here are some things to think about:

- Copyright applies, or is capable of applying, to virtually everything in an archive or registry: written texts of all kinds, including business letters, accounts or diaries; maps, plans, drawings and photographs; sound recordings; films.

- It lasts for a long time: in the UK and many other parts of the world the standard term is for the life of the author plus a further 70 years. A drawing made by an artist aged 20 in 1865 could still be in copyright in 2012 if the artist died aged 97 in 1942. That's a term of 147 years from creation. Archivists in the UK have it even worse: an unpublished literary (written) work is in copyright until 2039 at the earliest, regardless of when it was created.
- The simple making of a copy can infringe, but there are exceptions to the rights of copyright owners. You need to be aware of what they permit and what requires permission.
- Users of archival services frequently wish to publish the results of their research. They rely on the archivist for advice on what they may do and how they should set about obtaining necessary permissions. You should be able to advise them on where to look for answers and you should be ready to give permission yourself if you have authority to do so.

These are the questions you should ask when confronted with a copyright problem:

- What kind of work is it: literary, artistic, sound recording, film?
- Are you being asked to supply a copy? If so, you need to know about the exceptions to copyright that apply to you and what they permit.
- Does the proposed use of the work infringe? You should be safe, for instance, if exhibiting an artistic work or quoting from a literary work in a review of it.
- Do you know, or can you discover, who created the work and when?
- Has copyright expired?
- Did the creator own the copyright, or was it perhaps owned by an employer?
- Is it possible to trace how the ownership has been passed through successive generations or to successor bodies, so that you can identify the current owner?
- Is there a licensing body that can issue a licence and do the work of tracing the rights owner for you? Sadly for archivists and records managers, this is not such an easy solution as it can be for librarians, but it is likely to work with artistic materials.

The biggest copyright problem for archivists is created by the biggest opportunity they have ever faced. Modern technology makes it possible to create a digital copy of virtually any document and to allow users to gain access to it online from a computer on the far side of the world. The demand for these services is immense, and as an archivist you are expected to provide them. May you do so?

There is no copyright problem if:

* copyright has expired
* you have authority from the copyright owner to give permission or to use the work. This will be the case if a copyright owner has assigned the rights or given a licence to the archive (so long as the terms of the licence permit). It should also be the case if the documents in question are the copyright of your employer or parent authority.

Otherwise:

* Digitization involves copying, which is an infringement. Making the copy available online is a communication to the public, which is an infringement. Permission is needed for both these activities.
* Most archival documents are orphans: they are copyright but the copyright owner is unidentifiable or untraceable, even if a 'diligent search' is carried out. What is the likelihood that you will be able to identify and trace the current owner of copyright in a private letter written by, say, a child's governess in 1870?
* Even if it were possible to trace the copyright owners, would it be economically viable to do it for every one of thousands of works to be digitized in an online project?
* Countries around the world are seeking to find satisfactory solutions to the orphan works problem, but even when they find one it tends to be directed at published works alone. Archivists remain out in the cold, but should encourage their governments to create exceptions or licensing solutions that will help them.

So, the message is: don't regard copyright as a dark river full of ferocious beasts and currents. Approach it like any other intellectual problem and you will find that the river is, if not a stream, at least navigable.

Conclusion

Ethics and copyright are areas which can seem particularly daunting to the new information professional. Remember that you don't have to learn every possible permutation of copyright law, or become a brilliant information ethicist. Learn enough to support you in your day-to-day work – and more if it interests you! Use the resources available to support your knowledge, and never be afraid to check your understanding, or look up points you are unsure of.

Remember, too, that your professional colleagues and organizations are there to help you. Talk to people in your networks – have any of them been faced with similar situations? Can they offer advice on what to do – and what not to do? Finally, don't be too scared of working with copyright or making ethical decisions. If you get something wrong, apologize and learn from the experience.

References and further reading

American Library Association (2008) *Code of Ethics of the American Library Association*, www.ala.org/ala/issuesadvocacy/proethics/codeofethics/codeethics.cfm.

Berman, S. (1981) *The Joy of Cataloguing: essays, letters, reviews, and other explosions*, Oryx Press.

Boles, F. (2009) *Enforcing Ethics*, www.archivists.org/news/ethics09.asp.

Buchanan, E. A. and Henderson, K. A. (2008) *Case Studies in Library and Information Science Ethics*, McFarland.

Cook, M. (2006) Professional Ethics and Practice in Archives and Records Management in a Human Rights Context, *Journal of the Society of Archivists*, **27** (1), 1–15.

Danielson, E. S. (2010) *The Ethical Archivist*, Society of American Archivists.

Davis, M. (2006) Freedom of Access to Information Post September 11, 2001, *ALIA New Librarians' Symposium, Sydney*, http://conferences.alia.org.au/newlibrarian2006/programme_files/davis_m_paper.pdf.

Dingwall, G. (2004) Trusting Archivists: the role of archival ethical codes in establishing public faith, *American Archivist*, **67** (1), 11–30.

Foskett, D. J. (1962) *The Creed of a Librarian – no politics, no religion, no morals*, Library Association.

Gorman, M. (2000) *Our Enduring Values: librarianship in the 21st century*, ALA Editions.

Hauptman, R. (1988) *Ethical Challenges in Librarianship*, Oryx Press.

Hauptman, R. and Hernon, P. (2002) *Ethics and Librarianship*, McFarland.

Larson, M. S. (1977) *The Rise of Professionalism: a sociological analysis*, University of California Press.

McMenemy, D. et al. (2007) *A Handbook of Ethical Practice: a practical guide to dealing with ethical issues in information and library work*, Chandos Publishing.

Sturges, P. (2003) Doing the Right Thing: professional ethics for information workers in Britain, *New Library World*, 104, 94–102.

Codes of ethics/conduct

American Library Association, www.ala.org/ala/issuesadvocacy/proethics/codeofethics/codeethics.cfm.

Archives and Records Association, www.archives.org.uk/membership/code-of-conduct.html.

Association of Canadian Archivists, http://archivists.ca/content/code-ethics.

CILIP Code of Professional Practice, www.cilip.org.uk/sitecollectiondocuments/PDFs/policyadvocacy/CodeofProfessio nalPracticeforLibraryandInformationProfessionals.pdf (2004).

CILIP Ethical Principles, www.cilip.org.uk/sitecollectiondocuments/PDFs/policyadvocacy/Ethicalprinciples forlibraryandinformationprofessionals.pdf

IFLA, www.ifla.org/en/faife/professional-codes-of-ethics-for-librarians (has an extensive list of library association professional codes, which may be out of date, so check associations' websites).

IFLA Committee on Freedom of Access to Information and Freedom of Expression, Principles of Freedom of Expression and Good Librarianship, www.ifla.org/en/faife/mission.

Information and Records Management Society, www.irms.org.uk/member-accreditation-code-of-ethics.

Ethics: case studies and resources

CILIP ethics blog, communities.cilip.org.uk/blogs/ethics/default.aspx (registration required).

CILIP resources for the information ethicist, www.cilip.org.uk/get-involved/policy/ethics/resources/pages/default.aspx.

IFLA, An ethical framework for professional practice, www.ifla.org/en/node/5714.

Lifelong Education @ Desktop: Ethics in the Real World: library case studies, www.leadonline.info/catalog_detail.php?oid=57&tab=objectives (paid online course, $25 in autumn 2011).

Copyright

Bently, L. and B. Sherman (2009) *Intellectual Property Law*, 3rd edn, Oxford University Press.

Cornish, G. P. (2009) *Copyright: interpreting the law for libraries, archives and information services*, 5th edn, Facet Publishing.

Garnett, K. M. et al. (2011) *Copinger and Skone James on Copyright*, 16th edn, Sweet & Maxwell and Thomson Reuters.

Holland, C. (2010) The Digital Economy Act: what are the implications for libraries?, *Legal Information Management*, **10** (3), 170–4.

Laddie, H. et al. (2011) *The Modern Law of Copyright and Designs*, 4th edn, Butterworths.

Padfield, T. (2010) *Copyright for Archivists and Records Managers*, 4th edn, Facet Publishing.

Pedley, P. (2008) *Copyright Compliance: practical steps to stay within the law*, Facet Publishing.

The National Archives (2010a) *Copyright and Related Rights*, www.nationalarchives.gov.uk/documents/information-management/copyright-related-rights.pdf.

The National Archives (2010b) *Using Materials from the National Archives*, www.nationalarchives.gov.uk/documents/information-management/use-of-tna-materials.pdf.

Copyright resources

Berne Convention, www.wipo.int/treaties/en/ip/berne.

Copyright Licensing Agency: beta title search, www.cla.co.uk/licences/titlesearch (allows you to search by title or ISBN for CLA licence coverage).

Design and Artists Copyright Society, www.dacs.org.uk (will give licences for orphan artistic works).

IFLA Copyright for Library Associations, http://learning.ifla.org (online course, available to members of IFLA member organizations).

Public Domain Calculator, outofcopyright.eu/ (tells you whether a work that originated in an EU member state is still in copyright).

UK Copyright Designs and Patents Act 1988,

www.legislation.gov.uk/ukpga/1988/48/contents.

Writers, Artists and Their Copyright Holders (WATCH) database, www.watch-file.com (gives contact details for many copyright owners).

UK Intellectual Property Office, www.ipo.gov.uk.

WIPO Copyright Treaty, www.wipo.int/treaties/en/ip/wct.

WIPO Lex website, www.wipo.int/wipolex/en (access to copyright legislation of member states around the world).

➡ Over to you . . .

Think about a situation where you have had an ethical choice to make. Was it a professional situation? Was it personal?

Write it up in the form of a case study. Present the background and circumstances, changing or removing any names or identifiable personal details. Include three or four responses to the situation (including the one you chose at the time). Would you still make the same choice? Why?

If you are comfortable doing so, share your case study with professional colleagues for discussion. Before doing so, make sure you have removed all details that could be used to identify people or places.

CHAPTER 10

Upskilling and professional development

Introduction

Continuing professional development (CPD) is an important part of being a professional. It is a commitment to keeping your knowledge and skills up to date; without it, your development will stagnate, and you will fail to provide the best service possible to your users.

There are various aspects to professional development. One of the first things to do is to assess the skills you already have (carry out a skills audit). You should then look at the skills and knowledge required by your current role, and see which areas you need to strengthen. You can follow this with a more aspirational assessment – look at the positions you might like to occupy in the future, note which skills you need to develop, and plan your CPD accordingly. This will help you develop as a professional, as well as aiding your career planning.

A commitment to CPD is important because:

- it ensures you have the right skills to give your users what they need
- it makes you more valuable to your current organization
- it makes you more employable when it's time to move on
- it can keep you energized and engaged
- it can lead to further qualifications (such as CILIP Chartership)
- lifelong learning can be enjoyable
- it can extend your professional network through contacts made at courses, conferences, etc.

You can build continual skills assessment into your professional life. Deborah Dalley, a freelance consultant who specializes in personal and group development, gives you some tools to help plan your development.

🔧 How to . . .
Assess yourself

I have been a management trainer for the last 20 years and one thing I've observed is that successful people are proactive, not reactive, about their career planning and personal development. They take responsibility for their learning and recognize that it requires an investment of time and energy.

Personal development planning involves asking yourself three key questions:

- *Where am I now?:* What skills do I have? Can I identify things that I have achieved that demonstrate those skills? What do I enjoy doing most at work? What motivates me?
- *Where do I want to be?:* What would I like to be able to do that I currently don't feel I have the knowledge or skills to? What have I tried to do in the past that I have not succeeded at or felt I could have done better? What feedback have I received from my manager, colleagues and customers that has shown me that I need to improve my skills? Where do I want to be in two years' time? Where do I see myself in ten years' time?
- *How will I get there?:* Consider opportunities for learning and development like training courses, conferences, coaching, delegation, job rotation, secondment, job shadowing, giving presentations, sitting on working parties, reading, online tutorials, internet research, journals from professional bodies, evening classes, mentoring, attending meetings, chairing meetings, writing reports, social media, action learning groups, networking, volunteering and seeking feedback from colleagues.

It is important to identify the ways that you learn best and develop your plan to suit your learning style.

Take action

Remember the importance of taking action. This may sound obvious but a lot of people are good at identifying goals and discussing them, and not as good at turning those goals into action. This is usually because they have not identified the first steps. These are critical because if the action appears too big in our mind then we fall at the first hurdle.

First steps need to be:

- very specific
- something that will move you toward the goal
- things that can be done within five days (preferably within 48 hours).

These are some quick tips:

- Keep your CV up to date.
- Start collecting job advertisements of roles that interest you – this will help you to identify the skills and traits that you might need to develop to apply for those posts in the future.
- Keep your CPD file current – keep copies of training attendance certificates; make a note of achievements; and keep any e-mails of thanks or recognition for work.
- Regularly review your career goals – as our lives change so do our aspirations.
- Seek feedback from others regularly.

⊘ **See the website (http://lisnewprofs.com/assessyourself)** for an example of how this helped one person improve their skills and job satisfaction.

Bodies of Professional Knowledge

Deborah has given us a helpful set of tools that you can use to think about your skill set in any circumstances. As well as looking at your skills in general and in relation to your organization, you might find it useful to assess yourself in the context of the information profession as a whole.

There are several resources that aim to frame the knowledge of an information professional. Some seek to generalize all the skills needed for a role in the profession; others (such as that of the Library and Information Association of New Zealand Aotearoa, LIANZA) talk about the role of an information professional within a specific cultural context. You don't have to stick rigidly to every skill outlined in these documents! Some will be more applicable to your role (and desired future roles) than others, and it is important to be able to assess which skills and competencies are most relevant to you. Likewise, don't discard or disdain your other skills just because they're not mentioned – one of the most exciting things about the information profession is that you will find a use for all your skills, no matter how specialized or esoteric. Professional competency documents include:

- CILIP Body of Professional Knowledge, www.cilip.org.uk/jobs-careers/qualifications/accreditation/bpk/pages/default.aspx (currently being revised)
- the Government Knowledge and Information Management Professional Skills Framework, www.nationalarchives.gov.uk/information-management/gkim/gkim-professional-skills.htm
- ICA 'About records, archives and the profession', www.ica.org/125/about-records-archives-and-the-profession/discover-archives-and-our-profession.html
- LIANZA Body of Professional Knowledge, www.lianza.org.nz/resources/professional-registration/resources/body-professional-knowledge
- SLA Competencies for Information Professionals of the 21st Century, www.sla.org/content/learn/members/competencies/index.cfm (currently being revised)
- SLA Future Ready Toolkit, www.sla.org/content/resources/toolkit/index.cfm.

Now Dee Magnoni, Library Director at Franklin W. Olin College of Engineering in Needham, MA, and past chair of the SLA Professional Development Advisory Council, discusses SLA's Competencies for Information Professionals of the 21st Century, and how to relate these to your role.

⚲ How to . . .
Meet contemporary challenges in the information profession

Today's information professionals are entering an evolving profession filled with challenges and opportunities. Many traditional roles are in decline, while more hybrid and non-traditional roles are emerging. How do new information professionals find their way through market possibilities? How does an individual decide if a role is a strong fit? And, once in a role, what steps should an individual take to maximize success?

There are several lenses that can be used to answer these questions. No matter what lens is used, information professionals must understand their personal strengths and potential areas of growth, and the mission and culture of an organization of interest. On the broadest level, there are critical soft and hard skills that are needed in the industry:

- *soft skills:* creativity, being innovative, being flexible, undertaking lifelong learning, communicating, being able to work in a team, being self-motivating
- *hard skills:* writing, understanding maths, handling social media, knowing job-specific technology, marketing.

There are also behaviours that are so basic that they are taken for granted, such as showing up on time, doing the work and providing excellent service.

A targeted lens: SLA's Competencies for Information Professionals of the 21st Century

This broad lens is not very useful for specific self-analysis. Another lens is outlined in the revised edition of *Competencies for Information Professionals of the 21st Century* (www.sla.org/content/learn/members/competencies/index.cfm), published in June 2003 by the Special Libraries Association (SLA). This document outlines three categories of competencies that information professionals need to succeed. Augmenting the competencies are applied scenarios, which provide working examples for specific competencies.

The three competency categories are professional, personal and core. The professional competencies relate to the following four areas of a practitioner's knowledge: managing information organizations, managing information resources, managing information services, and applying information tools and technologies. The personal competencies reflect an individual's attitudes and skills, working together across professional and personal areas of life. Personal and professional boundaries are much more fluid than in the past, and a whole life approach to development and success is critical. Finally, the two core competencies address the essential values of sharing knowledge and adhering to the ethics of the profession.

The purpose of the document is to provide a tool for individuals to use to assess their areas of strengths and target areas for development. For each target area, decide if the competency is emerging, developed, excelling or not relevant. Once ranked, provide a brief sentence or two outlining your plan for that competency, and, where possible, include comments from co-workers, your supervisor or friends and family. This can help you to get a rounded view of your competencies and development needs.

Figure 10.1 gives an example of how one might evaluate a single competency area.

Professional Competencies: A. Managing Information Organizations. A.1: Aligns the information organization with, and is supportive of, the strategic directions of the parent organization or of the key client groups through partnerships with key stakeholders and suppliers.			
Emerging [ ]	Developed [ ]	Excelling [ ]	Not Relevant [ ]
Competency plan:			
Comments:			

Figure 10.1 *An example of how you might evaluate a single competency area*

Relating the competencies to your role

Becoming familiar with the competencies and performing a personal assessment is the first step in applying the competencies to a professional role. The second step is to understand your organization and its mission, and then align your competencies with those of your organization.

Using Franklin W. Olin College of Engineering in Needham, Massachusetts, as an example, consider the College's mission and aspiration:

- *Mission:* Olin College prepares students to become exemplary engineering innovators who recognize needs, design solutions, and engage in creative enterprises for the good of the world.
- *Aspiration:* Olin College seeks to redefine engineering as a profession of innovation encompassing 1) the consideration of human and societal needs; 2) the creative design of engineering systems; and 3) the creation of value through entrepreneurial effort and philanthropy. The College is dedicated to the discovery and development of the most effective educational approaches and aspires to serve as a model for others.

These are the mission and aspiration of Olin College Library:

- *Mission:* The library furthers Olin College's mission by selecting, developing, deploying, and managing resources, services and knowledge discovery tools that foster independent thought, learning, and innovation while cultivating the human element in engineering design and pedagogy.
- *Aspiration:* The Library strives to embody Olin's philosophy of innovation in

engineering and continual improvement by 1) designing systems for the cultivation of independent thought, research skills, the human element in engineering design and pedagogy, and lifelong learning; 2) creating new and strengthening existing partnerships to broaden the scope of the library's resources; and 3) leveraging emerging technologies and practices to serve Olin and the broader learning community. The library seeks to create transparency in resource discovery and facilitate the educational goals of the College and engineering education.

The Library's mission and aspiration are developed from and support the College's mission and aspiration. Similarly, using the competencies, an individual would look at their role and the mission of the library and college, then choose the professional and personal competencies necessary to succeed and advance in that role.

For instance, a new professional starting at Olin College Library might look at point 3 of its aspiration, and decide they need to address competency D.1: 'Assesses, selects and applies current and emerging information tools and creates information access and delivery solutions.' The core competencies will always be applicable to any role.

Optimally, this competency assessment can be built into the review process, and the organizational review process and competency assessment will work together over time.

Bridging library and i-school to the competencies and professional roles

Information profession students receive a broad education that serves as a solid foundation for many roles. No graduate has every competency necessary for a role, nor should they. The information profession demands life-long learning. Some new professionals have gaps that graduate school was not meant to fill. Weak writing or maths skills may be a personal gap. Both of these skills will become important in almost any role, and individuals should seek opportunities to grow through courses, groups, mentoring or online resources. Technology will continue to evolve, and everyone must keep up to date with relevant changes. Many competency skills can be developed through volunteer roles in associations and other groups. Process skills are often not taught in school, and becoming familiar with how work flows in a specific organization, then how to improve that flow, is an example of bridging general project skills to more specific

THE NEW PROFESSIONAL'S TOOLKIT

organizational process competencies.

Using the *Competencies for Information Professionals* for personal assessment within a role provides a strong framework to succeed in almost any information profession role. Additional tools for personal assessment and lifelong learning augment the Competencies, and some are listed below.

SLA Competencies for Information Professionals,
  www.sla.org/content/learn/members/competencies/index.cfm
SLA Future Ready Professional Development Toolkit,
  http://wiki.sla.org/display/future/Professional+Development+Tools [wiki registration required].

Training and development

Once you have an idea which skills to develop, you will need to identify some training and development opportunities. You might immediately think 'conferences' or 'training courses', but there are plenty of other ways to develop yourself. As training budgets shrink alongside other budgets, and demands on your professional time increase, you might need to be creative when identifying development opportunities. Laura Woods, Information Services Adviser at Addleshaw Goddard LLP, tells us of her experiences of doing CPD that 'could be hidden in the stationery budget'.

Case study
CPD on a shoestring

Many information professionals struggle with finding the time or funding for CPD, particularly if their employers are unable or unwilling to support them. It is however vital that each of us take responsibility for our own CPD, with or without support from our bosses.

After library school, I started a job with a commercial law firm, a sector I had little experience in. I found myself working on many different aspects of library provision, some of which I had only been aware of in theory. It was of immediate importance that I find ways of supplementing my on-the-job training with CPD. My workplace had no budget for training opportunities for support staff, so I either had to foot the bill myself or find free development opportunities.

What types of training and development can you do?

CPD can encompass many different activities, from formal continuing education courses through to reading and commenting on fellow librarians' blogs.

Formal training and funding

Attending professional development and continuing education courses is an excellent way of keeping your skills up to date. Unfortunately, it is also one of the most expensive! If you are lucky enough to have funding available for this kind of formal learning, there are many library related courses available from providers such as CILIP (www.cilip.org.uk/jobs-careers/training/pages/default. aspx) and TFPL (www.tfpl.com/training). For those in far-flung locations, or struggling to get time away from work, it is worth looking into online learning and webinars, such as SLA's Click University (www.sla.org/content/learn/ index.cfm).

Conferences are an unbeatable source of information on current hot topics, as well as a great way to get to know other information professionals. Unfortunately, they are probably even harder to get funding for than short courses! There are ways and means to attend conferences on a shoestring though – see Chapter 12 for tips.

Informal learning

CPD doesn't have to take place in a formal setting. It is easy to fit learning opportunities into your daily work – perfect if you have time and budget constraints! One of the easiest ways to keep your knowledge up to date is reading professional literature – including professional journals and library and librarian blogs. Not sure where to start with blogs? Try the UK Library Blogs Wiki (http://uklibraryblogs.pbworks.com), which lists blogs written by librarians and libraries in the UK.

To find professional journals, start with your professional body, which might publish or provide access to a variety of professional journals and databases.

Want to learn about other jobs in librarianship? Try job shadowing. This could involve visiting other organizations, or shadowing people within your own workplace – a great way to learn how your library as a whole functions. You could also read the Library Day in the Life (http://librarydayinthelife.pbworks.com) and the Library Routes project (http://libraryroutesproject.wikkii.com).

Volunteering on professional body committees is a perfect way to build up your experience outside your job description, and acquire new skills you may not have a chance to learn in your current role.

Proving the value of training

Even if your employers aren't supporting your CPD financially, it is still important to demonstrate to them what you are getting out of it – apart from highlighting your professionalism, proving the value of CPD may increase your chances of getting funding later on.

Shortly after starting work for a law firm library, I saw an advert for the Legal Foundations course of the British and Irish Association of Law Librarians (BIALL). I knew that my employer wouldn't pay for me to attend – I'd already been told that we didn't have a training budget, so the firm would only fund something for us 'if it was cheap enough to hide in the stationery budget'!

I asked anyway, emphasizing to my boss that improving my legal knowledge would make me more efficient at my job, saving the firm time and money. We agreed that I would be able to have time away from my work to study the course materials, and could leave early on the days the course ran, to get there on time.

During the course, I kept records of the times when something I'd learned on the course came up at work and allowed me to answer an enquiry with more speed and accuracy. My manager was impressed, and after some budget wrangling offered to contribute half the costs of the course when the invoice arrived. I would never have got that partial funding without taking the time to apply my learning to my work, and recording how the course had improved my skills.

As well as giving some interesting ideas for ways to find development opportunities, Laura touches on the other key point about CPD – follow-up. It is not enough to simply attend a training course or read a book: to get the most out of your development activities, you need to reflect on your learning, and incorporate it into your work. This applies especially when it is difficult to find time and money for CPD: the scarcer development opportunities are, the more valuable they become. Gil Young, CPD and Partnerships Manager at Health Care Libraries Unit, NHS, shares her tips for making sure that you wring every last drop of value out of your training and development opportunities – formal or informal.

🔧 How to . . .
Get the most out of training and development

Personal development plans

A personal development plan can help you to think about what you want to gain from training and development activities. You can create your own, or use a formal template such as your organization's appraisal process or CILIP Chartership.

The format of your plan – such as table, mind map or list – is up to you, but don't duplicate work or effort. If there is a formal framework available that suits you, then use it. However you put it together, start by considering the following questions:

- What do I want to learn?
- Why do I want to learn it?
- How will learning about this make me better at my job?
- How will attending this event benefit my service or organization?
- How will attending this event develop me professionally?
- What would be the best way for me to undertake this learning? Think much wider than formal training courses.
- How will I put the learning into practice?

Set your aims and objectives

Writing your aims and objectives for each learning experience will help you clarify why you are attending and ensure that it is the right event for you, assist you in your reflections after the event, and help you put the learning into practice. It may also help you answer the frequently asked icebreaker 'why are you here?'

The learning cycle

Using the learning cycle (Figure 10.2) can be a good way of ensuring that an activity has resulted in learning taking place. If you have attended a course, reflected on it, but failed to think about how you can put the learning into action then you have not developed and the opportunity has been wasted.

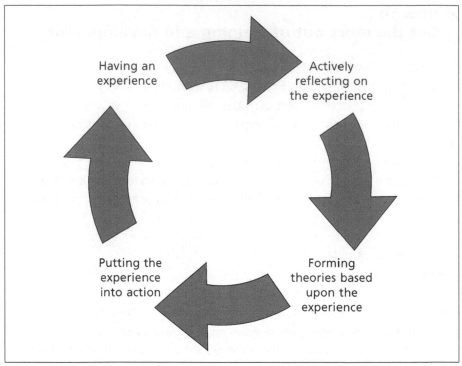

Figure 10.2 *The Experiential Cycle of Learning (based on Kolb, Rubin and McIntyre, 1984)*

Say 'yes' to everything (within reason)

In my previous role in the academic library sector I investigated which skills senior library managers looked for in new professionals. Flexibility was mentioned by them all as a key skill; demonstrated by individuals' attitude to change and their ability to take on challenges and projects outside of their defined job role. So, when you are asked to do something new – attend a meeting, write an article, speak at a conference, update a website, take on a new project – unless there is a very good reason why you shouldn't do it, your default answer should always be 'yes'.

Scary is good

If you are frightened of something then try to find opportunities to do it – scary activities often turn out to be the most interesting and the ones that really provide us with opportunities to develop both personally and professionally. For instance, many people say they don't like presenting, but it is a part of many jobs and you will often be asked to do it at interview. The more you do it, the better you will get at it. It doesn't have to be a big deal in the first instance: resolve to speak out a meeting; or join in a training session or a presentation by doing the introduction or moderating questions.

Do the same things differently

We all have our preferred ways of learning and working, but sometimes we need to take a different approach to tasks we've done many times before. I love writing lists and the creativity of mind mapping doesn't appeal to me. However, I recently struggled to write an essay for a course I was undertaking, until I tried mind mapping the plan. It wasn't the greatest mind map in the world but it broke the deadlock and really helped me get going with the essay.

Participate fully in the event

These are some suggestions for how you can get the best out of events:

- Complete any pre- and post-course work.
- Actively listen to others and respect their opinions even if you don't agree with them.
- Be friendly to everyone. You never know when you might meet them again.
- Put what is going on in the workplace to the back of your mind. Constantly contacting the office doesn't look professional, and will be distracting to you and other attendees.
- Take business cards and pass them out.
- Fill in the feedback form honestly and constructively.

Reflect and review

Always take the time to reflect after a learning experience has taken place – not just courses but all work-based activities. Remember to reflect on positive experiences as well as negative ones.

You could use this as an opportunity to develop other skills: if you want to learn more about Web 2.0, consider using a blog to record your reflections. If you want to develop your writing or presentation skills, write an article about the event for an internal newsletter or give a five minute talk at a team meeting.

Make the most of statutory training

I recently had to attend an event which showed me how to wash my hands when working on a ward, even though I'm office based and never go near patients. If you have to attend a statutory training course where the subject isn't relevant to you, try to turn it into an opportunity to see what you can get out of it. Can you use it as a networking opportunity, or to market your service to staff that you might not normally reach? Does the way the trainer presents the information give you ideas for your own presentations and training sessions?

Training and development are lifelong activities

As a professional you should never stop learning or developing. Some of the most meaningful learning experiences I have had in recent years have come from mentoring CILIP Chartership candidates, many of whom were younger or less experienced than me. As a result of their enthusiasm for the profession and the different ways they approached their own learning and development I frequently got more out of the relationship than they did.

Continuous learning and development are the hallmarks of being a professional. Stop doing them and your career will quickly stagnate.

Mentoring

We've mentioned the importance of support from fellow professionals, but how do you find this support? There are a number of ways to link yourself with fellow professionals. Participating in a professional body and building peer networks are great ways (more about these in Chapters 11 and 12), but for formal support you could also consider mentoring. A mentoring relationship can help you at any stage of your career, but new professionals might find them particularly valuable. A mentor will offer support and encouragement, give you a different perspective on issues, listen to your concerns, and keep them confidential. They're also someone to celebrate success with, and a good mentoring relationship can often lead to long-term friendship.

As with training, mentoring can be formal or informal. Your organization may have a mentoring scheme in place – these can range from simple 'first-week-in-the-job buddy' schemes, to long-term formally recognized schemes. If there is no formal scheme in place, you may still be able to create an unofficial mentoring relationship.

You may also be able to get involved with a mentoring scheme through a professional organization. Many of them encourage mentoring, and in some circumstances (such as undertaking CILIP Chartership or Registration with the Archives and Records Association) it is mandatory.

Mentoring relationships have traditionally been built around personal contact, and thus choices of mentor/mentee have been at least partially based on geographic proximity; the CILIP mentor directory, for instance, is still arranged by region. This may not be the pattern for mentoring relationships of the future, as social media continues to make it easier to build and maintain personal links with people in other regions and countries. In this case study, Emily Hopkins, Health Information and Resources Library Manager at Manchester Mental Health and Social Care Trust, tells us about how she had a successful long-distance mentoring relationship.

📁 Case study
Long-distance mentoring

Like many other candidates, I approached CILIP Chartership as the natural next step after qualifying and starting a professional post. I dutifully set about reading regulations, completing forms, and eventually looking through the list of mentors and wondering who to inflict myself on! I must admit I probably didn't give much thought to why I needed a mentor, other than because the regulations said so. It wasn't until later that it became clear that it would have far-reaching benefits for my professional development. As a new professional, having an excuse to pick the brains of an established professional and learn from their knowledge and wisdom is not an opportunity to be missed.

Chartership can be a slightly daunting process and it can be easy to get immersed, lose perspective, and focus solely on the portfolio. A good mentor will help you put it all into context, and get the most out of your experiences to help your CPD overall.

I was very fortunate to find a mentor with whom I built a successful mentoring relationship with embarrassingly little effort on my part. I glanced through the CILIP mentors list and – after a minimal look into the company Richard worked in, which I thought looked intriguing and very different to my own – I sent off a quick e-mail. At our initial meeting we talked about professional issues and CPD in general, as well as Chartership and how mentoring contributed to it. I think a shared enthusiasm for the profession, and a realistic view on the bigger picture of changes in my sector (the NHS) and how that related to his (private sector), made me realize that this was the right mentor for me: someone who was going to challenge me and my perceptions of what was going on in my organization, but also be able to offer advice and expertise. Establishing a common ground and an understanding of how you will work together is an important part of building a successful relationship with your mentor.

Being mentored was extremely beneficial to my personal and professional development as it helped me question not only my pieces of evidence, but also my day-to-day work. It taught me to not accept everything at face value and to step back and look at the bigger picture. This was probably related to our respective sectors; the NHS often looks to the private sector for inspiration, so it seemed fitting. It also made me understand the climate within my own sector better, and how information professionals can contribute to the NHS in an era of efficiency savings and productivity targets.

We had a slightly untraditional mentoring arrangement as we made use of Facebook as part of the mentoring process, supported by regular phone calls. It was Richard's idea, and largely a practical one to address the logistics of distance – I'd never even thought of it, assuming only face-to-face meetings would meet the criteria but as I readily used social media sites, I happily agreed.

Mentoring in this way may not be for everyone, and I've had horrified looks from some people when I've mentioned it, but it worked for us. It gave the mentoring process a very instant and fluid feel to it – we could have brief chats about small issues, as well as setting an agenda for a formal meeting. It also meant that we often talked about things other than my portfolio, keeping in touch informally. This could be something LIS-related in the news, or something completely off-topic. Sharing things – whether a frustrating day at work or a piece of good news – as and when they happen, rather than weeks later, can help give a supportive yet relaxed and friendly feel to the mentoring relationship. And knowing that I could send a quick message saying I was going to write something up by a particular date, helped motivate me to actually do it! I use social media sites to communicate with friends and colleagues, many in the LIS-sector, and these tools can help your mentor become part of your wider network; and encourage more interaction than just using e-mail.

Mentoring doesn't have to just be a formal process consisting only of scheduled meetings; having contact with your mentor, particularly as part of a wider network of LIS professionals, can be a huge support to your professional development. Being able to share your enthusiasm and interest with another professional, who's also willing to offer you advice and guidance is a hugely valuable resource, and I recommend all new professionals take as much advantage of it as possible!

As Gil mentioned earlier in the chapter, the benefit flow in a mentoring relationship isn't all one way! Being a mentor can be very rewarding – you can feel re-invigorated by contact with enthusiastic professional colleagues, learn new ideas, and gain listening and communicating skills.

There is no minimum experience requirement to be a mentor, and new professionals can be effective mentors, too. It might seem intimidating, but remember that your key roles are to listen and to support. The mentor doesn't always have to be in a more senior job role, or have more professional experience – we all have different experiences, and can use these to help others.

Being a willing ear is important – but there is much more than that to building a truly successful mentoring relationship. Jenica Rogers, Director of Libraries at the State University of New York at Potsdam shares her experiences of the attitudes and capabilities that help to make an outstanding mentor.

🔧 How to . . .
Be a mentor

Participating in mentoring relationships is one of the most rewarding things I do as a librarian, but mentorship isn't easy. Not everyone can be a good mentor, and not every good mentor is a good match with everyone seeking a mentoring relationship. Sometimes, two people just don't hit it off, or can't find the trust to go past superficial, or simply don't have enough in common. Some of the best mentoring relationships in my professional life have had simple things that connected them, though, which any of us can emulate.

Be available

Mentoring relationships are often crucial in the moment when a crisis or dilemma presents itself. The most useful of my own mentors have been the people who had the capacity and empathy to say, 'Yes, of course I have five minutes to talk. Would it be better if we took half an hour and got a cup of coffee?' In short, it is easy to ask for advice from someone who makes you feel welcome.

Know yourself

A good mentor has empathy about others and about themselves. You need to be able to understand your mentee's strengths and weaknesses, but also your own. If your mentee has a weak grasp of institutional politics, and you know that you do too, you may not be the best mentor for that individual. But if you are aware of your own challenges, perhaps you can be a strong supporter for that person because you can speak from the wisdom of experience in similar circumstances.

Be honest

Honesty is crucial for successful mentoring partnerships because they are all built on trust. Why would any of us tell our insecurities, doubts or challenges to someone we don't trust? Part of building that trust is communicating with unvarnished honesty. As a mentor, your successes and your failures are the models that others will use to model their own course forward. If you are embellishing or diminishing your experiences, positive and negative, you are doing a disservice to anyone coming to you for advice, but if you are confident enough to share relevant but unpleasant experiences from your career, you can build the trust that your mentee needs to bring their own struggles to you.

Be open to serendipity

I call on many people when I struggle or need a gut check, some of whom don't know that I see them as mentors. Several think of themselves as junior to me because of our divergent responsibilities, and several others are entirely outside of libraries. The thing that they all have in common is a willingness to help me when I ask for help, and the empathy to understand my concerns. I try to be open to the same kinds of requests for help when others come to me, because you never know which of your casual conversations will become the basis for something greater.

Be a smart expert

A crucial part of choosing the story to tell and the advice to give is in finding the balance between saying what you know that your mentee needs to hear from you, and telling them what they're asking for. Sometimes when we're asked for advice, the concern seems off-target, or like the person is asking the wrong questions. As a mentor, part of the role is to ask yourself how you can be most useful. Sometimes that means redirecting their energy to the thing that is the unseen root of their problems.

Be brave

Being a mentor isn't all encouragement and support. In addition to cheerleading, it is imperative that the mentor take a deep breath and teach hard lessons as well as easy ones. A mentor is uniquely positioned to be the impartial observer who can frankly say, 'I would have had the same negative reaction as your supervisor did to the approach you just described', or 'Whoa. You are not in a good situation. That job is just a bad fit for you.' But always follow up with advice or assistance when you feel you must critique – negative feedback without follow-through is just sniping, and won't facilitate a constructive partnership.

Listen as much as you talk

Since mentoring is so hard, one might wonder why people do it. I believe it's because mentoring is such an amazing learning experience for both people in the partnership. In the abstract, mentorship is the embodiment of the notion that you can't teach without learning. Rooted in the practical, mentorship makes it clear that you can't assess an individual and their fit in the profession or their institution without relearning the profession and the institution for yourself. Helping someone else find goals, connections and learning opportunities opens your own mind to those possibilities, and talking someone through their challenges and their dreams helps you think about your own challenges and dreams. The whole experience opens you up to new involvement in your career, your profession and your organization, and introduces you to people who can have a deep impact on your life.

Conclusion

In this chapter, we've looked at some of the many ways you can develop yourself professionally, and why it is so important to do so. CPD doesn't need to be a formal activity that you separate from your day-to-day work; if you are committed to developing yourself, and have the right mindset, you can turn any activity into a development activity. Remembering that you have opportunities to learn every day will help to keep you engaged with your job and with the profession. In Chapter 11, we will look at how your networks can help you to learn, and in Chapter 12 at development outside the workplace, and what you can give back to the profession.

References and further reading

Self-assessment and skills

Bolles, R. N. (annual) *What Colour Is Your Parachute? A practical manual for job-hunters and career-changers*, 10 Speed Press.

Dority, K. (2006) *Rethinking Information Work: a career guide for librarians and other information professionals*, Libraries Unlimited.

Duranti, L. (1993) The Archival Body of Knowledge: archival theory, method, and practice, and graduate and continuing education, *Journal of Education for Library and Information Science*, **34** (1), 8–24.

Kolb, D. A., Rubin, I. M. and McIntyre, J. M. (1984) *Experiential Learning: experience as the source of learning and development*, Prentice Hall.

Rath, T. (2007) *Strengths Finder 2.0*, Gallup Press.

Rosenstein, B. (2009) *Living in More Than One World: how Peter Drucker's wisdom can inspire and transform your life*, Berrett-Koehler Publishers, Inc.

Training and development

23 Things for Professional Development (2011) www.cpd23.blogspot.com.

Doessel, N. (2008) Librarian – Library = ? Professional development for non-traditional librarians, *4th ALIA New Librarians' Symposium*, Melbourne, http://conferences.alia.org.au/newlibrarian2008/Abstract.html.

Farkas, M. (2006) Skills for the 21st Century Librarian, Information Wants To Be Free, blog, http://meredith.wolfwater.com/wordpress/2006/07/17/skills-for-the-21st-century-librarian.

Mentoring

Benn, J. and Brennand, M. (2008) Why Mentoring Matters: a personal journey that created professional success, *4th ALIA New Librarians' Symposium, Melbourne*, http://conferences.alia.org.au/newlibrarian2008/Papers/Benn.doc.

Stephens, M. (2011) The Role of Mentoring: office hours, *Library Journal*, (15 September), www.libraryjournal.com/lj/community/libraryeducation/891738-272/the_role_of_mentoring_.html.csp.

Resources

OpenCourseWare Consortium, www.ocwconsortium.org.

The Open University, www.open.ac.uk and Learning Space,

http://openlearn.open.ac.uk.

Riley Guide, *Self-Assessment Resources,* www.rileyguide.com/assess.html (includes links to classics such as Myers-Briggs Type Indicator and lesser known tools such as MAPP – Motivational Assessment of Personal Potential).

➡ Over to you . . .

1. Perform a simple goal-setting exercise, by answering the following questions thinking about your current job:

   - What is it that you most enjoy at the moment?
   - What would you like to do more of?
   - Identify one action that will help you get more of what you enjoy. (Thanks to Deborah Dalley for this exercise.)

2. Perform a skills audit on yourself. You can use one of the resources or toolkits suggested above, or use your organization's (or potential future organization's) aims and mission.

   Think about one area of improvement you would like to see, and identify three actions you could take to address it (such as finding a formal training course, reading a book, or talking to a contact in a relevant area). Evaluate the potential:

   - cost
   - time commitment
   - effort commitment
   - accessibility (can you travel to the course or borrow the book from a friend?)
   - return (will this action teach you everything you need to know? More or less than you need?).

   Decide what action will give the best return for your effort.

3. Think about a formal or informal learning experience you have had recently and reflect on:

   - what you learnt
   - how you will put it into practice

- what difference it will make to you as a professional (in the workplace or other professional involvement)
- whether you are now aware of any other gaps you need to fill
- what further three actions you will take as a result of this learning; draft a timetable for them, and identify any resource needs.

CHAPTER 11
Networking and promoting yourself

Introduction

In Chapter 4 we covered how promotions and marketing are a vital part of providing the best service possible to your users. It is not just your organization and services that need promoting: you also need to promote yourself, and for many of the same reasons. This isn't about boasting about how great you are, but about making people aware of your unique skills and expertise, so they can call on them as necessary.

Just as your users won't know how your service can help them unless you specifically tell them, people won't know what you personally have to offer unless you make it obvious. In the workplace, you as a person can inspire trust and reliance in a way that your library or archive as a service can never do. Your users are much more likely to connect with your personal expertise: 'The information service can do that. I read it on a leaflet' is a much less powerful message than 'Bethan can do that. She was talking to me about it last week.' Your knowledge, expertise and personal skills can be a very valuable asset to your organization.

Personal promotion isn't all about raising your profile, and that might never be a conscious part of your actions. Your 'brand' will often grow naturally out of the work you are doing and sharing with the community. As you share your learning, thoughts and insights, professional colleagues will build up a picture of your skills, knowledge and personality. This will help in all aspects of career development – the more people know about what you can do, the more likely they are to ask you to do it.

Think of it as conservation of energy – you are making the most you can out of the activities you do, and allowing others to share in the benefits too. A reputation for professional generosity is an excellent one to have! Making sure that you have a good professional reputation and brand is also good for your employer, as their name will be associated with all the interesting and innovative work you do.

Branding and marketing yourself

It can be difficult to take the first step towards promoting yourself, especially for introverts, who might see it as being pushy, or boasting. But it is an important aspect of professional involvement, and as Michael Stead said at the 2011 CILIP Cymru Welsh Libraries, Archives and Museums Conference, 'It's not boasting if it's true.'

Kathy Ennis, Career and Business Development Mentor and International Speaker at Envision Training, gives some tips about why and how to build your personal brand.

🔧 How to . . .
Approach personal branding

When I was young I loved Bazooka Joe bubble gum. What I wanted more than anything else was a pair of the Bazooka Joe x-ray spectacles; imagine being able to see through walls! The only problem was you had to collect hundreds of tokens for your 'free' set of x-ray specs, which meant an awful lot of bubble-gum chewing.

I was so happy on the day my x-ray specs arrived – until I opened the package. What I actually received was a pair of glasses with black lenses each with a white skeleton painted on it. What a swizz! I never bought Bazooka Joe again.

Many people have had similar experiences with a whole variety of products and services – that feeling of disappointment when it doesn't live up to your expectations. Our disappointment comes from our emotional investment in the product or service.

When you start to talk about personal branding, people often feel that what is being created is an image aimed at fooling people into buying into something that isn't quite true. In fact it is the opposite – with personal branding you are using the principles of branding in their best and purest form to provide yourself with a framework for how you live your life, progress your career or build your business.

Branding is often associated with the physical manifestation of the brand – a trademark or logo. But a brand is far more subtle than that: it is an identity.

A brand can take many forms: a name, a sign, a symbol, a combination of colours or even a slogan. From its early beginnings – a shape seared onto cattle using a red-hot iron to tell one farmer's herd from another's – the word has evolved to encompass identity. It is the 'thing' that gives a product, company or service a personality; in essence it is what creates in the customer a collection of thoughts and feelings about a particular product, company or service.

The idea of creating the right impression is not new – 'Clothes maketh the man' (Hamlet) – how many people who never wear suits decide they are the appropriate clothes for an interview! But the use of the term personal branding is relatively new and is about much more than wearing the right clothes.

Tom Peters wrote in 1997:

> Regardless of age, regardless of position, regardless of the business we happen to be in, all of us need to understand the importance of branding. We are CEOs of our own companies: Me Inc. To be in [work] today, our most important job is to be head marketer for the brand called You. . . . . The good news – and it is largely good news – is that everyone has a chance to stand out. Everyone has a chance to learn, improve, and build up their skills. Everyone has a chance to be a brand worthy of remark.

The power of personal branding is that it uses all the principles of product branding and applies them to the individual.

It is essential that the key elements of the personal brand are applied consistently. This is achieved by ensuring that the message you are sending – the sensation transference you are creating – and the way you are sending it through words, actions and visual attributes are in alignment. In coaching and personal development terms this is known as being congruent. Congruency is consistency, alignment and harmony. Congruency builds credibility. Credibility builds trust, respect and loyalty and is an absolute requirement for all professionals. This convergence of congruency and credibility is the cornerstone of personal brand development.

Building a personal brand is an objective process of discovering a set of key personal and professional assets which are then communicated consistently and passionately in person and across all media. Over the years I have been working in this area I have designed a step-by-step programme that ensures the individuals build a personal brand that is both consistent and congruent – I call this method The 4Vs Principle©.

V1 is values

Congruency flows from this V; it is the bedrock as it defines your personal beliefs and core philosophy; it determines your attitudes and behaviours; it is your unique selling point.

So, what do you believe? What do you stand for? What will you stand up against? See the 'over to you' section for a short exercise that can help you understand yourself.

V2 is visuals

This V is visual identity; it determines the look, appearance and actions of your personal brand and must be used consistently.

Stereotypes

Many library and information professionals obsess about how their profession is seen by others and often take exception to those well meaning people who say, 'You don't look like a librarian.'

Get over it. Every profession has a stereotype – estate agents, lawyers, used car salesmen. The power of the stereotype is that it is based in truth. For every information professional you find who doesn't conform to being female, middle-aged, glasses-wearing you will find ten who do.

Within the visuals element of your personal brand you use your values as the starting point for your visual manifestation – not your profession.

V3 is vocals

This is the V that deals with what is said and how it is said; from formal presentations and the elevator pitch to the 'hello' in the corridor.

Presentation skills

Presentation skills, the clue is in the second word – skills.

The ability to present confidently and coherently to ensure your audience is informed and entertained is a skill you need to learn and develop.

A good presentation is not a good PowerPoint show; a good presentation is *you* – building rapport and adding value to your audience, whether it consists of one person or 100 people.

V4 is verbals

This V deals with the written part of your personal brand. It is about having a view that you express in the magazine articles you write, your blog, your Facebook account and all the other forms of social media and social networking you use.

I Googled you

More and more employers and human resources professionals are admitting that they are using Google searches as part of their candidate selection processes. The consequence is that many people who are using social media are missing out on opportunities because their online profile reflects them in a less than positive light.

Does your online presence do you justice? Does it really reflect who you are? Is there anything you are doing and saying today that could have an impact on you when you are job hunting?

Taking the time and making the investment of developing your personal brand at the beginning of your career will enable employers to recognize a potential employee; create immediate recognition; build a loyal following; communicate core personal and professional values; and demonstrate your personal and professional relevance.

Much of what is written about the importance of personal branding centres directly on its importance when job hunting, or for career development or job security. However, there is a more fundamental reason for developing a personal brand. Personal brand development is essential because it celebrates individuality and uniqueness; putting it simply, it demonstrates your personal and professional value – it is your unique selling point.

Kathy has given us some great advice on how to build your brand. But how does it work in practice? Ned Potter, Academic Liaison Librarian for Music at the University of York, and founder of the LIS New Professionals Network (LISNPN), tells us about how he became known professionally as The Wikiman.

📁 Case study
Ned Potter: The Wikiman

How did you become 'The Wikiman'?

As there are two Ned Potters who already figure prominently online I wanted a nom-de-2.0 that was unique to me. I was just about to create a wiki for the digitization community, and I could see the possibilities of having a wicker man logo – so The Wikiman was born.

Why did you decide to create your own brand?

I'm not sure that I did. To paraphrase Bohyun Kim (2011) building a brand was largely a byproduct of my pursuing my interests in librarianship, and doing so publicly and in as networked a fashion as possible.

It is important to remember that when you talk about a product or a company, the brand is the sum total of everything that is thought about them, said about them, written about them and so on. It exists independent of the company – in effect the brand is the world's collective experience of that company.

I don't think it is quite like that for an information professional's brand as the demographic for the brand is much smaller and far more concentrated than it is for a commercial consumer product. But you don't control the brand completely – you just try and influence it as positively as you can. Just as people will Google you whether or not you have consciously shaped your online presence, your brand is out there whether or not you are branding yourself.

How have you promoted it?

I have a logo or avatar, which is a picture of a wicker man. I found it on Flickr, and got permission from the photographer to use it. It is useful to have something distinctive like that to use in multiple ways. It is on my website, my social media presences, my business cards; it shows up when I comment on other people's blogs, and I put it into presentations.

Everything I do links back to the blog – and that includes publications, and my accounts for Twitter, YouTube, SlideShare, NetVibes and the LISNPN. I try only to use a new platform of social media if I really see a need for it, so I don't spread myself too thinly – if you are going to take part in a conversation, you need time enough to say something interesting.

What effect has it had on your personal and professional development?

It has had every effect on my professional development. It has given me a voice, and a platform to allow people to get to know my views and expertise, and from that comes amazing opportunities I wouldn't have dreamed of two years ago. Nearly all of the interesting things I've been asked to do, from writing a book to speaking at some amazing events, can be traced back to my online identity.

🔧 How to . . .
Build your information professional brand

Be yourself

While part of branding is to put the best of yourself forward, it is more important to find the demographic that is happy to accept your professional activities as they are than to modify the way you behave to suit a demographic that isn't for you. But be careful! If being yourself involves being massively controversial, remember there is little point in building a great brand that gets you speaking at gigs and earns you respect as a maverick if it also alienates you from the kind of organizations that will actually pay your wages.

Building a brand and marketing yourself as an information professional isn't a one-way street: it is all about multi-way communication. You are not just telling people about yourself; you are positioning yourself as part of a dialogue about librarianship, and trying to offer something meaningful to the conversation. This involves not only giving advice, but also taking it; passing on others' expertise as well as your own; and being open. This is what stops brand building from being an empty exercise in self-promotion. You should aim to be a resource, not to be a hero.

Find something distinctive about yourself on which to build your brand (an interest in emerging technologies, for example, or expertise in ancient manuscripts), which can provide a focal point with which people can find and engage with you. If you don't have one particular area that defines you, you can still engage, but you might find it takes a little longer to establish yourself in an already crowded market.

Collaborate

It is a great experience and exposes you to new things, new views and new audiences. Just ask people if they'd like to work with you – it is surprising how often they'll say yes!

Attribute everything you do that is remotely inspired by or related to someone else's work. It is important to give credit, and it opens up the channels of communication.

Don't write cheques with your online brand that your face-to-face brand can't cash. If you portray yourself as an expert in something then eventually you will get asked to talk about it in person. Whenever you are doing something online, imagine saying it to the same audience in the flesh. Can you back it up?

Link everything together

Every online presence should link back to every other – every slide-deck should link to your blog, every blog home page should have links to your YouTube channel, and so on. Anyone who has even the slightest bit of curiosity to find out more about you should be able to do so without any barriers at all.

As the great Phil Bradley says, give as much of yourself away for free as you can, because reputation is everything. Get out there, add something of value to the conversation, and make yourself and your output available to all.

Ned has built a highly successful and influential brand, by sharing what he knows and thinks about with his professional networks. These good relations with your professional networks are key to many aspects of personal and professional development.

Networking

Your professional network is made up of all the people you have contact with. Some of these will be close friends, others will be people you have met once, or never met at all, except virtually.

Professional networks are important for a number of reasons. They can help you get informal training, share good practice and ideas, and give and receive advice. You can congratulate others for their successes, and commiserate and support people when things aren't going so well. They can be a knowledge curation tool: one Twitter-using librarian says, 'I use Twitter to find out what I should be reading. If several people re-tweet an article, I know it's a must-read.'

Having a good peer network can help you feel a lot less isolated. This is very important for new professionals, but it is also important at all stages of your career – continued involvement in peer groups can help you to stay connected and up to date, can support you through changes and developments in your career, and help that career progress.

How do you make the initial connections with people that enable you to become part of a network, and how do you develop and make the most of those networks? Maria Cotera, Branches Relationship Manager, Chartered Institute of Taxation, gives us her top tips for professional networking.

⚒ How to . . .
Network professionally

Professional networking is the art of meeting and building solid, long-lasting relationships with people who can be of help to us, and who we could help in return; it is about building reciprocal connections.

Developing a good network of professional contacts helps us to:

- *Build up interpersonal and communication skills:* We develop our influencing skills and our ability to approach new people, present ourselves in a positive light, deal with possible rejection, and communicate clearly and assertively.
- *Exchange ideas, get inspiration, build alliances:* No man is an island. I always get my best ideas from communication with colleagues whom I value and trust. They provide me with fresh perspectives, renewed enthusiasm, inspiration and encouragement.
- *Let others know which type of opportunities we are after:* This makes it much more likely that these opportunities will find us. For example, some jobs are never advertised, so those who get them often find out about them through their professional networks. I recently found out about a job via Facebook – a former fellow committee member saw it advertised and thought of me. It was my dream job, and I applied for it.
- *Find the right person for the job:* I knew I'd developed into a good networker when I realized that even when I couldn't help those in my professional network with a particular issue they were still coming to me for help getting in touch with the right person. I do the same all the time; for example, when organizing a conference, I'll ask others in my network for advice on who may be the best speaker on a particular topic.
- *Find information, seek expertise:* Whether inside intelligence about a job you

are interested in, tips on how to tackle something new, or information about a particular person: who do you trust most? I always trust those I already know – I write an e-mail, pick up the phone or send a quick tweet to the right people in my network. The wider your professional network, the greater the chances someone will be able to help.

• *Get a mentor:* All my mentors, peer mentors and mentees are colleagues with whom I have developed strong relationships through professional networking. One of my CILIP Chartership mentees came to me after her relationship with her previous mentor didn't work out – they hadn't got to know each other to see if they'd be a good fit before starting the mentoring relationship.

Building a network

With the rise in popularity of social networking sites such as Twitter, LinkedIn and Facebook, it is more vital than ever to remember the importance of effective face-to-face networking. This isn't about going to lots of different networking events, or collecting a business card from every person we meet, but about understanding who is relevant to us, and connecting with the same people regularly in order to establish ongoing relationships.

It is likely you are already establishing your own professional network, but as career goals change and we develop professionally it is always important to keep re-evaluating and expanding our networks. Joining a professional committee, for example, offers great opportunities to network with like-minded professionals.

Networking exercise 1

Draw a mind map of your current network, including work colleagues, contacts from voluntary work, societies and so on, and other people with whom you share interests. This exercise will help you to reflect on your existing networks, think about how to make the most of your current contacts, and identify gaps you may need to bridge.

Figure 11.1 shows how rich an existing network can be, providing many opportunities to learn from our existing colleagues and other contacts.

Networking exercise 2

Make a list of people you consider good networkers and think about what they have in common. Those on my list are:

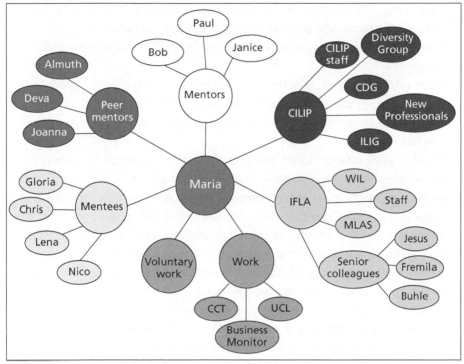

Figure 11.1 *Maria's network*

- self-confident
- good listeners
- curious (they enjoy finding out about others)
- friendly and approachable
- able to establish personal relationships before 'talking business'
- natural in displaying positive body language, including eye contact
- not judgemental
- good at remembering names, important facts and dates
- able to move on gracefully
- generous with what they have (support, information, skills, etc)
- reliable
- good at following up communications
- grateful for anything received.

Learning from them has helped me to be a better networker.

These are my top tips for successful professional networking:

- Make every effort to attend events where you know you are likely to find interesting people who you would like to add to your network.
- Create a positive first impression; look smart and present a professional image.
- Enter with confidence; take the initiative and approach others; introduce yourself and say something positive to start conversation.
- Smile, shake hands firmly, make eye contact, repeat and try to remember people's names.
- Show genuine interest; listen, be curious, ask open questions that allow the conversation to grow; remember key facts about others.
- Be yourself, don't boast or try to impress or you will risk appearing arrogant.
- Make up your mind whether you are interested in pursuing a contact or not within the first few minutes of conversation. If you are not, don't be afraid to end the conversation (for example by offering to introduce them to someone else) and move on. If you do want to maintain contact, exchange details and say how much you have enjoyed your conversation and that you would like to keep in touch, and gauge the person's reaction.
- Take notes about the people you are interested in on the back of their business cards so you remember key points about them.
- Follow up with an e-mail or on LinkedIn a few days later – remind your contact of who you are and where you met; send something you believe to be of genuine interest to them (a link to a useful website, a contact for someone else relevant to them, and so on).
- Concentrate on developing a unique relationship for each new contact, adding personal touches.
- Show appreciation for things others do for you.
- Be generous with your time.
- Retrieve people in your network who have drifted away.

Supporting yourself

Your colleagues can be one of the most useful advantages of getting a job. They are a ready-made network, and can help you to develop as a professional. But what if you don't have any professional colleagues? Small organizations are often more likely to employ a single information professional, and school librarians are often solo practitioners; see Farkas (2007) and McIntosh (n. d., 5).

While being a solo practitioner can be daunting, it has its benefits, too. Two solo practitioners tell us of their experiences below.

📁 Case study
Solo librarian at Cafcass

Jo Wood is Librarian at the Children and Family Court Advisory and Support Service (Cafcass) Library, which was established in April 2009. The Library was run solely by the Librarian until June 2010, when a library assistant was appointed.

The Cafcass Library has two core functions:

- to support the development of evidence-informed practice and to assist practitioners in using research in their front-line work
- to support the CPD needs of Cafcass staff.

The Library provides all Cafcass staff (mainly qualified social workers) based in c.90 offices around England with a comprehensive remote library, information and research service with free access to more than 14,000 books, journal articles, multimedia kits and links to government publications and research briefings.

What's it like working as a solo new professional?

It's a mixture of daunting and liberating. As a solo librarian, the buck stops with you and there is no one to share the workload. It is hard even to take annual leave – I took long weekends for a time rather than weeks of leave, because we couldn't afford to shut down the Library for a week or more as the social workers were reliant on the service for their work.

I established a brand new library single-handedly in April 2009, which is an unusual thing for a (reasonably) new professional to do. I had six years' experience of library and information work to fall back on, but it was a challenging time. I'm the only information professional in the organization so it was down to me to know my stuff and if I didn't know something, I had to learn it pretty quickly! I relished the opportunity to shape the service to fit the specific needs of the organization and it was great to be trusted with such a big responsibility so early in my career.

How does it affect your personal/professional development?

You don't have any opportunity to do CPD in work time. All of your energies are focused on developing and delivering a high-quality library and information service. As a solo librarian, I did everything from managing the library budget and reporting on expenditure to photocopying articles and everything else between, including acquisitions, journal subscriptions, cataloguing and classification, outreach work and promoting the Library.

There simply isn't the time to do professional reading or any form of professional networking (online or in person) during working hours. My organization's computer systems have disabled the majority of social networking tools and only selected external e-mail clients work on our secured networks. Our internet use is monitored and we're expected to keep to work-specific websites in work time.

I've attended one conference in the last two years. With the squeeze on public finances, many opportunities to take part in training courses have vanished. Moreover, because of my heavy workload I can't just take an afternoon out of my working time to attend an event, free or otherwise.

The only opportunity I have to do any CPD is in the evenings or when I'm on annual leave, and with a young family it is hard to justify extra time spent on professional development.

What do you like most about it?

Not having anyone to answer to! Not strictly true, but there are few 'dissenting voices' to challenge my ideas. I can come up with an idea to promote the Library, or improve the collections, and enact it the same day. It gives me a huge amount of flexibility and freedom that I wouldn't get if I worked in a team.

What do you miss most about working with professional colleagues?

Having someone that 'gets it' to bounce ideas off. It is extremely wearing to constantly explain what your role is in an organization, why it matters and why your role should continue to exist. You sometimes feel like a lone voice in the wilderness, trying to shout your importance from the rooftops and being ignored. Having a team of professionals would provide that support.

I'm concerned that I might get stuck in a rut and become stale because I'm so focused on ploughing a lonely furrow that I forget to look up and see what's happening in the profession. A team structure would allow me to focus on particular aspects of the Library, rather than being a jack of all trades and fearing that I'm rapidly losing touch with my professional colleagues.

Lee Pretlove is records management officer at TWI, a technology engineering company.

📁 Case study
Solo records manager at TWI

Prior to 2007, when I joined TWI, there was already an embedded administrative culture that had understood the importance of retaining important records, although management of these records varied from department to department. The organization moved buildings in 2003 and a Records Manager was employed to design and implement a central Records Centre but moved to another role within the organization shortly after its establishment. The running of the Records Centre was then temporarily placed under the remit of the Deputy Librarian. In 2007, I was originally employed to consolidate and digitize around 20,000 confidential reports, but after six months in post, the Deputy Librarian handed over her records management responsibilities to me.

Over the last four years I've tried to establish a comprehensive records management programme, whilst at the same time studying for a diploma, and also attempting to complete consolidation and scanning of the organization's report archive.

The idea of a centralized records management function is fairly new to TWI, and other business support functions, such as finance and information technology, are better understood and traditionally accepted as business support functions. 'Records Management' (RM) is sited within Information Services, commonly referred to as 'The Library'. This perception has made it a challenge for me to demonstrate the unique skills and function of a records manager.

Attempts to overturn this perception have helped to sharpen the advocacy and the influencing skills I acquired during my qualification period. Working and communicating with colleagues at all levels in the business, who are from various professional backgrounds in IT, systems development, marketing and engineering, has helped me learn to adapt my approach in order to get RM higher up the corporate agenda. I've learned to adapt tones and methods of communication to help staff understand what RM involves, and how it can help them achieve their organizational aims.

Initially I found it very frustrating that staff didn't understand what RM was, and why it was needed. It was through sheer persistence, patience and the valued support of my line manager that it was generally realized that RM was not just an 'add-on' job, and that it could actually enhance organizational working practices and assist in ensuring compliance with relevant information laws.

While advocating RM and information law compliance, there was of course also the necessity of answering everyday records enquiries and retrievals. When working alone, it becomes very difficult to plan a day and stick to the plan, however much you build in time to devote to enquiries. Quite often the retrievals have a high degree of urgency.

I've found that, working as a solo unit, the records manager will always be occupied. Whether you are rushed off your feet completing many small tasks in one day, or have some long periods of uninterrupted time to plan much needed projects, you will hardly find an idle moment. My tasks range from strategic planning to answering short enquiries and records accessioning; there is always something new to do and you must be flexible in your approach. One moment you can find yourself in meetings with Executive Board members and the next covered in dust, emptying and slinging around filing cabinets, or rushing around retrieving records. At the moment I'm putting the finishing touches to the digitizing of the technical report archive project and I am looking forward to working with all levels of staff in finally implementing a company-wide RM programme.

The luxury of setting your own agenda is perhaps one of the best aspects of working solo. Only you know the detail of work involved in any given project, and you are able to call on the specifics of a relevant piece of legislation for best practice. Accordingly, you can use your professional judgement to advise colleagues on a course of action. This all helps to build up professional trust and value.

I do sometimes wish that, whilst working towards my qualification, I had been working in an established team, under the wing of an experienced records manager, to assist my development. There are times in my present post when a professional sounding board would be useful: quite often it's a case of just wishing to check whether I'm proceeding along the right lines. However, solo working helps you to gain conviction in your decisions, and you have free rein to interpret RM theory within the workings of the organization.

In order to fill the void of fellow professional company at work, it is really good practice to network with fellow professionals in other organizations. I'm Training

Officer for the ARA (Archives and Records Association) Eastern Region and a member of the Section for Records Management Executive Committee. This has helped me stay in touch with the broader archives and records community, and also helped me in times when I've needed someone to talk to about professional issues. I've not yet had the privilege of working with fellow professional colleagues in post. If I get the chance to do so in the future, it would feel good to have people who I could talk 'shop' with and know that they understand.

Tips for coping with working solo

- Have an end vision to be achieved through a set of specific goals: this will help to keep you focused and motivated.
- Make professional contacts: they are invaluable for the solo professional and they can help you by giving advice.
- Break your workload down into bite-sized chunks: understanding the basics of both time and project management will help with this.

Jo and Lee have highlighted many of the same aspects of working as a solo practitioner, and much of what they say echoes Reece's case study on embedded librarianship from Chapter 4: by working more closely with your users you will find it easier to communicate value, and to build a personal profile as a trusted professional colleague. They have also shown the value of professional networks and mentors in supporting solo practitioners.

Conclusion

Building your brand and your professional network are both aspects of professional development, and will benefit you and the profession. They take some effort, but to be really effective they should flow naturally from who you are and what you do – be congruent and authentic. You don't have to echo every aspect of your personal life in your professional persona, but do be authentic in your interactions with other professionals.

This authenticity will help to build the trust necessary to have a flourishing professional network, to help and be helped throughout your professional life. In Chapter 12 we will discuss some of the ways you can get involved in the professional community, and give back to your network and the profession.

References and further reading

Personal branding

Alcock, J. (2011) Thing 3: consider your personal brand, 23 *Things for Professional Development*, blog, http://cpd23.blogspot.com/2011/06/thing-3-consider-your-personal-brand.html.

Bates, M. E. (2011) Creating Groupies: info-pro guerilla marketing, *SLA Annual Conference Philadelphia*, www.batesinfo.com/extras/assets/groupies.pdf.

Gladwell, M. (2005) *Blink: the power of thinking without thinking*, Penguin.

Kim, B. (2011) Surprise! A personal brand is a by-product!, *Library Hat*, blog, www.bohyunkim.net/blog/archives/1048.

Peters, T. (1997) The Brand Called You, *Fast Company*, 31 August, www.fastcompany.com/magazine/10/brandyou.html.

Networking

D'Souza, S. (2010) *Brilliant Networking: what the best networkers know, say, and do*, 2nd edn, Prentice Hall.

Heye, D. (2006) *Characteristics of the Successful Twenty-first Century Information Professional*, Chandos Publishing.

Kollermann, N. (n. d.) *Effective Networking Inspiring Perspectives: finding a job in tough times*, http://inspiringperspectives.com/job-search-advice-dealing-with-recruitment-consultant-customising-a-cv-or-cover-letter/effective-networking.

Ruddock, B. (2010) Proving the Value of Peer Networks: plugging in to your peers, *CILIP CDG New Professional's Conference*, www.slideshare.net/bethanar/proving-the-value-of-peer-networks-final.

Zack, D. (2010) *Networking for People Who Hate Networking: a field guide for introverts, the overwhelmed, and the underconnected*, Berrett-Koehler.

Solo practitioners

Farkas, M. (2007) 2007 Survey of the Biblioblogosphere: results from the solo librarian filter *Information Wants to be Free*, http://meredith.wolfwater.com/survey/solo%20librarian.pdf.

Lang, J. (n. d.) *The Proverbial Lone Wolf Librarian's weblog*, http://lonewolflibrarian.wordpress.com.

McIntosh, S. (n. d.) *School Library Staff Progression Framework*, www.sla.org.uk/school-library-staff-progression-framework.php.

Peacock, J. (2011) Working with Burnout, *Libhat's blog*,

http://libhat.wordpress.com/2011/06/30/working-with-burnout.

Library RX. (2010) Going Solo in the Library, *Closed Stacks*, www.closedstacks.com/?p=2716.

Siess, J. A. (2006) *The New OPL Source-book: a guide for solo and small libraries*, Information Today.

Smallwood, C. and Clapp M. J. (eds) (2011) *How to Thrive as a Solo Librarian*, Scarecrow Press.

➡ Over to you . . .

Personal branding: a five words exercise

Brainstorm all of the words and phrases that you feel describe the person you are – honest, trustworthy, courageous, fun-loving, helpful and so on – and then prioritize the top five. Ask some of the people around you to come up with the five words they would use to describe you. Choose a variety of people: friends, colleagues and family members. Compare their lists with your list. You will find (if you are being honest with yourself) that there is a core set of words and phrases that not only describe 'you' but the characteristics that you exhibit, because others see them in you too.

If there is a mis-match between the terms you have identified and what others are seeing you need to question how honest you are being with yourself.

Thanks to Kathy Ennis for this exercise.

Networking

See Maria's case study earlier in this chapter for two exercises on networking.

Reflect on a recent networking experience, either face to face or online. Ask yourself:

- Was it a comfortable or enjoyable experience?
- What went right?
- What went wrong?
- How can you follow up to make the most of the experience?
- Would you do or say anything differently next time?
- What did you gain from the experience?
- What do you think the other person (people) gained?

CHAPTER 12
Professional involvement and career development

Introduction

Though it might not feel like it for those vital first few weeks in a new job, there is professional life outside the workplace. Although work-based activities and development are interesting and important, you will also find personal and professional value in other professional involvement.

This might be attending conferences or other learning or networking events; or joining a professional organization, and getting involved as a member, volunteer, or committee member. You could find interesting and innovative ways to share your professional thinking and insights with other members of the profession – do you have a passion for haiku? A knack for communicating through cake?

All of this involves learning new skills, and honing your existing ones. While you are doing this, you might start thinking about the future of your career: where you would like to go next, and how you are going to get there. Career planning can seem intimidating, but it doesn't have to be. As an information professional, you will already have most of the skills you need to think about how to develop your career.

In this chapter we will look at all these types of professional involvement and planning. It isn't a prescriptive guide to how to get involved – there are as many ways to get involved in your profession as there are types of information professional, and we hope the case studies in this chapter will inspire you to come up with some of your own.

Conferences

Conferences are a fantastic opportunity for development. They give you opportunities to increase your knowledge formally, through attending sessions, and informally, though sharing ideas with other delegates. They are one of the best networking opportunities you will encounter, and they usually have time set aside specifically for networking, often over meals or drinks. This is a great way to get to know people in a social (yet professional) environment.

Attending conferences can help you improve your listening skills; learn how to network; develop your presentation skills; teach or facilitate workshops; and get writing practice by blogging or writing-up the conference. All of this looks great on your CV, and can be good fun, too.

Conferences are inspiring. It can be rejuvenating to spend time with infectiously enthusiastic fellow professionals, and to hear about the great projects they are running or the innovations they are making.

It can also be valuable to attend conferences outside your sector – or out of the information profession altogether. If you are working in a particular subject area, attending a conference on that subject can be a fantastic way to deepen your knowledge, make good contacts, and raise the profile of your profession.

The drawback is that conferences can be expensive. Your organization might fund you to go, but with training budgets tightening, you might have to think up other strategies to be able to attend the conference of your dreams.

One of the ways to attend a conference on a budget is to speak at it. Speakers are often given free (or reduced-rate) attendance. This gives you all the benefits of attending the conference, as well as building up your personal skills and portfolio, and allowing you to share your work with the profession. Chris Rhodes, an economics specialist in the House of Commons Library, was on the conference panel for the first two CILIP Career Development Group (CDG) New Professionals' conferences. Chris highlights some common mistakes which should be avoided, and sets out some key ways that a proposal can be made to stand out from the crowd.

🔧 How to . . .
Write a successful conference proposal

There are few better ways of extending your professional network, demonstrating your value to the profession, or acquiring the essential skills of presentation and reasoned argument than speaking at conferences. Competition to speak at conferences is fierce and your proposal must be arresting and insightful.

The basics

Conference proposals are usually divided into two sections: biography, normally in the form of a CV or short personal statement; and the presentation proposal. Both sections are equally important, and should be considered as one document, which can be read as a coherent whole.

Make sure you keep content to the appropriate section. Don't assume that the content section is another opportunity to describe anything about yourself: it is frustrating to be reminded of someone's CV when you are trying to ascertain what they will talk about.

Avoid practical mistakes. These will result in an amateurish application, which will be overlooked. Make sure you are eligible to submit proposals – there may be restrictions that disqualify you from applying. Submit by e-mail or print, as required by the conference committee, and use a single, standard font, as a straightforward presentation of your ideas is required. Check for spelling and grammatical mistakes, stick to word limits, and make sure you include all the required information.

Style

You are applying to present at a professional conference, so the style and content of your proposal should be professional. Use formal language, and try to avoid phrases that could be construed as 'chatty'; they are conspicuous in a formal setting like this and will make your proposal stand out for the wrong reasons.

There is a tendency among information professionals to write about their childhood and their formative experiences in libraries. This is a mistaken attempt to demonstrate some kind of innate connection to the profession. Doctors applying to medical conferences feel no need to describe their first experience in hospital. Information professionals should refrain from describing their first memories of libraries. Never say that the career 'chose you'. This phrase is essentially meaningless, inelegant and surprisingly popular in this profession.

Content

You should tailor the section about yourself (normally a CV or personal statement) so that it is clear how your career makes you suited to present at the conference. Highlight achievements that are relevant, just as you would when applying for a job. Demonstrate that your professional experiences make you the ideal candidate to present on your chosen topic.

Find out as much as you can about the organization hosting the conference and make sure you address issues that are important to them. You should be familiar with previous conference content (if there is any available), make reference to any recent successes that the organization has been involved with, make clear that you would value the opportunity to be associated with their name, and demonstrate how you will enhance the reputation of the organization.

Information professionals like to read about their own profession – what it is, what it can be, what it will be. Make it clear that you understand the professional context in which you seek to present; demonstrate that you understand the profession and how your ideas will contribute. Don't apply to present conferences on subjects you are not interested in. If you are not fully enthused, there will be rival applicants who display more passion and dedication.

To be successful in a proposal to present to a conference you must demonstrate a commitment to the profession and confidence in your own abilities. If you manage to convey commitment and confidence then you are likely to make a lasting impression and secure the opportunity to make your arguments to a larger audience.

If your proposal to speak is unsuccessful, how about volunteering to work a conference stand? This could either be for your organization, or for an external exhibitor. It is hard work, but it does get you through the doors for free. Experienced exhibitor Lisa Charnock, Development Officer, Mimas, shares her top tips for making it through with your feet and mind intact.

🔧 How to . . .
Work an exhibition stand

When I qualified and took up my first professional post, I didn't think that working on exhibition stands at conferences and events would be something I'd be expected to do. From my limited experience of such things, I assumed that conference stands were for sales people – more akin to my previous jobs in retail than the career I had subsequently chosen. I couldn't have been more wrong. From internal careers and freshers' fairs to major corporate conferences, I've spent a lot of days working at events. It is different every time, but there are some key things that you can do to make sure that your event is a success.

Set your objectives

If you do nothing else on this list, make sure that you ask yourself one question: 'Why am I attending this event?' There are many reasons for exhibiting, but they tend to fall into three main areas:

* promoting something new
* connecting with existing users
* trying to attract new users.

Everything you do to plan your event will depend on your main reason for being there. For example, if you are there to attract new users, you might need something eye-catching and unusual on your stand to entice people over.

Do your homework

You should always have a main contact at the venue. This person is a goldmine of information, so get in touch with them as early as possible. These are some of the things you should find out: delegate numbers (to know how many leaflets and giveaways to take), delivery information (if you need to post anything), and what equipment and facilities are included. There are conferences where you have to pay for everything, including your plug sockets, so it is always best to be prepared.

Know your audience

Would you take a supply of lollipops and novelty freebies to an event where the delegates are managers and heads of department? Probably not. But those lollipops would be popular during a Welcome Week event for undergraduates. If you want to pitch things at the right level, it pays to know who you will be talking to on the day. Having the right giveaways on a stand can be a great way to attract people – Mimas once created quite a stir on Twitter with some blue cupcakes, and people still ask about them two years later.

Get the right people to help you

Although it is never advisable to work an exhibition stand on your own, budget restrictions might mean that this is unavoidable. Staff are valuable, so choose them carefully, and make sure the right people are at the event. If you are launching something new, make sure you have someone with you who knows the product or service well – you never know what someone might ask you on the day. Remember, you can't know everything. It is fine to take someone's details and get back to them.

Think about the practicalities

Working at events usually involves long, tiring days so make sure you and your colleagues have scheduled comfort and lunch breaks. Often, the times when the event delegates are having their own breaks is when you will be working hardest, so it is important to make sure you can get away from the exhibition at other times. Exhibition halls can also be vast, draughty spaces so make sure that you are wearing something comfortable which you can adapt to changes in temperature.

Make a good first impression

How do you get people to speak to you? Well, when you go to a fair or an exhibition, do you approach the stand with the person sitting behind a desk, checking e-mails on a laptop, eating a sandwich and drinking a cup of coffee? No? Most people wouldn't, but it is surprising how many people run their stands like this. Make sure that you smile and make eye contact with people as they walk around. Many will just walk right past you unless you make the first move, so be friendly, welcoming and ready to talk to anyone.

Ask questions

People approach exhibition stands for all kinds of reasons. Some will have no idea what you do, others will have a specific question, and some will just want the free pencils. Ask open questions to find out what they're interested in and start a conversation with them – don't just launch into a speech about your service without finding out a little bit about them.

Get in touch

So, you have spent all day talking to people, the leaflets are packed away, and you are heading home. Job done? Actually, there is still a lot to do if you want anything useful to come out of your hard work. Within a week, look through the business cards and contact details that you collected and contact anyone who had specific questions, or who you promised information or materials. The delegates will have spoken to a lot of people, and if you don't contact them quickly, they may not remember who you are.

Ask for feedback

I have a standard set of questions that I circulate a few days after every event to help me evaluate how successful it was. A simple, 'what went well, what didn't go well, what would you do differently next time' evaluation will help you to reflect. You could also ask:

- Do you think it was a successful day?
- What kind of comments did you receive?
- Did you meet any useful contacts?

It is worth putting all of this information into a brief report. It doesn't have to be detailed, but documenting the successes and failures of the event will help you to plan the next one.

Revisit your objectives

Go right back to the beginning and look at your reasons for working on the exhibition stand. Did you achieve your objectives? When deciding whether the event was a success this is a key question to ask, but you might need to wait a few months before you can answer this properly.

Tip

Next time you go to an exhibition, find a stand that you like and ask yourself why. Is there something about the way it is dressed or presented? Is it the attitude of the staff? Do they have nice giveaways? Now find one that you don't find welcoming and ask yourself the same question. I do this at every exhibition I attend, and it is a great way to get ideas, and to find out what I shouldn't be doing!

No chance of working a stand? There is still another route to conference attendance. Laura Woods, Information Services Adviser at Addleshaw Goddard LLP, has attended five conferences after winning awards, and shares her tips for finding and winning awards and bursaries.

🔧 How to . . .
Apply for awards

Attending conferences is a fantastic way to broaden your professional experience, but they are usually out of the budget of most new professionals. Luckily, there are numerous awards and bursaries available from various professional bodies to sponsor attendance at conferences. Some of these are aimed specifically at students or new professionals.

Finding awards to apply for

Most awards are publicized on mailing lists, lis-link such as (https://www.jiscmail. ac.uk/cgi-bin/webadmin?A0=LIS-LINK) and lis-awards (https://www.jiscmail. ac.uk/cgi-bin/webadmin?A0=LIS-AWARDS). Organizations also advertise awards on their own websites and mailing lists. Look at your professional body's website, to find out details of its annual conference and any awards or bursaries to support attendance.

If no awards are advertised, it is always worth getting in touch with the conference organizers or sponsors, or your professional body, to see if they are willing to support your attendance.

Some conferences will waive at least part of the attendance fee in exchange for your volunteering to help out at the conference – this is a great way to witness first-hand the work that goes into organizing a professional conference!

Applying for awards

Applying for conference awards can be highly competitive, with many people applying for the same award. You should approach applying for an award in the same way as applying for a job:

- Make sure you read the application instructions carefully, so you know that you are supplying all of the information asked for.
- Tailor your application to the specific award – just as you wouldn't send the same application and CV for two different jobs, don't use the same application for two different awards.
- Familiarize yourself with both the conference programme and the organization you are applying for an award from.
- Make sure you are clear about what you hope to learn and take away from

the conference. If there is a particular session, speaker or theme that's caught your eye, mention it.
- Demonstrate an understanding of the goals of the organization sponsoring the award: they will want to know that you will be a good ambassador for them.

Making the most of your award

There are many general tips and guides for first-time attendees at conferences, but here are a few specific pieces of advice helpful for those who have won awards to support their attendance:

- Talk to your sponsoring organization to see if they have any specific advice for you – they will want you to get as much as you can out of the conference too.
- If any vendors or other organizations sponsored your award, try to attend any sessions they are running, and/or stop by their stall in the exhibition hall to thank them in person.
- Get in touch with any other sponsored attendees. Meeting other award winners can give you someone to chat to, and share ideas and tips with before, during and after the conference.

Post-conference write-ups

After the conference, you will often be asked to write about your experience for your sponsoring organization's newsletter, journal or blog. Make sure the write-up reflects well on you, and your sponsors:

- Don't try to write down everything that happened – this will lead to a very dull write-up! Focus on the general themes of the conference, what your main takeaways were, and what you plan to put into practice.
- Try to tailor your write-up for the intended audience: will it be a professional journal read only by members of the organization, or a blog open to the general public?
- Finally, and most importantly, remember to thank the organization that gave you the award, as well as any other sponsors.

Unconferences

If you can't find a conference that's relevant or affordable, how about organizing your own? Over the past few years, there has been a growth in the number of library and archive unconferences. These are conferences without a set agenda: they usually set a general topic, and then the agenda and format largely arrange themselves on the day. The idea is to get a critical mass of people together, and let them decide what they want to talk about. It is designed to encourage unconventional thinking, brainstorming and risk-taking in a welcoming, informal environment. They are usually free to attend, which helps bring in attendees who can't go to normal events.

Anyone can organize an unconference. All you need are an idea, a venue and some attendees. You can then add as many extras as you like. If you can get sponsorship and provide a lovely (and geographically accessible) venue, then that's great! If not, an unconference can just as well happen in your local park or pub.

As well as unconferences providing a great collaborative learning and networking event for your professional community, organizing one can help you to develop high-level skills. Pursuing sponsorship, in particular, can help you to understand financial negotiations and the esoteric art of asking for money – skills which will be useful as your career progresses and you find yourself pursuing funding for your service or organization.

Professional involvement

There is no one easy definition of 'professional involvement'. Attending and organizing conferences is one form of it, but it can encompass all sorts of activities: from attending conferences to writing articles; from being a member of a professional organization to taking up a professional office. Broadly speaking, we can define professional involvement as 'engaging with the profession in any way that is beyond the normal demands of your job'.

Why would you want to do it? It can open up new opportunities, help you gain skills and experience that you might not be able to get within your workplace; build your professional reputation, which can lead to increased employability; help you do your job better by keeping you informed and honing your skills; benefit the profession by developing yourself and sharing your ideas with others; and give you chances to have new experiences and meet new friends.

Lauren Smith, PhD student at the University of Strathclyde, tells us about some of the benefits she's felt from professional involvement.

📁 Case study
Professional involvement for personal development

In 2010, while studying for a Masters in Librarianship, I helped to found Save Doncaster Libraries (http://savedoncasterlibraries.wordpress.com) and Voices for the Library (www.voicesforthelibrary.org.uk), while I was working and studying full time. It has been of great benefit to my personal and professional development, and I have developed skills which I might not have been able to within an ordinary workplace environment. Professional involvement outside work has allowed me to develop in a safe way; there is far less chance of me losing my 'job' as a campaigner if I take a risk and it fails.

Although the grass-roots and voluntary nature of campaign groups usually develop according to the skills and interests of those involved, there are some tasks which are new to everyone, but still need doing. I had no experience of liaising with the media, but I knew that some of my skills and previous experience – such as being involved in music performances, debating societies and public speaking – could be put to good use and give me a good foundation to build on. If you are keen to develop your skills and experience, it may be useful to consider which areas you want to develop and think of specific ways you could do this through advocacy or activism.

Table 12.1 lists some examples of how skills or strengths can be developed through carrying out particular activities.

Benefits

The wide range of skills you can develop from involvement in advocacy and/or activism can have a positive effect on your career; for example, I was named a Library Journal Mover and Shaker 2011. My experiences of involvement gave me confidence to run for Vice-President of CILIP. The skills outlined above are transferable and can strengthen your CV and job applications. Similarly, opportunities to have your work published can be used in applications for further study; I was able to use articles I had written as advocacy pieces in my application for PhD funding. Articles are also considered valid for inclusion in CILIP Chartership applications and can add variety to your portfolio.

Table 12.1 *Skills and strengths gained from various activities*

Activity	Skills developed or strengths gained
Holding public or committee meetings	Leadership, teamwork, acting as chair, minute-taking, time management, diplomacy
Organizing protests and events	Leadership, co-ordination, event management, promotion and advertising, designing publicity, knowledge of civil and political rights
Analysing legal documents for an understanding of the key issues	Critical thinking, summary writing skills, reporting
Analysing council documents to understand decision-making processes and assess where there may be flaws	Critical thinking, developing complex arguments, communication
Writing letters and sending press releases to newspapers	Writing press releases and content to catch journalists' interest
Blogging about events, news, updates, opinions and so on	Self-confidence, time management, organization, credibility, demonstration of knowledge, development of network of interested people, practical social media skills
Writing articles for journals and magazines	Writing skills (including writing to word counts and deadlines, and for specific audiences)
Giving guest lectures at universities	Lecture planning, designing presentations, encouraging discussion, public speaking, awareness of developments or changes in academic discipline or LIS research
Taking part in cross-disciplinary discussion panels	Reputation as knowledgeable in field, cross-sectoral involvement, networking
Giving newspaper, radio and television interviews (local, national and international)	Interview skills, self-confidence; expert knowledge in that particular field – you become the authority on it; keeping calm under pressure or when frustrated – managing emotions; being able to memorize statistics, access and use them under pressure
Networking and promoting at conferences, festivals and other events	Self-confidence, networking, subject knowledge
Developing websites as a source of information for the public and the media	Social networking skills, website building, information architecture, information retrieval

Table 12.1 *Skills and strengths gained from various activities*	
Activity	Skills developed or strengths gained
Helping newspaper journalists research articles	Working to tight deadlines, information retrieval, presenting information in a meaningful way
Helping lawyers put legal arguments together; giving background and history	Information retrieval, ability to manage large amounts of information
Asking for sponsorship and statements of support	Pitching proposals, writing convincing requests
Dealing with councillors and MPs	Diplomacy, advocacy, pitching your aims to meet interests and values of people with different priorities, interests and values

Challenges

Professional involvement isn't all plain sailing! Maintaining a sensible work–life balance is important – this may come naturally, but I found I needed to make sure I was aware of how much I was taking on. Although the workload can be high and there is always a lot to be done, you can pace this depending on whatever other pressures you have to contend with. Good time management skills are important, and you will soon find yourself getting better at prioritizing and managing your workload. Some people find it helpful to take time away from everything for short periods; others prefer to keep at least a low level of involvement in projects – taking a step back rather than completely removing themselves.

Another challenge is to stay positive when things go wrong or when there is bad news. In-built resilience is useful, but, again, taking a step away to recharge can be helpful. Building a strong network of other people who are involved in similar activities can play a significant part in maintaining energy and momentum.

Professional organizations

The first real professional involvement for many information professionals is through a professional body. You might start off by attending events, which gives you a chance to get to know people; you hear about an opening on the committee – next thing you know, you are organizing events!

A professional organization will do most or all of the following:

• run events, conferences and training courses

- provide opportunities for networking
- provide opportunities for structured professional development
- provide chances for a mentoring or peer support programme
- publish journals, magazines, newsletters and blogs
- have committees staffed by members.

All of these provide opportunities for you to get involved. Finding the right professional body for you is important, too.

In the next ase study, Fiona Bradley of IFLA, and co-ordinator of the Australian Library and Information Association (ALIA) New Librarians Symposium 2006, tells us more about professional organizations – what they do, and how you can get the most out of membership.

💼 Case study
Building skills and networks and contributing to the profession through professional organizations

Library and information organizations play an essential role in the development of LIS services on behalf of users, and the standing of the profession locally and internationally. Professional organizations set standards, develop guidelines and advocate for the value of library and information services to decision-makers. A strong membership is necessary for organizations to have a strong voice.

Why you should join a professional organization

Membership of professional organizations can have an impact on you individually and as a member of the profession. New professionals are important – they bring new perspectives, ideas and practices to associations. In turn, associations provide opportunities for professional development such as training, networking and conferences. Networking provides the opportunity to see beyond your workplace and sector to how others are tackling (often the same) issues, and to find solutions together.

There are more ways than ever to become involved. CILIP, the Australian Library and Information Association (ALIA), American Library Association (ALA) and other organizations provide opportunities for new professionals to contribute. The New Professionals Special Interest Group for example, is a group within the International Federation of Library Associations and Institutions (IFLA) that works through the association and uses social networking to connect with professionals globally. Associations are providing more opportunities to participate online through event streaming and social networking, broadening access even if you can't physically attend events.

Finding the right organization for you

A great time to explore your options is while you are still a student, or soon after graduation. Many organizations such as CILIP, the SLA, the American Society for Information Science and Technology and IFLA provide reduced membership rates to students. Some associations have developed programmes to provide mentoring and sponsored membership to students and new professionals to help you find your place.

Finding the right organization for you will depend on what you want to get out of it. You may be seeking a place to turn for advice; professional development, such as training courses or joining a committee; or having a say in advocacy for library and information services, and contributing to standards. Many organizations provide all of these, and your choice may be based on what organizations colleagues in your sector have chosen to join. But don't feel that you should necessarily choose the same organization – each one has a different approach, and you may find benefits from branching out.

Making the most of your membership

Consider your goals, budget and how the organization may be able to help. As a new professional, make the most of your membership by taking advantage of opportunities such as:

- access to grants to attend conferences, such as Umbrella in the UK, and the international IFLA Congress
- awards, such as SLA Europe's Early Career Conference Award
- new professional information days offered by CILIP
- events such as New Professionals in the UK, BOBCATSSS (an annual symposium organized by LIS students) in Europe and the New Librarians' Symposium in Australia for relevant, affordable professional development and networking
- new professional positions on branches and committees.

Professional organizations can provide a forum to develop skills that you may not have the opportunity to develop in your current role. Conferences such as the New Librarians' Symposium (Australia) and New Professionals Conference (UK) are run by new professionals. The IFLA New Professionals Special Interest Group (NPSIG) hosts pre-conferences and other events at each World Library and Information Congress.

Attending conferences for new professionals can be the gateway to broadening your perspective beyond your workplace or sector. These events strengthen connections and development throughout both your career, and benefit the sector in the long run.

Committee members develop essential transferable skills in project management, communications and budgeting that can give a new professional the boost they need in their current or next role. These skills are highly valued by employers, but can be difficult to gain early in your career.

The organizers of the IFLA NPSIG satellite meeting in Borås, Sweden, in 2010 came from more than seven different countries, and organized the meeting online using a working wiki, a blog and other collaboration tools. They gained skills in conference management and had the opportunity to connect to an international audience and to recruit new members to the group. Similar events are already planned for the upcoming IFLA Congress in Finland. At the same time, the NPSIG is hosting various sessions and workshops at other conferences such as the annual BOBCATSSS symposium. This kind of ongoing work in a global environment provides much inspiration for the daily work of everyone involved and leads to a rich personal and professional network which is essential, especially in the early career of an LIS professional.

The work and the outcome of the NPSIG's activities also have an impact on the wider LIS profession, providing feedback and input to the IFLA network.

Special thanks to Sebastian Wilke, convenor of IFLA's NPSIG for contributing to this case study.

Other professional involvement

Professional involvement doesn't have to be formal, or require membership of any particular group. You can engage and express that engagement with the profession in any way that suits you.

Sarah Wachter became an LIS celebrity with the 2010 release of her video, *Librarians do Gaga* (www.youtube.com/watch?v=a_uzUh1VT98). Based on the Lady Gaga hit 'Poker Face', the lyrics were written by Wachter, and the singing and dancing talent were provided by members of the University of Washington's iSchool students and faculty.

Wachter's aim was to 'sing, dance, and educate', and there is a serious teaching message behind the fun and glamour:

> I worked hard to make the lyrics educational as well as funny. One of the iSchool's mottoes is 'We make information work' and it was important to me that I live up to this. . . . I thought of including Mike Eisenberg's Big Six information literacy skills in the rap at the end. The response to this has been enormous. I've received requests from teachers at all educational levels to use the video in their information literacy instruction.

Wachter also enhanced the image of the profession, by showing librarians as 'enthusiastic, passionate, friendly people', with creativity and a sense of humour. Wachter's personal and professional development has also benefited, giving her 'professional exposure beyond my wildest dreams', and a network of mentors and established professionals.

Her advice to new professionals?: 'Love what you do. Let your creativity shine. Use all the talents you have from your life and your professional training to make something you are proud of. Become part of the conversation. You are the future of librarianship – so let your voice be heard!'

   ∂ **Read the full story of Librarians do Gaga on the website (http://lisnewprofs.com/librariansdogaga).**

Rebecca Goldman caught the attention of the archive community with her webcomic, Derangement and Description (http://derangementanddescription. wordpress.com), started when Rebecca was new to archive work and teaching herself Encoded Archival Description (EAD) – see Chapters 5 and 6 for more on EAD. There weren't any other archives webcomics, and Rebecca decided to fill the gap, improve her own learning, and inform and entertain the archives community.

Rebecca says: 'I saw it as my professional contribution to the field. I didn't yet have the education or experience to publish papers or present at conferences, and I thought EAD jokes and drawings of talking doc boxes would be an easier way to start.'

Derangement and Description has become popular in the archive community, and tackles serious issues such as sexism in the LIS professions and the difficulties facing new archivists trying to enter the field, as well as providing humour, puns and parodies. Rebecca's comics have been used by other professionals in teaching and presentations, and have helped her gain professional recognition – and a professional post.

This is Rebecca's advice for new professionals:

> Don't wait until your content is perfect to start blogging. I was so self-conscious about my comics that I didn't even put my name on the blog until after it won an award. As with More Product, Less Process, tell yourself you can always go back and fix things later – and then don't. Learn from your mistakes, and implement your improvements starting with your next entry. It can take time to find your own style, but you won't find it if you never publish anything.

 𝒪 **Read Rebecca's full story on the website
    (http://lisnewprofs.com/derangement).**

Career development and planning

It is never too early to start planning your career. While you don't have to have a clear idea of where you want to be in five, ten or 20 years, it does help to have some idea of which area you want to go into, and which skills you need to develop. It is a good idea to look at job descriptions for roles you might be interested in pursuing in the future, take note of the skills and experience needed, and use that to plan your personal and professional development. Even if you end up going in a different direction, learning and development is never wasted – you will always find a way to apply the skills you have to whatever role you are filling.

Planned or unplanned, at some point you will need to start thinking about job hunting, CVs and interviews. You may dread this, and feel uncomfortable promoting your skills and achievements, but there is no room for self-effacement in job hunting. That doesn't mean it has to be too painful. Sarah Johnson, electronic resources and reference librarian at Eastern Illinois University, has maintained Library Job Postings on the Internet (www.libraryjobpostings.org, a meta-index to library job sites) since 1995 and explains how to make career planning easy.

✦ How to . . .
Make career planning easy

In today's difficult job market, as libraries worldwide experience budget cuts and competition for positions remains fierce, it becomes increasingly critical to make yourself and your qualifications stand out. Although jobs in popular locations and/or specialties can attract hundreds of applicants, only a fraction of these people will be a good match. Below are nine tips, based on my experience with search committees and as a long-time resumé reviewer, which can help with career planning and building a stronger case in the job search.

Know your environment

Make a comprehensive inventory of your skills and abilities, looking back on your employment history and accomplishments and classes in library school (and include relevant details on your resumé). Do your best to prepare for commonly asked interview questions in advance so you will have an answer ready. If submitting CVs for jobs at an academic research library, for example, expect to be asked questions about your own research programme. Familiarization with the work environment at places where you are applying will also help. Study the organization's website, examine its organizational structure, and see where its strengths lie – and where you might fit in.

Learn a variety of skills

While many librarians assume a specialty, it can also help to have diverse skills to draw on. This can begin while in library school and extend throughout your career. Reference librarians can better serve their clientele if they have some knowledge of cataloguing, for example, and knowledge of management principles can be useful regardless of your focus (and will make it easier to become a supervisor at a later time). Also, some career changes are planned, while others happen unexpectedly; having a broad range of experience will make it easier to adapt to something new.

Cast your net widely in the job hunt

Some job sites are more useful than others, but none is comprehensive. To find the greatest number of positions, consult a variety of sites, from national, regional and specialist job banks to recruiters to local newspapers. For UK residents, CILIP's LIS Job Net (www.lisjobnet.com) and Jinfo (www.jinfo.com) are excellent sources, as are recruiters like TFPL, Sue Hill and Glen Recruitment. For those outside large cities, visit local newspaper and university websites. In the USA, the ALA JobLIST (http://joblist.ala.org) posts dozens of jobs every week. Libraryjobpostings.org and LISjobs.com, meta-indexes to job sites worldwide, can save you time in finding relevant sites.

Tailor your CV or resumé and cover letter to each position

This is common advice given to new professionals – for a good reason. Examine the job requirements and duties in the advertisements you read and compose your resumé or CV and cover letter accordingly, making it clear to employers that you possess the necessary skills. Also, your cover letter should present a strong case for your candidacy, building on rather than repeating word for word the information in your resumé. Finally, take time to proofread the end result!

Consider writing for publication

Only a small number of librarians choose to write for publication, so those who do stand out. Contributing to the literature demonstrates your willingness to share ideas with a larger community, and good written communication skills will be needed wherever you work. Don't feel you have to tackle a lengthy research-based piece right away (or at all). Start out small by writing for a local library or association newsletter. Library journals rely on book reviewers and other contributors, so look for calls for reviewers or proposals on e-mail lists. Visit journal websites to see their guides for authors. Opportunities abound.

Emphasize technology

Whether you are working as a systems librarian, reference or information specialist, or archivist, information technology will have an impact on your work life. Are you savvy about using DreamWeaver or InDesign? Or are you an expert in searching EBSCO or Gale Group databases? Consider including a separate section on your CV in which you name technology applications in which you are well versed – anything from database interfaces to spreadsheet software to operating systems. Brainstorm what to include; you never know if an employer will be using a similar system and take note of your expertise.

Quantify your accomplishments

To turn a generic resumé into a unique one, include specific, quantifiable details when writing about your previous experience. If you managed a decent-sized budget (for a collection or an entire library), list the amount. If you were an instructor for workshops or library training sessions, provide details on the number of classes, and the number of students you reached. And so forth.

Join associations and committees

Joining associations and serving on committees can be very beneficial. Working with other librarians from across your region (or country) will help you form a professional network of people you can call on for advice, partner with you on projects, or help you co-author an article or book. CILIP (www.cilip.org.uk/get-involved/ways-to-get-involved/pages/default.aspx) gives details of ways to get involved; these days, much committee business is conducted online. Within the ALA, the New Members Round Table division (www.ala.org/nmrt), geared toward newer professionals, guarantees committee placement.

Be open to new possibilities

The information field is incredibly diverse, both within traditional library settings and outside of it. When job hunting, keep your eyes open for positions that would be a good match for your skills, regardless of whether they have the 'library' name or are located in a library proper. Businesses, technological ventures and government agencies all need individuals skilled in organizing information. (Searching using the word 'information' will often give better results in a UK-based job hunt than using the word 'library'.) Keeping your options open, and being flexible, will serve you well in the long run. Best of luck!

⚷ How to . . .
Make sure you are successful when applying for jobs

So you know where you might want to go – how do you make sure you can get there? Suzanne Wheatley of UK-based Sue Hill Recruitment gives us her top tips for CV and interview success:

- Make your application eye-catching – for the right reasons. A recent survey

219

showed that 71% of hirers might only skim read applications. Make sure the relevant points clearly stand out, and remember that your CV might go to the human resources department, or be scanned for keywords using scanning software.

- Make sure you proofread. One of the recruiters surveyed said, 'I toss any resumé or letter that has a spelling or grammatical error on it, without regard to any other qualifications. To me, it means the person is not resourceful (not knowing anyone that can proof?), lazy, unprepared, disorganized and a danger to my company.'

- Prepare for interview. Don't just rely on the information the organization gives you: use your information professional skills and contacts to find more information about the organization. Make sure that you know exactly what you can offer them.

- Be smart for interview, but above all, be comfortable. Take time to breathe from the diaphragm, using your full lung capacity, imagine you are slowly inflating and deflating a balloon. Being able to control the rate at which you exhale will let you control your airflow and thus speak at your normal pitch and with your usual enthusiasm and vibrancy, rather than that raspy, shallow voice we get when nervous. It will also give you precious time to formulate your answers.

   🔗 **Read more advice from Suzanne on the website (http://lisnewprofs.com/applyingforjobs).**

How did we get here?

So, now you have got some ideas about your career – still need a bit more inspiration? The information professions are varied, open, creative and give you a wide range of areas to choose from. Here we hear from three information professionals with slightly unusual career paths.

📁 Case study
From Story Time to the Society of Advocates

With squeamishness disbarring her from her early ambition to be a vet, Maria Robertson decided to be a librarian, as she 'loved books, computers, and people'. After a BA in Information and Library Studies at Robert Gordon University in Aberdeen, she had a six-week work placement in the House of Commons Library.

This fuelled her desire to work in special libraries, yet her first professional post was Children's Librarian for Clackmannanshire, based in Alloa Public Library. Maria admits, 'I wasn't good with children', but she learned some valuable lessons, including 'If you aren't sure of something you need to ask about it, ignoring it and hoping it goes away doesn't work, and ends up being very horrible.'

Faced with a choice between a job at the Advocates Library and a better paid post as teenage fiction librarian in a private school, Maria went for the greater potential of the Advocates Library position, where promotion eventually led to her 'dream job'. A move back to Aberdeen prompted a change of position, to Executive Secretary and Librarian for the Society of Advocates in Aberdeen. This role includes such non-traditional librarian activities as arranging and attending wine tastings and theatre trips, and arranging CPD events for the solicitors.

    ℰ **Read Maria's full story on the website (http://lisnewprofs.com/maria).**

📁 Case study
Archivist – at last!

Linda Butt's career started in the Radio Times Hulton Picture Library in London – a fascinating place to work, which ran on the accumulated knowledge and expertise of the picture researchers. After a career break, she went to work at de Montfort University Library as a library assistant, and gained her library qualification on the archives-focused archive administration and records management course at Loughborough University.

Ten years later, the institutional archive was discovered in an underground safe, and Linda started lobbying the university to promote proper care and use of the archive. In 2010, Linda gave up her post as a senior assistant librarian, and took on the role of archivist, in a dedicated archives and special collections repository.

Linda's story shows that you never know where your career will take you, and it is never too late to pursue that dream job. You can be a new professional at any age: 'So how does it feel to have achieved the dream job after all this time, at a point in my life when others are looking at retirement? Amazing!'

    ℰ **Read Linda's full story on the website (http://lisnewprofs.com/linda).**

📁 Case study
4000 miles towards professional happiness and success

'Who knew that in order to find myself I had to cross the ocean? Be brave, and dare to be adventurous, fellow and future librarians! Take pride in your profession. It is a noble one!'

Aileen M. J. Marshall moved continents to find her place in her dream profession. Born in Germany, she started volunteering at her local public library shortly after moving to the USA in 2007. Her first paid position as a librarian was working for Peumansend Creek Regional Jail. While working here she decided to qualify as librarian, and enrolled on the MLIS at the University of South Carolina. Aileen has an impressive resumé, with an internship in the Business Reference Section at the Library of Congress, and her current position as Information Specialist and Librarian at the National Transportation Library, US Department of Transportation, DC.

These are Aileen's top lessons to be learned:

- Volunteering can help you build skills and find positions.
- Don't be afraid to try something new.
- You might have to travel to find your perfect job.
- Apply, apply apply! Even if you think you won't get the job.

    🔗 **Read Aileen's full story on the website (http://lisnewprofs.com/aileen).**

Conclusion

There is no how-to guide for professional involvement – it is up to you to find the levels and types of professional involvement that work for you. This may well change throughout your career, as your skills and development needs change. Don't think of any form of professional involvement as a life-time commitment – in fact, you may find it helpful to put a time limit on your involvements. Committees especially need new blood to help keep things moving forward.

Whatever professional involvement you choose to undertake will help to develop both you and the profession, and will help you to write your own unique career story.

References and further reading

Career development and planning

Arnott, J. (2011) Job Hunting Retrospective: index, *A Modern Hypatia*, http://modernhypatia.info/2011/08/job-hunt-index/.

Benjes-Small, C., Ackermann, E. and Hyde, G. (2011) Job Hunting: what search committees want you to know, *ACRL 2011 Conference Proceedings*, www.ala.org/acrl/sites/ala.org.acrl/files/content/conferences/confsandpreconfs/national/2011/papers/job_hunting.pdf.

Chisholm, J. (2006) Skin of Your Teeth Library Management: how to survive falling up the career ladder, *ALIA New Librarians' Symposium*, Sydney, http://conferences.alia.org.au/newlibrarian2006/programme_files/chisholm_j_paper.pdf.

Dority, K. (2006) *Rethinking Information Work: a career guide for librarians and other information professionals*, Libraries Unlimited.

Doucett, E. (2010) *What They Don't Teach You in Library School*, ALA Editions.

Driscoll, L. (2006) Acting the Part: the opportunities of taking higher duties, *ALIA New Librarians' Symposium, Sydney*, http://conferences.alia.org.au/newlibrarian2006/programme_files/driscoll_l_paper.pdf.

Giles, N. R. and D. J. Hamid (2008) Brave New World: breaking barriers and embracing opportunities outside the library, *4th ALIA New Librarians' Symposium, Melbourne*, http://conferences.alia.org.au/newlibrarian2008/Papers/Giles.doc.

Gladwell, M. (2005) *Blink: the power of thinking without thinking*, Allen Lane.

Gordon, R. S. (2008) *What's the Alternative? Career options for librarians and info pros*, Information Today.

Hodge, M. (2011) New Perspectives in Leadership: how to be a library leader even if you're in school or underemployed, *Library Leadership & Management*, **25** (3), http://journals.tdl.org/llm/article/view/3289/2957.

Lawson, J., Kroll, J. and Kowatch, K. (2010) *The New Information Professional: your guide to careers in the digital age*, Neal-Schuman.

Leung, D. (2008) Any Old Library Job Versus The Job You Really Want, *4th ALIA New Librarians' Symposium, Melbourne*, http://conferences.alia.org.au/newlibrarian2008/Papers/Leung.doc..

Pantry, S. and Griffiths, P. (2003) *Your Essential Guide to Career Success*, 2nd edn, Facet Publishing.

Ruddock, B. (2011) *Alternative Careers*, Webinar, http://vimeo.com/34984523.

Shontz, P. K. (ed.) (2004) *The Librarian's Career Guide-book*, Scarecrow.

Shontz, P. K. (ed.) (2011) *LISCareer: Career Strategies for Librarians*, www.liscareer.com.

Totterdell, A., Gill, J. and Hornsey, A. (2005) *An Introduction to Library and Information*

Work, 3rd edn, Facet Publishing.

Yeo, G. and Ander, E. (2008) 'My First Professional Post': students' expectations of the job market in archives and records management in the United Kingdom, *Journal of the Society of Archivists*, **29** (2).

Unconferences

Library Camp UK, www.librarycamp.co.uk.

Library Success Wiki, www.libsuccess.org/index.php?title=Library_Camp.

LIS wiki liswiki.org/wiki/Library_Camp.

Stainthorp, P. (2011) Let them tweet cake: why Library Camp was unconferencing done right, Paul Stainthorpe: technology in the library, http://paulstainthorp.com/2011/10/08/let-them-tweet-cake-why-library-camp-was-unconferencing-done-right.

Professional involvement

ALIA New Graduates Group, www.alia.org.au/groups/newgrad.

Bradley F., Dalby A., Spencer A. (2009) Our Space: Professional development for new graduates and professionals in Australia, *IFLA Journal*, **35** (3), Big6, www.big6.com.

CILIP Career Development Group, www.cilip.org.uk/get-involved/special-interest-groups/careerdevelopment/Pages/default.aspx.

Greene, M. A. and Meissner, D. (2005) More Product, Less Process: revamping traditional archival processing, *American Archivist*, **68**, 208–63, http://archivists.metapress.com/content/c741823776k65863/fulltext.pdf.

Hack Library School, http://hacklibschool.wordpress.com.

IFLA NPSIG, https://npsig.wordpress.com.

LIS New Professionals Network, www.lisnpn.spruz.com.

Watson, K. (2008) Bang for your buck: getting the best experience and value for money from your library association investment, *4th ALIA New Librarians' Symposium, Melbourne*, http://conferences.alia.org.au/newlibrarian2008/Papers/Watson.doc.

➡ Over to you . . .

Conferences

Identify three conferences within the next year that you would like to attend. For each conference, consider:

- How well do the themes of the conference fit with your interests and development needs?
- Would your organization send you as a delegate?
- Are there likely to be any awards or bursaries available? (Reports from previous conferences are a good place to start looking.)
- Are you eligible to submit a paper? Would you like to speak at this conference?
- Is there an exhibition? How big is it? Is your organization likely to exhibit? If not, can you identify any other exhibitors who might be looking for help?

Write a proposal identifying which of the conferences you think would be most beneficial for you to attend, and how you might finance it. Don't forget to include travel and accommodation costs.

Career planning

Look at job adverts, and find a job that you might like to apply for in the near future (two to five years), and one for the medium term (five to ten years).

Produce a CV and covering letter for each job. Which skills are you lacking? How might you gain them?

Ask a colleague or friend to 'interview' you for the job. Ask them to consider how well you have tailored your application to suit the job and the needs of the company.

Conclusion

This book has given you the tools to thrive in your first professional role: to manage projects, money, users and your own development. You should have a clear view of how to move forward in the profession, and to make sure that you, your users and your professional peers get the most out of what you do.

You should understand how to think about project management, and how to make sure that you are using the most suitable tools for the job.

You should be more confident in measuring and communicating success in all forms of communication. While communicating well is very important, don't worry if you are scared of it. Practice helps to build confidence, and peers will support you, and provide useful feedback. Remember that all forms of communication feed off each other, and learning to communicate with peers in writing can help you to have more confidence when communicating verbally with users.

Place the needs of the user at the centre of your role. This is easiest to do if you align yourself with them – understand their values, use their vocabulary. Knowing what they really want will help prove your value, too.

Remember that marketing is a vital part of providing a good service, and strongly connected with meeting your users' needs. It can take some special effort, but can also be part of your everyday activities. Just being the most professional person you can in all your interactions is great marketing. You could take this to its furthest extent, and become 'embedded'. Think about the extent to which place defines your role.

Meeting users' needs is likely to involve working with technology. The advent of technology hasn't changed what the fundamentals of our job are, just how we do it. The more you know about technology, the more you can get involved in using it to deliver cool and innovative services.

You don't have to learn to code – though it's great if you want to! There are applications and services you can use, without having to understand all of the technology behind them. You should know enough to support your users, and to collaborate with IT specialists and coders. You also need to understand the fundamentals of digital preservation, for future information curation and retrieval.

Social media provide a great way to interact with users. You can connect with existing users, and attract new ones. Using social media and opening up your data and services is about having an open mindset, willing to share and connect. Web 2.0 and social media tools move very quickly – learn to rely on principles, not platforms.

As a result of economic pressures we all have to think about alternative funding and ways to do more with less. You should now have an idea of what alternative funding streams are open to you, and how to plan and deliver a successful bid. You should also know how to manage your money once you get it, and to make the most of your money through careful budget handling and negotiation.

What to do if you suspect financial – or other – mismanagement? Ethics and codes of conduct are vital parts of a profession. Ethical problems are never easy, but familiarize yourself with the ethical guidelines, think about case studies and situations, and honestly do your best. Upholding copyright and intellectual property laws is a big part of the ethics of the profession, and it is not as scary as it seems. Inform and educate others, and use available resources to educate yourself.

By reading this book, you are already showing a commitment to continuing professional development. CPD is professional lifeblood – do it to keep active and stop stagnating. It doesn't have to be official training courses – you can find learning opportunities everywhere if you start looking. Make the most of these by reflecting on your training and applying it to your professional activities. There is guidance available for the competencies and skills you are likely to need, and you should know how to relate these to your organization. Remember that mentoring relationships can be very valuable – for mentor and mentee. Support, learn, encourage.

Personal branding is just another aspect of marketing your service – you and your skills are a huge part of what you can offer, so you need to let people know. You are not being pushy! You should have some ideas of how to do it with grace. You should also have some ideas on how to network with confidence, and how to make the most of and follow up your networking. Reflections from solo practitioners should help to reinforce the importance of an external professional network, and help you to understand what being a solo practitioner involves, and how you can cope if you have to be one.

We have discussed why conferences are important, and how you can attend, even without a budget. You have advice to refer to if asked to work a conference stand or submit a paper. You should know more about the value of professional organizations, and what you can get out of membership, along with some innovative ideas for other types of professional involvement, and what you can gain from them. Finally, we looked at where you might want to go next, and how you might get there. You should now be equipped to plan your career, make a success of your first professional role, and progress within the profession. Go for it!

Appendix: Budgeting example spreadsheets

	Jan-12	Feb-12	Mar-12	Apr-12	May-12	Jun-12	Jul-12	Aug-12	Sep-12	Oct-12	Nov-12	Dec-12	Total 2012
Books													0.00
Periodicals													0.00
Library materials													0.00
Staff salaries													0.00
Payroll expenses													0.00
Office supplies													0.00
Repairs and maintenance													0.00
Marketing and promotion													0.00
Telephone													0.00
Utilities													0.00
Insurance													0.00
LMS subscription													0.00
RFID system service agreement													0.00
Miscellaneous													0.00
Totals	0.00	0.00	0.00	0.00	0.00	0.00	0.00	0.00	0.00	0.00	0.00	0.00	0.00

Table A.1 *Example of a form that monitors expenditure over 12 months*

	Jan-12	Feb-12	Mar-12	Apr-12	May-12	Jun-12	Jul-12	Aug-12	Sep-12	Oct-12	Nov-12	Dec-12	Total 2012
Books	450.00	540.00	640.00	345.00	354.00	456.00	546.00	687.00	485.00	542.00	235.00	254.00	5,534.00
Periodicals	12,000.00												12,000.00
Library materials		45.00			17.00					85.00			147.00
Staff salaries													0.00
Payroll expenses													0.00
Office supplies													0.00
Repairs and maintenance													0.00
Marketing and promotion													0.00
Telephone	10.00	10.00	10.00	10.00	10.00	10.00	10.00	10.00	10.00	10.00	10.00	10.00	120.00
Utilities			100.00			100.00			100.00			100.00	400.00
Insurance													0.00
LMS subscription			2,000.00										2,000.00
RFID system service agreement	1,450.00												1,450.00
Miscellaneous													0.00
Totals	13,910.00	595.00	2,750.00	355.00	364.00	583.00	556.00	697.00	595.00	637.00	245.00	364.00	21,651.00

Table A.2 *Example spreadsheet that monitors expenditure in one department over 12 months*

	Budget	Actual spend	Balance
Books		0.00	0.00
Periodicals		0.00	0.00
Library materials		0.00	0.00
Staff salaries		0.00	0.00
Payroll expenses		0.00	0.00
Office supplies		0.00	0.00
Repairs and maintenance		0.00	0.00
Marketing and promotion		0.00	0.00
Telephone		0.00	0.00
Utilities		0.00	0.00
Insurance		0.00	0.00
LMS subscription		0.00	0.00
RFID system service agreement		0.00	0.00
Miscellaneous		0.00	0.00

Table A.3 *Example of a form for budget monitoring*

	Budget	Actual spend	Balance
Books	10,000.00	5,534.00	4,466.00
Periodicals	11,000.00	12,000.00	-1,000.00
Library materials	500.00	147.00	353.00
Staff salaries		0.00	0.00
Payroll expenses		0.00	0.00
Office supplies	50.00	0.00	50.00
Repairs and maintenance	800.00	0.00	800.00
Marketing and promotion	400.00	0.00	400.00
Telephone	150.00	120.00	30.00
Utilities	500.00	400.00	100.00
Insurance	1,000.00	0.00	1,000.00
LMS subscription	1,800.00	2,000.00	-200.00
RFID system service agreement	1,400.00	1,450.00	-50.00
Miscellaneous	100.00	0.00	100.00

Table A.4 *Example spreadsheet that monitors expenditure in one department*

Index